LIST

T0155085

ROCHDALE

THE RUNAWAY COLLEGE

DAVID SHARPE

First published in 1987 by House of Anansi Press. This edition published in
Canada in 2019 and the USA in 2019 by House of Anansi Press Inc.
www.houseofanansi.com

House of Anansi Press is committed to protecting our natural environment.
As part of our efforts, this book is made of material from well-managed FSC®-
certified forests, recycled materials, and other controlled sources.

23 22 21 20 19   1 2 3 4 5

Library and Archives Canada Cataloguing in Publication

Title: Rochdale : the runaway college / David Sharpe.
Names: Sharpe, David, 1949- author.
Description: Originally published: Toronto : Anansi, ©1987.
Identifiers: Canadiana 20189067063 | ISBN 9781487006648 (softcover)
Subjects: LCSH: Rochdale College—History. |
LCSH: Free schools—Ontario—Toronto—History.
Classification: LCC LE3.T5692 S53 2019 | DDC 378.713/541—dc23

Library of Congress Control Number: 2019930412

Series design: Brian Morgan
Cover design: Patrick Gray
Text design and typesetting: Sara Loos

 Canada Council   Conseil des Arts   ONTARIO ARTS COUNCIL
for the Arts   du Canada   CONSEIL DES ARTS DE L'ONTARIO

We acknowledge for their financial support of our publishing program
the Canada Council for the Arts, the Ontario Arts Council, and
the Government of Canada.

Printed and bound in Canada

MIX
Paper from
responsible sources
FSC® C103567

The seven years of Rochdale took seven years to bring into print. I was supporting a fiction career by working as a security guard at the Royal Ontario Museum when I began the book in 1980. The project first involved a year of interviews and research, notably a day-after-day sifting through the archives in the Thomas Fisher Rare Book Library, helped enthusiastically by library personnel Luba Hussel and Margery Pearson. The book itself went through three versions — each one made possible by the patient and vital assistance of the Ontario Arts Council. The final version was completed during summer break while teaching creative writing at Brown University and Connecticut College. The project would have died after the second rewrite if not for John Robert Colombo, who helped find the right publisher at last.

The people I contacted for information about Rochdale were all intent that the story be brought into permanent and comprehensive form. As representatives of those many sources, I would like to single out Aulene Maki and Mark Buckiewicz, who offered photographs and friendly conversation. Essential to this one treatment of the story is material generously provided — in the spirit of Rochdale — by Alex MacDonald. Though I have tried to be even-handed, the subject of Rochdale College cannot be exhausted by one book and one perspective. Wherever this story is inadequate or confused by the jumbled, contradictory records, it points towards further accounts yet to be written.

If not for a teacher-and-student who influenced me greatly during my undergrad years at the University of British Columbia, who polished my interest in alternative education and thus, indirectly, turned my eyes in 1968 to the runaway College halfway across the continent, I would not be able to say:

Dedicated to Father Gerald McGuigan,
teacher-and-student.

CONTENTS

Part Four: The Rocking Cradle

Part Five: The Fall

INTRODUCTION BY STUART HENDERSON

From 1968 to 1975, a brand-new Toronto high-rise was taken over by a couple thousand hippies, draft dodgers, dreamers, intellectuals, Vietnam vets, drug dealers, free lovers, addicts, artists, anarchists, and runaways.

For seven turbulent years, Rochdale College served as perhaps the largest drug distribution warehouse in Canada, a home to untold numbers of drop-outs from the "straight society," a complex and multifaceted experiment in alternative living, and a never-ending orgy of partying, sex, and invention.

I am, let's say, a fan.

I first learned of Rochdale College almost twenty-five years ago, when I picked up a copy of the book you're now holding. I recall being utterly entranced by David Sharpe's reconstruction of the story of this improbable building, its confusion of residents, its shape-shifting community of communities. The idea that a place like this could have existed at all, let alone survived and even thrived for so long, captivated me. Full of youthful idealism, a reflexive respect for "the counterculture," and a healthy interest in drugs, sex, and hedonism (I mean, I *was* seventeen), Rochdale loomed large in my imagination. It has ever since.

Sharpe's great accomplishment in this book is that he imposes a structure on what is inherently a structure-free story. To relate the history of a building — comprising multiple floors, each themselves comprising multiple rooms, each filled with a mutable collection of individuals — is a daunting task. But to reckon with all of the competing narratives in *this* building — a revolving door of thousands of people, agendas, experiences, perspectives — is to impose order on chaos. It takes a keen imagination and a dexterous hand to make sense of this pretty mess.

Truth is, for many Rochdalians, the key to understanding the high-rise is that it *began* as a mess. As an always already unfinished space. A place that was, every day, being built, rebuilt, and built again.

After a summer of construction hassles and strikes, Rochdale College opened its doors in September 1968, when it was only barely fit for habitation. The noble idea that it was to be a progressive Free School, a kind of antidote to the "multiversity" system, was imperiled rather immediately. The simple fact that the building was still in some ways a construction site may have deterred many of the students who were attracted to the idea of the hip, alternative education envisioned by its founders, torpedoing the *raison d'être* for the enterprise on day one.

Toronto's hippies were undeterred by the dust and debris. Following the month-long hepatitis scare that had swept through their nearby Yorkville scene and looking towards the long winter to come, they weren't exactly picky. They poured into this apparent haven by the hundreds. Overcome by "crashers" (non-paying residents), increasingly menaced by hard-drug users and dealers, and burdened by thousands of "tourists" dropping in at all hours looking for an endless party, the whole Free School idea fell apart within the year. The garbage piled up, rent was hard to collect, and, increasingly, disorder reigned. A group of core residents attempted to institute some structure, establishing a governing council. But nothing really calmed things down until they made the politically tricky decision to evict the heavy-drug dealers, ban amphetamines and most narcotics, and crack down on non-permanent residents.

That's why 1970–73 is the period that has always interested observers of the College most. Sharpe dives deeply into these years, elucidating the sustained attempts at building the truly functional alternative social structures, communities, and facilities that characterized the period. Residents, realizing that they were edging towards a kind of separate society right there in the building, founded a health clinic (where babies were born!), a library, a range of food services, a child care centre, an in-house radio and TV station, a vibrant newspaper, and a series of floor-wide communes. It is often claimed that some inhabitants didn't go outside for weeks and months at a stretch, since they could access everything they needed right within the building.

There were feminist contact sessions, Black Power meetings, and Marxist book clubs. For a time, there was a Hare Krishna community on one floor, a group of evangelical Christians on another, and much cosmic spiritual exploration throughout the building. Of course, there was also a lot of sexism, macho male posturing, and bad behaviour. To pretend that this community was anything other than a microcosm of the wider society would be a mistake. Rape, addiction, unwanted pregnancies, violence, mental illness, casual racism, and sexual exploitation were all part of the Rochdale mess. As Sharpe demonstrates, Rochdale may have approached its problems differently than other communities, but it clearly did suffer the same problems. This was no utopia.

Through the early 1970s, it may have looked to residents like things could work out — that maybe Rochdale really could be sustained. But new people kept coming to party, and they were sometimes underage or unwell, and it was always hard to control their numbers. And then came the numerous drug overdoses, bad trips, and several deaths by suicide — particularly by way of people jumping from the building's windows. The relative quiet was shattered as media and police attention intensified. Sharpe carefully reconstructs this dark chapter, and reminds us at every turn that education — the original idea behind the building — never really disappeared from Rochdale. It had certainly taken on a new and more amorphous character, but this was always a space filled with hungry minds, open learners, and creative energies alongside the revolving door of partiers, runaways, and tourists.

By the end of 1974, the writing was on the wall, and Rochdale had entered its period of decline. Out of money, and struggling through complex legal battles, the governing council was exhausted. Surrounded by "Green Meanies" (green-jacketed security guards put in place by the receiver of the building), hundreds of Rochdalians tried to maintain their community, to rebuild yet again out of this new muddle. But it was getting harder. As the evictions ramped up, the building began to empty, and the end came into sight. Rochdale would be cleared out, shut down, scrubbed, repurposed. Its once boundless energy dispersed into the wind.

Thanks to David Sharpe's efforts, you have an opportunity to dig into the rich history of one of the counterculture's most extraordinary creations. Fifty years on, as we continue to negotiate hegemonic approaches to community, sexuality, living arrangements, property, identity, and education, we could do worse than to consider what was learned on these eighteen floors, over seven wild years.

STUART HENDERSON is an award-winning Canadian historian, cultural critic, filmmaker, and musician. He is president of 90th Parallel Productions, an independent film and television production company based in Toronto, and the author of *Making the Scene: Yorkville and Hip Toronto in the 1960s.*

PART ONE:

THE RISE

1

The Seven-Year Itch

In the late Sixties, young idealists and rebels, 800 at a time, were given full control of an eighteen-story highrise in the heart of English Canada's largest city. Rochdale College it was, this untested, bold idea on Bloor Street at the edge of the University of Toronto campus, a ten-minute walk from the Ontario Legislature. Rochdale College — a twin tower of raw concrete and straight lines in its second year of operation in 1970, the largest co-operative student residence in North America, the largest of the more than 300 free universities in North America, and soon to be known across the country as the largest drug supermarket in North America.

At that point in the decade, social gestures had become broad. Youth was a "movement"; the Americans were at war. The young idealists and rebels in the heart of Toronto had said they wanted to change — even revolutionize — education, but when the federal government gave them the money to do it, what they tried to challenge and change was society itself.

In August 1970, police staged a series of well-publicized raids against the College. Immediately, the public confirmed a suspicion that this was no ordinary building. Although there were many perfectly normal, responsible citizens within those walls, some of the young people there were holding a festival of dreams that the public didn't share, couldn't share, and they were holding those dreams in a fortress. Nothing short of an armed invasion — or a long war of attrition — would get them out. It was a set-up that surprised everyone, including the people who found themselves set up. It had never happened on that scale before, and — judging by the furor it caused — it will never happen again.

Rochdale College could have begun only in that experimental decade. In the Sixties, society had become, like a marriage, tired of itself, and Toronto, like a fretful spouse, searched for a lover. The city was feeling a Seven-Year Itch, a sort of menopause in which the pasture dries up and husbands seek new wives or runaway affairs. When Rochdale College arrived, it was as if Marilyn Monroe had moved in down the block.

By popular mythology, the Itch recurs every seven years. But with Toronto, it came only once — and lasted seven years. Indeed, for the seven years of its lifespan — from September 1968 to September 1975 — Rochdale became the itch that Toronto couldn't scratch.

Through all the twists and turns of the story, the times took Rochdale seriously. The College received detailed press coverage, with frequent, impassioned letters to the editor. When Rochdale diplomas became available, payments came in the mail from all over North America, and some from Europe. Reports entered national magazines and national TV news, and as the word of mouth and media spread, young people loved what they heard. At least 5,000 lived in Rochdale at some point in their impressionable years. They came from, and went to, all parts of Canada. And in the States, Rochdale was an address contemplated by young men with draft-dodging or deserting on their minds.

The following pages document the way both the larger society and the Rochdalians themselves turned a community into a symbol and destroyed it. The Rochdale story has features which lift it from the local, Toronto scene into the continent-wide examination of the Sixties which has begun in the Eighties. Many in the group now holding positions in the social and business establishment were exposed to the ideological challenges of the Sixties and decided either for or against the social protest, the radical conservatism seen in health foods and communes, the killing of categories, the drugs. Rochdale played out a pure form of those challenges-in-action. The reader will find that, if he thought the Sixties were good, they were better inside Rochdale, and if he thought they were bad, inside they were worse.

Much of the following has been taken from internal publications, papers, and interviews — material not carried by the public press. However, looking behind the scenes carries some consequences. Surviving collections of internal publications, for example, are disorganized and partial, and the incidents recorded in the publications are just as disorganized and partial. Items in the internal newspaper, the *Daily*, are often anonymous and almost never representative of anyone but the writer. In general, the *Daily* staff printed whatever was submitted. Unattributed quotes, of which there are very many, come from "the man in the elevator." Both spoken and written language often break into erratic "fucks" like flatulence. I've saved some for atmosphere, and deleted many for the sake of the air. Likewise with errors in typing, grammar, and spelling. Once the material is seen to be so loose that it hangs over all the edges in the English language, little is gained by reproducing every slip.

Unavoidably, interviews and scattered source papers select, almost randomly, some participants, and ignore others. The people who affected the community often did so without having any definable position, and often without having a name they cared to release. Rochdale prided itself on its brand of urban anarchy and its blunt democracy. This combination of anarchy, democracy, and secrecy allows no orderly retrieval of events, and permits no tidy history of leaders and individuals.

As well as de-emphasizing leaders, I have often had to leave aside another demand commonly made by a history: an accuracy that will stand up in court or classroom. Rochdale refuses to co-operate. As an example, Alex MacDonald, an articulate, alert former resident whom you will hear often in the pages to come, replied to a question about medical facilities by saying "there was a big — not one of those damn hippie street clinics — a fully functioning, three-room, eight-doctor clinic." Eight doctors? That seems a lot. MacDonald shrugged: "I invented that number. Lots of doctors."[1] And when inventing doesn't play with the facts, impairment might. As one interviewee put it: "I've destroyed my memory cells with acid and whiskey. A good combination."

I am saved from one form of distortion, however, since none of this book is memoir. In 1973, I bought a loaf of raisin bread in the Etherea store at ground level as I passed through Toronto on my way to Europe, and that was as close to the living Rochdale as I came. For me, Rochdale did not need to be more than an idea. During the two years that I attended an experimental program at the University of British Columbia, Rochdale was the remote, full-scale example of what we were trying by half-steps.

Despite all the full-scale pain and confusion we are about to see, Rochdale was one of the brightest mindgames in a decade of mindgames, and none of it makes sense without a sense of fun. As longtime resident Bill King said, "It's impossible to understand Rochdale without the boogie."[2]

2

An Ideal Beginning

The founders wanted a reputable name for a co-operative. They chose "Rochdale" in honour of an enterprise in 1844 in Rochdale, Lancashire, England. In that long-ago Rochdale, twenty-eight weavers, disciples of Robert Owen, had formed a co-op grocery on the ground floor of a cotton warehouse in Toad Lane. This prototype extended its alternative system into retailing, wholesaling, insurance, and welfare, all within twenty years.

The twentieth-century Rochdale might have lived twenty years as well and would be operating in Toronto today if the Rochdale building, as in the original plan, had become nothing more than a highrise housing students. The scale of the project was unusual, true, but large as it would be, it expected only to become a sober — and co-operative — university residence. Instead, in a moment of innocence, the building welcomed a passing spark, a quickening germ.

A new kind of college, found mainly in the heads of educational idealists, was looking for a home — and found this spacious one in the early, ovum-sperming stage of a plan. The Rochdale Affair began by the coming together of a college on a residence, an ideal of education finding and occupying a structure that would be wonderfully concrete. While the residence was being raised, it became unique by the raising of its consciousness.

In the forefront of that consciousness was educational idealist Dennis Lee, in his late twenties and in the early years of a teaching career at the University of Toronto. At this point, Lee had written challenges to the education system published in small-circulation journals, and had not yet achieved his success as a writer for children and a poet.

It had taken Lee a long time to decide what was wrong with the university system. In the mid-Sixties, he realized that the university had replaced liberal education with other goals: "It was this shift of focus that had stymied me for so long — the shift to recognizing that the university was functioning quite adequately, but in a different educational universe from the one I thought it occupied. I had kept on asking why no one shot the puck, but it was easy: we were all playing basketball." [1]

Lee proposed a return to hockey. He wanted a renewed "liberal education," but one that would not lack structure or rules. Under Lee, a student would be encouraged "to steep himself so deeply in a discipline — philosophy, say, or economics or theology — that his mind and imagination came to recapitulate the structures and categories and models that inhered in that discipline; at that point his mind had a new order accessible to it — not as an object of study, but as itself." [2]

The purpose of the new ideal, as it came to be expressed in the *Rochdale College Calendar* of 1967–68, was to "create an academy: a place where men and women who love wisdom can pursue it under the forms and by the avenues which seem best to them." By Dennis Lee's vision of a liberal college, Rochdale would provide "an idealized Oxbridge education — immersion in the subject, testing conclusions against the mind of a tutor, re-immersion in the subject by which that initial liberation could be repeated and extended as he pushed into new disciplines or deeper into one which became his vocation."[3]

This was not new. As *Toronto Life* pointed out: "Lee is in fact describing the constant academic dream. It is not far removed from the raison d'etre and functioning of some medieval universities, and describes the same aspirations of nineteenth-century educationist Cardinal Newman."[4] Rochdale was said to derive from eleventh-century Oxford and Cambridge Common Houses. If it worked, Lee said, Rochdale would be "a place where people of a particular temperament could do the university's work better than at the university."[5]

Such a dream could be entertained in the prosperous times of the mid-Sixties, and seemed to be the answer to a suspicion that was circulating among the most skeptical of academic minds: experience could be richer than study, the suspicion whispered; knowledge may not be wisdom. Teachers with the most suspicion decided that they were students as much as their students. Whole fields of knowledge were being questioned, and as a consequence, the owners of dubious knowledge became roughly equivalent to those who had none at all. To these newly humbled educators, education became a sharing of poverties, rigorously democratic, in which everyone was, in a relative sense, wealthy. Like mendicant monks, the members of the new order would sacrifice expertise for the possibility of wisdom.

The first vow of these monks of wisdom was to despise job-training. Education should promote a disinterested curiosity. In terms of disinterest, the monk resembles the aristocrat; the one is free of gain by wanting nothing, the other is free by having wealth already. The style of education being proposed was aristocratic, the style that wealthy nineteenth-century landed gentry could pursue, when an amateur was as serious an expert as a professional. Charles Darwin was one such amateur, developing over decades his theories while secluded on his estate. For the educational idealists of the Sixties, the society had become rich enough to support amateurs, and democratic enough that anyone could aspire to become one. Conveniently, because of the residence being built on Bloor Street, at least one set of these gentry would become landed in the twentieth-century, in an eighteen-story estate.

Within this new order of education, anyone could be a teacher since the subjects for teaching had expanded to embrace whatever special learning one had picked up. If origami wasn't better than linguistics, it was at least equal. A person became a teacher if at least one other person reciprocated and became, temporarily, a student. That would happen only if the teacher earned, moment by moment, the student. Certification, qualifications, none of that mattered if the teaching didn't work. With the doubts being raised about expertise, it was a small step to cross the usual academic disciplines and adopt a generalist instead of a specialist approach. Biology could be tied to economics, number theory to novels and sociology.

The experiment in an experimental college was a deliberate and risky rejection of control, and in this, academic experimenters shared attitudes with young people who were furthest from organized education. The one ideal that overshadowed the others, and seemed to be universally held by the generation, was an ideal of the Open. If one is sufficiently open — by rejecting the imperfect, unhealthy controls of the current society — one could begin again, perhaps without the mistakes. This ideal hinged on a trust in natural and human forces, a reliance on a white kind of anarchy, an anarchy assumed to be, ultimately, gentle. As such, the people involved in setting up Rochdale, as well as the people who inherited it, had the innocence associated with the young. The effort to establish the new College was not unlike a Children's Crusade, and just as the medieval Children's Crusades were too gutsy and mortal to be slighted, what later proved to be naivete should not be dismissed. The cradle being set up would try to nurture something vulnerable, messy, and new.

One control had been identified and labelled for extermination, and that was labelling itself. Rigorously, the new thinkers took the forms that molded thought for practical and approved ends and made them anti: anti-category, anti-status, anti-name, anti-hero, anti-establishment. To be pro was to be locked into what was being promoted; to be anti was to be released to continue to look. Skepticism had reached a new worth, with the greatest skepticism applied to the boundaries of law and convention.

Curiously, because religion often finds itself outside the modern categories, the new education discovered allies in priests who wanted a paring back to essentials that they trusted would be, if not holy, at least respectful. A Basilian Father co-founded the experimental program I attended at the University of British Columbia; Rochdale College had, at the beginning, a Dominican and an Anglican. Though the steps being taken were called forward ones, they stepped far back — at least to the medieval, perhaps to the early church, to a less-organized, more mystic time.

From all the possible ways to step out of the contemporary style of education, the experimental programs that found homes established a rough consensus — in a typical free university, classes were replaced by "meetings" or seminars, subjects were multidisciplinary, assignments were replaced by voluntary projects, testing was rejected as irrelevant, and no syllabus was pre-planned. "What Rochdale is all about is having a system flexible enough to fit people, all kinds of people, rather than trying to make people fit a structured system inherited from somewhere and someone else. It is a place where people must create their own environment, make their own decisions, learn to face themselves — because the basic truth everyone must face is about himself — and learn to live and be complete, rounded people."[6]

Or so Dennis Lee put it. Lee serves in the Rochdale story as a figurehead for the many heads who contributed. Dissatisfaction with the standard university was neither new to the region, nor patented by Lee. A student survey at the University of Montreal, for example, called 43 percent of the faculty unfit for teaching, and student leaders at Toronto's Glendon College were calling for a month of "people-generated classes."[7] The times were encouraging action for whatever causes seemed right, and not only intellectual ones. In addition to the anti-war, civil rights demonstrations of the post-graduate, non-graduate world, tents were being pitched in battle at Queen's University in Kingston and at the University of Toronto to protest a shortage of student housing.

Meanwhile, the highrise student residence in the heart of Toronto was being prepared to ease that shortage, initiated by an experienced group called Campus Co-op. Campus Co-op began the adding of education to co-operation, "College" to "Rochdale," by incorporating Rochdale College in 1964 as an educational institution and electing a "Rochdale Council" in April '66 to oversee preparations for the high-rise. However, whatever educational ambitions the Council might have begun to entertain were modest compared to the larger forces that were at play. As Rochdale co-founder Howard Adelman relates (in his book, *The Beds of Academe)*, the student anti-nuclear movement of the early Sixties had scaled down to the Student Union for Peace Action (SUPA) by mid-decade. "Remnants of SUPA" approached Rochdale Council and offered to develop a radical educational side to the new co-op. At first, they were "rebuffed for their arrogant and undiplomatic manner," but later, with help promised by the Company of Young Canadians (a federal social service program), the Council agreed to research the possibilities.[8] Chosen for that research was Company of Young Canadians worker and University of Toronto lecturer Dennis Lee.

Late in December '66, Rochdale Council decided to pursue that research by opening a preliminary version of its college, to "establish Rochdale College as an operative institution beginning this fall, a year before the College proper opens."[9] The planners of this "continuing educational laboratory" felt a mixture of nerve and caution. The committee spoke of "the risky and demanding task of front-line experiment," and reminded themselves that their expensive asset "demands stability and sobriety."[10] Quite naturally, they wanted a year to try out a smaller version.

The smaller version began as planned in September '67, and can best be referred to as "the Rochdale Houses" to distinguish it from the highrise that opened a year later. Offices were shared with the parent organization, Campus Co-op, in a house that also held the editorial staff of *This Magazine Is About Schools*. By the spring of 1968, the Rochdale Houses had commandeered six rented buildings scattered over four areas of downtown Toronto, and had enlisted eighty-six residential members, eighty external members, and two full-time organizers, Dennis Lee and John MacKenzie, who were paid $10,000 a year by the Company of Young Canadians. Thirty to forty of the Rochdale members were classed as full-time.

Lee's vision had found many visionaries. One early resident realized that "while I am getting my B.A., I should be learning the rest of the alphabet."[11] In the enthusiasm of the early days, it seemed that a freeform education would be possible even in the sciences. Rick Waern, honours student in physics and chemistry, recent drop-out, and College registrar in the first year, intended to "apprentice myself to someone I respect, wash his test-tubes."[12] Rochdale would educate "without the habits that b(l)ind most educational institutions."[13]

Intellectual students enjoyed an intellectual free-for-all during these smaller days of the Rochdale Houses. We can see them in a seminar in the front room of the Rochdale office on Huron Street in 1967: "While rejecting the formalized education, they all seem to have mastered its discipline of logical progression and precise use of words — 'transcendental affirmative impulse,' the difference between 'systems and systematics,' careful distinctions between the 'esoteric and exoteric' approach to a problem... But sometimes it seemed like an empty exercise in phraseology. Or like the English seminar gone wild, when lack of preparation leads to a camouflage of deep terms, and an attempt to impress with discussion of Underlying Universals."[14]

These were the people who asked on the 1967 application form for Rochdale: "Can you love the people and govern the state by non-action? Can you regulate the breath and become soft and pliant like an infant? Can you open and shut the gates of nature like a female?"[15] One of the first *Rochdale Dailies* advised its readers that "you were the George who learned from Mr. Fred. Now you are Mr. Fred. Be a McLuhanite professor. Be an IBM know-boy. Be a vacuum cleaner in reverse in re-verse."[16] Not only were these students esoteric when they were serious, but also when they laughed. Look at these samples of early academic humor from 1967, inserted at random into the Bulletin: "It is not known whether Sir Edward Tupper ever slept at Wawa;" "To pullulate in groups of more than 11, is worse than pullulating alone;" "The word 'brob' was first used in 1784. It has seldom been used since."[17]

While still enthusiastic about finding ground for his ideals, Dennis Lee described the unsystematic, contemporary student that he hoped would do the work of the university: "This new student doesn't really believe in anything before 1945 because of the combination of his own affluence and the total shambles that history has produced. He works intuitively, in fits and starts without much method. He moves sideways — not backwards and forwards like the rest of us. Sometimes he explodes and takes up 31 vantage points simultaneously. Often he is the most brilliant or most interesting mind about."[18]

In this restless time, under the early urges of the Itch, the city was eyeing foreign turf, and like societies everywhere, the young would be sent to do the occupying. The leaders, however, didn't realize that the troops were carrying into the affair a wisdom more extreme than the wisdom of the generals, and that wisdom said: if it itches *anywhere*, scratch. With intellectual orders and anti-intellectual disorder, some of the youths in the new College would try a newer, greener grass, and touch every untouchable they could uncover.

3

The Rock

The residence about to welcome interesting minds was an organizational and financial coup for the leaders of home-grown Campus Co-op. As a provider of student co-operative housing, Campus Co-op of Toronto was aggressive, successful, and ambitious. From a beginning in 1937 with seven members, it grew to 450 members and occupied thirty houses by 1967. In 1966, Campus Co-op set its sights higher than its collection of houses. It wanted a student-owned residence in a highrise.

But how could it afford a building that would eventually cost, after its construction was complete, $5.8 million? By a loan, of course. But Campus Co-op was student-owned, and not attractive to real estate investors aiming at profit. Could Campus Co-op find a large, comfortable, mild-mannered rich man, a kind of loan-guppy as opposed to a loan-shark? Yes, indeed. A loan for close to $5 million could come from the federal government. The federal government would be pleased to shoulder 90 percent of the capital cost for a time.

The purse had first been opened in 1964 when the Canada Mortgage and Housing Corporation (CMHC) was authorized to make loans to, not only university-owned residences, but co-operative and charitable residences as well. This was accomplished by a change in the National Housing Act, a change that was years in coming and had been watched closely by Campus Co-op. At last, affordable housing would be available under enlightened legislation. "The day after the legislation was passed, [Campus] Co-op — which had lobbied it through — bought ten houses."[1] Now the way was clear for the highrise, and only 10 percent of the capital cost would not be covered.

Campus Co-op had a chance for success because it had Howard Adelman.

When the Co-op hired Howard Adelman, it owned four houses and rented one. "[Adelman] was just 19 then, but proved sufficiently skillful and daring as an entrepreneur to out-fox Toronto's best real estate brains."[2] As Adelman said, "the old Co-opers just didn't know how to manipulate money around." Under his direction, in ten years Campus Co-op grew to twenty-two houses owned and ten rented.

Adelman's methods became known as "Joyful Capital." Joyful Capital and "Joyful Bureaucracy," said Dennis Lee, were attempts to learn the rules of the game so well that you could "subvert the values those rules usually serve... [for] human and lively ends."[3] The methods resulted in low, low costs. Massey College, a graduate student residence at the University of Toronto, cost $30,000 per unit. In contrast, each unit of an Adelman co-op at the University of Waterloo totalled $4,500. To his contemporaries, Adelman had a wizard's touch.

Co-operative College Residence Incorporated was formed by Adelman and personnel from Campus Co-op. A non-profit company, Co-op College had a specific target, namely, the development of new residences. The company's first project — and North America's first student-built residence — was the above-mentioned co-op at the University of Waterloo, Hammarskjöld House, completed in 1966. Without a pause, Co-op College moved on, doing developmental work across the continent, and primarily in Ontario. According to

Adelman himself, he was consulted for $100 million worth of student residences by June '69. By that time, Howard Adelman had been affectionately named "the founding father of a ridiculous number of co-ops."[4] "Rochdale might have existed without 'hoopies' [hippies]," says former resident Alex MacDonald, "but it would not have existed without Howard Adelman. He did the deals and the lobbying, and more than any other individual, he caused the building to exist."

With the help of Adelman, Campus Co-op had a solid record when it approached the CMHC for a mortgage for its highrise. For additional support, Campus Co-op turned to the University of Toronto. By now, the residence had begun to acquire its other role as a college. University president Claude Bissell wrote to organizer Jack Dimond in April '66 saying that "the University of Toronto has encouraged the concept of equality of opportunity for all foundations that are concerned with the discovery and spread of knowledge."[5] As MacDonald explains, the "U of T was desperate for student housing...they were running ads on the air about how the university is overcrowded. And Campus Co-op wanted to expand...it was going to strive and become the world vanguard student co-op. And the United Church got talked into it somehow — because they weren't paying attention, I guess. There were various attempts to haul in liberal academics with credentials in order to make the thing look nice for CMHC."

Howard Adelman, a man more comfortable with practicalities and deals than with fancies, approached the project with an enthusiasm as great as that of the educational idealists. "The College epitomizes democratic control," he said, "student initiative, small group settings for students within a high-density urban complex, and the intermixture of residential and academic life on the 5th Avenue of a booming metropolis."[6]

With many people saying "yes, let's do it," a 90 percent mortgage was routinely approved in July '66 under the revised Housing Act. The remaining 10 percent caused no difficulty. A developer, Revenue

Properties, not only controlled a parcel of land which was suitable, but was willing to reinvest — a fairly standard procedure — a percentage of the equity as a second mortgage. Then Campus Co-op mortgaged all its unmortgaged properties to raise $200,000 for equity in the building, and a fraternity, Nu Sigma Nu, completed the roster of investors. Construction began in December '66 with a projected completion in June '68. As the building was being constructed, however, the educational side was meeting obstacles. Rochdale College found that it couldn't seek financial aid from the Ontario Department of University Affairs. The provincial government believed that no more post-secondary schools were needed in Ontario and would grant no money for new ones. Neither would Rochdale be able to provide accreditation, since the province had no accrediting body that would approve or disapprove of its offerings. As the *Toronto Telegram* said, the most Rochdale could aim for was a reputation. [7]

And who would belong? Who would become owners of the building as well as its student body? By February '67, the Rochdale Council had expanded its bylaws to include non-residents and non-students as Rochdale members. Non-residents and non-students? Already the reach was exceeding the grasp of mainstream Co-op members, who were both resident and student. The Council approached the general Co-op members in March. "The Co-op members were aghast at our apparently nefarious activities and couldn't understand why they should turn over their skyscraper to such a bunch of questionable characters." Comments were made about "bearded, intellectual radicals." [8]

Because the majority of Co-op members were "upwardly mobile career-oriented students," according to Howard Adelman, they were quick to distance themselves from experimentation. They solved their doubts by voting independent existence to Rochdale "to prevent the new building from becoming the financial ruin of the old houses." [9] A most important step had been taken. The highrise would be owned, not by an established group of co-operative experts, but by the as-yet-unknown, as-yet-unselected residents.

With an early removal of "executive domination," amplified by a constant loss of the older members of the Co-op as they moved out of university life, little could be done to prepare for control and operation of the building in the year of the Rochdale Houses. In the Houses, as Adelman tells it, Rochdale spread rapidly "into more educational areas than any organization with effective conservative brakes would have permitted." [10] The College-to-be began to advertise for members.

The response was enthusiastic. With 800 spaces to fill, Rochdale had its pick of 2,150 applications by the time it opened, and in all, 4,000 applications would be received in its first year. However, in a chaotic start to what would be a chaotic year, the ones selected found that neither the College and its bureaucracy nor the building itself were ready when they arrived in September 1968.

The excavation for the highrise had begun in good time, but the worst happened: a sympathy strike by the cement haulers stopped construction for twelve weeks in the summer of 1967. By June 1968, the expected date of completion, only three of the eighteen floors were semi-finished and barricades were still up everywhere. During September, a sanders' strike stopped work once more. By September 15, when eighteen floors of residents were waiting for their rooms, ten floors were ready. Since the lower floors were finished first, the building filled from the bottom up for the next six weeks. By November, 718 of the maximum 800 residents had moved in.

As reported by *Change* magazine, "residents wove their way around workmen bobbing on air hammers and leaning on power drills. Live wires hung from gaping holes in ceilings, and piles of dust, broken concrete, cardboard boxes and rubbish were everywhere... There were serious floods from vandalized plumbing." [11] The rooms on the east side were to include meals, but no cafeteria could operate for three months. Some of the rooms were to be furnished, but beds, mattresses, desks, and drapes were late in arriving. Even eight months after the opening, some residents complained about their still unfurnished "furnished" suites. "We joined forces and decided to withhold our rent until an official statement was made. What happened? In our youth and naivete, we moved into our furnished (?) pads only to discover we'd been suckered. Are we being suckered again? Is there an official rent rebate committee? Am I fated to come home someday to find my door padlocked? If so, please remember to water my cat frequently. Our hands are getting tired of holding our rent (not to mention our suckers). Will the real rebate people stand up, please, and identify themselves? We promise to help you with the arithmetic! Rebatedly yours..."[12]

All of the windows were to be furnished as well, but "when the first ten floors of the building opened," said resident Sarah Spinks, "the glass in the windows wasn't installed."[13] Some of the windows gaped open until the cold weather. In September, the baths had no hot water "and you would get out of the bath to find a construction man putting the finishing touches to the baseboards in the hall." Caulking waited until freeze-up, and much of the finish in the building remained "defective or deficient" even after completion. The elevators "simply [refused] to function much of the time" due to concrete dust in the elevator room and the high volume of use.[14]

Occupying an unfinished building presumably violated more than a few codes and by-laws, but the scope and speed of the violations left the inspectors far behind. Just as a lie big enough may be believed, violations abundant enough may be ignored. Rochdale College did nothing official in response to what its new members were being forced into. Would it give out 800 hardhats for what was still a construction site? No. Would it arrange alternate housing? No. Would it absorb the chaos as an experiment in education and begin? Yes. Apart from a brief warning in the *Daily* that "the building inspector

is really serious about kicking us out," Rochdale College began by
living outside the small laws as readily as some of its members would
live outside the larger ones.[15]

Even when completed, the building they were moving into was
no beauty. The sides of raw concrete, the straight-line windows and
walls seemed sired by a battlement on nothing more alluring than a
cereal box, and received no kinder nickname than "The Rock." It was
part of Rochdale's resumé that the college had inherited the mission
of the original workers' co-operative at Rochdale in England; a lone
voice pointed out that "Rochdale is also reported to be the ugliest
town in England."[16]

Rochdale College fronted Bloor Street on the south side for all of a
city block between Huron and St. George, except for a service station
at the eastern corner. To the north, the Rochdale windows faced the
more decorative Medical Arts Building. Further down Bloor Street to
the east, the Ontario Institute for Studies in Education conducted the
traditional experiments that Rochdale wanted to surpass; "in a sense,
the [Rochdale] building was originally intended to be OISE's critical
counterpart."[17] To the west sat a much older College of Education
building, and soon, on the north side of Bloor, a smaller cousin of
Rochdale would be built with the same, pallid concrete, a highrise
student residence called Tartu, a building with fewer floors, no educational ambitions, no co-operative ownership, and a longer lifespan.
Behind Rochdale to the south, brick co-op and fraternity houses ran
for a block to the steep angles of "Fort Book," the Robarts Library
that had begun construction in 1968 in the heart of the University
of Toronto campus.

The Rochdale building consisted of two wings, an east wing
with sixteen floors and a west with eighteen. On the south side, at
the second-floor level, an open terrace awaited the sun. Two levels
of underground parking accommodated a total of 157 cars. The
basement included a dumbwaiter for deliveries to the kitchen; the

street-level floor was mostly reserved for leasing to stores; and the second floor was given over to a lounge, cafeteria facilities, and space for College offices.

Above the second floor, a wide variety of rooms had been designed for various degrees of shared occupancy. The east wing resembled a standard student residence. The single and double rooms in that wing were known as "Gnostics" on the north side and "Kafkas" on the south. In contrast, the west wing resembled a standard highrise. The full-scale apartments there featured a living room, kitchen, and bedroom if they were "Aphrodite" suites, and a second bedroom if they were "Zeus" suites. In between the two wings were the communal units — and the most experimental of the living arrangements. These units were called "Ashrams," one to a floor, and provided four double occupancy rooms plus four singles all opening onto a lounge next to the elevators and served by one kitchen and one "big bath." These Ashram, or house, units were "intended as an approximation of [the Rochdale Houses] system" that had preceded the highrise.[18]

If the rooms of Rochdale were distributed horizontally, Rochdale would equal in size a small town. There were ninety-eight Aphrodite suites, fifteen Zeus, sixty Kafkas, seventy-four Gnostics, and in the Ashrams, sixty single rooms, fifty-nine double rooms, and fifteen lounges — every one of them filling up with people in high gear. The place seemed designed to aggravate warm-blooded individualists. All the units, according to one critic, were "ugly, cramped, lacking in private study space and with poor acoustics between units."[19] Inside the rooms, the beds and desks were screwed down to make them part of the building and thus, eligible expenses to be included in the government mortgage that was making it all possible. One screwed-down arrangement in particular was hard to live with: the desks were built-in next to single-glazed windows, and although the temperature extremes could be enormous, the radiators — also next to the immovable desks — could not be regulated. Whenever any radiator was adjusted, it threw the heating system off balance across the building.

At first, carpets and drapes were provided. Ashram and Kafka units came equipped with sheets that were promised a holiday in a laundry once a week, and Ashram suites had free phones. However, whatever wasn't screwed down, and some that was, disappeared or migrated from room to room. The free phones were soon removed as well — by the telephone company. The long-distance calls added up to a phone bill that even Bell Telephone wouldn't want to pay. The walls in the rooms began white — elephant tusk white — but shortly after opening, the walls were written on, painted over, and claimed. One bedroom in the east wing was spray-painted completely black. Many of the apartment doors, left golden yellow by the contractors, were repainted and decorated.

According to sociologist and resident Kent Gooderham, the new tenant-owner "hated the building…which he considered to be anti-human in every respect."[20] The *Daily* knew the reason why: "The whole confusion at Rochdale is caused by the building being 18 stories high, instead of the original 19. This is enough to confuse anyone."[21]

But really, why? How did a conscious step towards an ideal come to land inside a dreary, conservative shoe? At the insistence of Revenue Properties, the second mortgage holder, changes were made to the original building design to "facilitate conversion to an apartment-hotel in the event of unforeseen difficulties."[22] In addition — and more importantly — "the shapes and sizes of individual rooms were determined for the most part by the structural grid system of the parking garage," as Adelman explained in *The Beds of Academe*. Pragmatic decisions such as these touched the living conditions of every resident: to save money and space, the parking spaces and thus, the rooms themselves, were reduced in size. "It is consoling to remember," said Matt Cohen in his review of Adelman's book, "that one of the officers of the corporation that developed Rochdale demolished a fender trying to manoeuvre into his parking space."[23] Cohen blamed Rochdale's difficulties, not on lifestyle or management, but on the building itself. It was designed to be too densely populated and "was never presented as a completed residence. For at least a year it was a work in progress — and offered as a natural theatre for anyone who cared to use it."

The physical deficiencies that existed at the beginning had to remain to the end. "A redesigner, remoulding fund to match the physical shell to its developing uses was never gotten for the building as a whole," Alex MacDonald explains, referring to a later period in Rochdale management, "because of the race to try and make the mortgage payments. It was done to some small degree by people in units or in communes. The only place that was developed very much was the roof. It turned into a summer paradise."

The design of the building promoted several results that became apparent as the use of the building continued. We can look ahead briefly to see what the architectural shell imprinted on the soft body that entered and inhabited it. The west and east wings, for example, differed by planners' fiat in matters of self-containment and density of intended occupation. As a result, the west wing attracted a population that was relatively stable, an attraction helped by one-year leases, while the east wing attracted more transient tenants. The west-wing units were more in demand, not surprisingly when the rent structure in the first years gave an Aphrodite for two at $135 a month in the west wing and a Gnostic for two, with less space, at $200 a month in the east. With this rent structure, for some time the east wing subsidized the "landed gentry" in the west. The west wing with its self-contained units tended to stay aloof from the east wing, and east-wing residents often were uninterested in the operations of the College. In a symbolic rather than a practical sense, a visible seal was put on this east-west division by a fire door that split the floors in half.

The divisions happened vertically as well. In the first year, residents of the eighteenth floor, west wing, screened applicants and admitted to the floor those who, like themselves, were older (twenty to thirty years) and more stable. The top floor collected a dentist, a psychiatrist, a printer, a theatre director, and a university professor. "We didn't socialize much with the rest of the building," said Registrar Jack Dimond, who would later be forced out as part of an unwelcome Old Guard.[24]

Friends were often spread among floors instead of along, and the elevators became more active for communication than the halls. This led to unusual demands on what should have been usual elevating, and impeded the sense of community that was being sought. "The elevator was at war with the plan for decentralized floor communes because it tied the residents to a vertical central street... it was a street, which instead of opening horizons to its inhabitants, closed in on them."[25]

Anyone who depended on the elevators needed uncommon valor in the face of an enemy. The four elevators were designed for ordinary apartments with two rush hour periods a day, but an estimated 70 percent of the building's traffic was constant and between floors. In addition, "the amount of construction dust in the atmosphere during the fall played havoc with the elevators' psyches."[26] In the first year, the elevators needed repair almost every day. Fortunately, repairs were covered by warranty until March, but even so, breakdowns added up to $5,000 a month in the first winter, and continued to cost $500 to $1,000 a month long after. As one account puts it: "The Otis men have taken out Rochdale memberships."[27] The *Daily* at the same time carried a scoop: "News item: Otis elevators headquarters is in a *one-story* building in Chicago."[28] A former maintenance helper, Ernest von Bezold, confirms that "the elevators were famous among elevator men in the city because the electric mechanical brain was the largest ever seen at the time for that kind of elevator and it had gone haywire. The man who fixed it for two or three years later moved into the building."

But dust and overuse accounted for only part of the break-downs. Vandals and unheroic people mistreated the "elevators and depressors" — probably in reaction to slow service — and passengers with flair caused more problems. "A usual trick," says a former resident, "was to punch the button for your floor with your foot." An open letter from a maintenance man says it all. "I spent a lot of Saturday runnin' around because some geek had kicked in the 17th floor buttons and alla cars were stopping onna floor and not going past, and folks were gettin' shocks from the thing and each of those touch tubes cost us $8 and the template assembly around $40 ... (it happens about twice a week)." [29]

Elevators were not the only facilities that were disappointing. Jack Jones, a vocal resident and sometime *Daily* editor, had another important complaint: the Rochdale highrise had "not even a fucking auditorium. A self-governing group without an adequate place to call a general meeting." [30] Nor did this College have a single classroom designed as a classroom.

Neither the developer nor the architect were responsible this time — it was the original Rochdale Council itself making a decision that mixed expedience and experiment. In September '66, the Council had to decide floor plans by the end of the month, but even with the deadline so close, it was necessary to be prompted by a suggestion from the University of Toronto president, Claude Bissell, before the Council went ahead and reserved the second-floor suites. The minutes of that meeting show that "previous to the University's proposal, it was not sure that we could afford to let this space go for seminar space." [31] When seminar rooms themselves arrived at the last minute in the planning, it is not surprising that an auditorium was overlooked. By May '67, when the concrete was about to be poured and the matter had become urgent, the use of the eleven suites on the second floor had still not been finalized.

For the next seven years, considerations of space for the college could only periodically include the units on the street level. A People's Art Gallery made an appearance, as did a low-cost record store and a twenty-four-hour cafe, but aside from the entrance, elevator lobby, and a room used for rentals or security people, areas were usually leased out to businesses of varying relevance. As an example, the street facade in the final year of the College featured a bank, a health-foods restaurant and store (Etherea), a travel agency (Friendly Travel), and the scm Book Room, a bookstore catering to University of Toronto students.

In the hybrid origins of the College, the residence gene had dominated the college one. The intended "classrooms" were the same size as the rooms above; the main lounge was no bigger than two one-bedroom Aphrodite units. But this shortage of meeting space seemed to fit the experiment: education should not be separated from residence, learning should not be confined to a special space at a special time. Seminars that couldn't find a home on the second floor would be held in apartment units.

And so we find The Rock as the first residents found it, a conglomerate wanting to become a gem. When the College opened in September 1968, its new owners, the Rochdalians, were an unpredicted part of the thousands of interested parties watching.

4

The Rochdalians

The late opening had an immediate effect on the selection of residents. The first thing jettisoned was selection itself. As Alex MacDonald tells it, "the building wasn't actually certified as complete until June of 1969... Now if you're planning on bringing 800 rent-paying bodies in on the first of September because that's when your debt structure starts and you haven't got anything at all for contingency and most of the assumptions you've made for utility payments have turned into a pile of crud and you've only got two floors open in the middle of October, you have a really serious problem. It's really, really important to get people in NOW. Please, anybody who looks like they might pay rent — because the whole student market was gone. You can't sell to students if you start in October."

"And along about that time, the police were beginning the task of cleaning out all of the property-depreciation 'hoopies' [hippies] over on Yorkville [a nearby Toronto street that had been the center of a low-rent youth community since the early Sixties]. It was 1968 and anti almost anything you could think of. There was this big empty building which was desperate for tenants and was a free college. 'Far out! Let's go there.' So there were a lot of people who moved in at the beginning who had absolutely nothing to do with any of the already conflicting machinations that had gone into building it."

Street people, cash poor and often hash rich, were claiming the same roof that students were finding half-built. The ideal that admitted any kind of study also admitted any kind of colleague. Indeed, the new college welcomed the experienced people who were joining the company. Organizers who may have felt resistance to the non-student student body that was moving in kept it hidden behind the new humility that the education idealists had achieved. But Dennis Lee was already beginning to doubt the results of his vision. He saw his idealized Oxbridge education becoming "dominated by the many with severe needs while the few who can give are simply numerically and energetically unequal to the task."[1]

Those becoming residents in order to be students mixed with those intending to be residents alone. Automatically, both groups became the loose form of student that the education ideal called for. The double nature of the highrise, both college and residence, now surfaced in its population, ambiguously both student and resident.

In addition to these fulltime Rochdalians, a large number of well-defined students joined Rochdale without committing themselves to its ideas of education. The 718 residents that had moved in by November '68 included 493 "extra-mural students" from the University of Toronto, Ryerson Polytechnical Institute, and the Ontario Institute for Studies in Education. By another count, Rochdale started with 400 U of T students, 50 from the New School of Art and the Ontario College of Art, 100-150 from Ryerson, and 100–150 fulltime Rochdalians.

In place of faculty, there were ten or twelve "resource people," who were paid a modest salary to be available for seminars, tutorials, and general guidance. Two of them were full time, while the eight or ten who were part time were given $2,000 to $7,000 in rent rebates or cash. Jim Garrard of Theatre Passe Muraille, for example, was excused from half his rent. The original resource people included an Anglican priest, a Dominican priest, an Odawa Indian, a philosopher, a poet, two writers, an actor, a chef, a printer, a filmmaker, and an artist.

Rochdale was trying to keep at least one of its feet in the academic world, but the street people, not the students, began to dominate. Into this garden where orderly rows of produce had been expected, entered a tangle of weed and bloom.

"Rochdale had an impressive variety," says one former resident. "You had the dumb, freaked-out, marginal people, and the artists, and even some straight people holding down jobs."[2] In 1969–70, resident sociologist Kent Gooderham found four types of resident: the Old Rochdalians, the Students, the Heads, and the Political Activists. The Old Rochdalians had set up artistic and social groups that we will look at later, and "walked through the halls with a proprietary air." The Students were simply unintegrated. The Heads "were illiterate — former graduate students [who] would stop reading anything except signs and notices…They danced. They fucked. They panhandled, dealt, and liberated needed articles from the establishment stores… They went to Vancouver, jail, mental wards, home, Europe, Asia, the island, a commune in the country. They came back."[3] These were the people one cabbie called "white men with black feet."

"The place was so determinedly casual," says the former resident, "people wandering in and out, constant noise. It seemed you were always running into assholes and idiots. It was very rare to come across a student. One heard they were in the building."

Both the very bright and very marginal were attracted to Rochdale, as a few examples will show. "Popper" from California wore a codpiece and a multi-colored jerkin. Kim Foikus came too, "the Vancouver Town Fool, flute-player, creative disturber, therapist-to-the-world."[4] And "Hank": "Hank was in the alley behind Rochdale flourishing his cape at the garbage truck yelling 'Ole'. A little girl passed by and remarked 'Hank the Bank.' 'Hank the Crank,' Hank responded and gave the ears of the garbage truck to the little girl"[5]

Then there was "The Meth Monster." Officer Dean Audley, a policeman who frequently entered Rochdale, relates that "one time I was walking with The Meth Monster and forgot to tell him the hallway was taking a turn. He walked into the wall and broke his nose." In a later year, "Jack the Bear" led a tour through a Rochdale Open House. A reporter asked him his real name. "Jack the Bear, friend, Jack the Bear. Look, my social security card, see?' (Great happy laugh). Sure enough, that's the name on it."[6] At that time, the Bear had been living for a month on the roof in an orange pup tent.

An early *Daily* reported that "we met the Zoo keeper and...he started talking about space people, flying saucers, and green sponge people with one eye the size of a baseball with a thing in the middle like the oil bubble in the carpenter's level. They only see light and dark, but see thru their whole bodies...Then he started talking about Quasi-Stellars and extracting ore from rocks by rays from space ships above the ground, and space people...some of them were already here and looked just like us except their heads were bigger and they had pointed chins and had...already interbred with us...the space people had answers to the Vietnam War and not to worry..."[7]

There were people with a criminal record and people flirting with one. "My first act on stepping into the building," says Syd Stern, one of Rochdale's prominent past citizens, "was to go up and see the President. I walked in and laid my police record down on the desk and said this is who I am so that there'd be no secrets. And 'I'm moving in. Like it says in the paper, Rochdale is a free college, and I'm moving in free.'" Stern was a self-professed drug dealer. In the final years of the college, he asked the property manager not to walk around rattling keys. "That's a habit most property managers get into," Stern said, "but I've been in jail, and an awful lot of the others have been in jail."

On the more innocent side, *Miss Chatelaine* reported on one "Shelley B.," "a pixy-faced 16-year-old from Edmonton...sitting outside in the sun, wearing blue jeans that are genuinely ancient and a sweaty T shirt...She's already one month behind in her rent because she was fired from her job as a salesgirl in a boutique when the owner caught her swiping a sweater. 'Christ, I was freezing to death; who the hell cares about one crummy sweater?'"[8]

The *Daily* suggested its own set of types for Rochdalians. "Many civic institutions are donating animals to [the new Metro] zoo — why not us? Why not ONE OF US?...We are sending two prime examples of human Rochdalians; we would encourage the other ethnic groups of Toronto to do the same." The contest to select the examples had categories for Hairy Brute, Brute, Jailbait, The Grooviest, The Intellectual, Witches and Wizards (black or white), and Old Moles.[9] But no matter how the population was analyzed, student or street, it remained mostly young and short on money. The low-rent people at Rochdale could appreciate the *Daily* cartoon of a businessman giving coins to a beggar and thinking, "\$9,842,731.50 − .40 = \$9,842,731.10."[10]

Questionnaires returned from ten of the floors in June '71 indicated that the residents were two-thirds male. Sixty percent of the total population were single, 20 percent were married, 5 percent divorced, and 15 percent lived common law. The average completed grade was half a year beyond Grade 12, with the upper two floors showing a concentration of residents with partial or completed university education. Just over 60 percent were from Canada, and just under 20 percent were Americans. Racially, the respondents numbered "fifty-eight Caucasians, two Negroes, two Orientals, and four Canadian Indians."

The average stay of a non-transient worked out to seven months, with one floor recording a lowest average of three months. A high proportion came from middle-class homes or above: nineteen counted their father's occupation as professional, fourteen had fathers who were managers or officials, twelve fathers were skilled workers or foremen. This contrasts with two fathers who were semi-skilled or unskilled and one farm owner and operator. Residents came from the city (thirty-nine) or the suburbs (twenty-three), not from farm (one) or fringe (seven).

A later governing council president, Peter Turner, saw Rochdale as "a focal point for youth. There is only limited occupancy, but thousands and thousands have come through here. Last year (1969–70), we estimated that nearly 100,000 people had visited Rochdale, 4,000 staying a month or more, and more than half of them from outside Toronto."[11]

The restlessness didn't end once the young people entered Rochdale. Another study — of movements within the building from September '69 to March '70 — showed that only thirteen out of the 150 people studied stayed in one room continuously. Thirty-two moved once, nine moved twice, thirty-six moved three times, and a full sixty moved four times or more. "If Rochdalers don't find Utopia on one floor," said *Change* magazine, "they look for it on another. Some have shifted as many as six times, like human sand."[12]

Rochdale began to exile itself from the surrounding community the more it filtered out the mediocre middle and kept the extremes. Appropriately, it also attracted genuine exiles — the American resisters. The Vietnam War was underway, and many young people, like resister and Rochdale resident Bill King, felt that "jail was the proper place for an honest man in Vietnamized America."[13] Many of those who didn't want jail or war, and were unlucky enough to be drafted, escaped to Toronto.

The Toronto Anti-Draft Program sent its *Manual for Draft-Age Immigrants to Canada* to U.S. campuses with a mention of Rochdale. From the date that Rochdale opened, the College had seventy-five U.S. students as residents, and at least twenty-five of them were dodgers. In November '68, a list was circulated in Rochdale naming "rooms for newly arrived draft-dodgers."[14] At all times, the American exiles were welcomed and encouraged. "You're allowed to fall behind in your rent for a reasonable length of time," *Miss Chatelaine* reported, "but individuals with extenuating circumstances, like draft dodgers, are rarely evicted for failure to pay."[15]

"Rochdale is offering a two-week residential education and counselling program for American immigrants," read part of an appeal for funds from Bill King.[16] "A free room will be provided along with a chance to meet new friends and learn about Canada at night while looking for a job during the day. All student-guests will live on the same floor, so the lounge of that floor can be set up as an education center." The plan would cost forty dollars per person per two-week period, and a coupon at the end invited contributions: "Here's $40 to aid a brave man of conscience. Here's $40 to get the cowards out of here." A brochure in March '69 assured "our American compadres: Forget Sergeant Preston. Toronto weather is similar to New York's. No snow and ice during the summer."[17] Circa March '70, Rochdale had been providing cheap or free rooms for two weeks for American immigrants, and wanted funds to expand that program to two east wing floors. The support could also be directly financial. In November '68, a benefit was held to support the Toronto Anti-Draft Program. The lounge featured a mock election and televised coverage of the U.S. presidential election, while the basement had a band, an auction, films, refreshments, and folksingers. The Rochdale Education Fund contributed $700 to the Anti-Draft group for the printing of new pamphlets and books.

The American presence transformed Rochdale. "There were large numbers of U.S. people," says a former resident; "their influence was pronounced. Very often they were in authority positions because they were bright or they had that American drive." Jim Garrard, a Canadian resident, saw the deserters and dodgers — "we didn't make a distinction between them" — as "superior individuals with superior leadership qualities. If they built cabinets, they really built cabinets... Toronto as a whole would have been far less interesting if not for that influx of good people at that time."

The leadership rising within Rochdale College had little to do with academia. In the first year, the intended leaders — "the few who can give," as Dennis Lee put it — were the "resource people" who stood in the place of faculty. However, the resource people were finding themselves just as isolated and vexed as Lee in the face of the unexpected characters who were arriving. They were prepared to lead in ways that the ones to be led ignored. "The concept of 'mastering' certain books or philosophies was alien to the new Rochdale residents," said Sarah Spinks. "Their orientation was toward sensual, bodily kinds of activities. The projects that gathered and kept them were the creative arts — batiking, photography... It was reflective, unfrenzied work, but it did not require as a prerequisite some experience in the world..."

"... [The resource people] were, unlike the Yorkville and Rochdale kids, in a twilight zone, between their parents who remembered the depression so vividly and the teenagers who were hitchhiking to pop festivals all across the country. Instead of joining a business or smoking grass, these people devoted themselves to a pursuit of truth and they chased it with the same rigorous competence [with which] businessmen twenty years ago had built their businesses. Unspoken but clear messages transmitted themselves to the stoned kids around them — most resource people expected intellectual rigor and competence."[18]

When their expectations were continually dashed, the resource people withdrew into their portions of the highrise and the residents picked up another unspoken but clear message — irrelevance. One resident complained in the *Daily* that "a 'drop in if you must' attitude, or the 'where can I best hide' thing... seems to characterize many so-called RPs [resource persons]."[19] Just as Adelman and the Co-opers had turned over the residence to strangers, Lee and the educational idealists were in the midst of turning over the college.

5

The Changeling

If the new residents were a problem to the resource people, non-residents were a problem to everyone. As Rochdalians claimed floor by floor in the fall of 1968, transients discovered wide-open areas on the upper floors and moved in — and out and in and out. As those areas became permanently occupied, the transients continued to wander and squat and wander again. Meanwhile, word of mouth, word of press, called out: A free college! A college so unlicensed that it offers, not freedom or license, but both. Freedom from parents, freedom from rent, freedom even from an address. Like a crowd to an accident, thousands of visitors and interim residents came from the roads and from the suburbs.

> Metro had a little school
> Its name was black as sin
> And day and night the Metro kids
> Were screaming to get in.[1]

During the winter of 1968–69, the weekends became tourist season and partytime for people passing through, while the building designed for 800 occupants gave shelter to 1,000 at the peak of the invasion. "In February," estimated a Toronto alderman who was one of the outsiders watching askance, "as many as 3,500 young people passed through Rochdale on a week-end."[2] Some of the overflow went into rooms that were considered crash pads. One of those had bunks used around the clock by shifts of sleepers. In some cases, the residents "created split level rooms to handle twice as many guests."[3] The rest of the overflow made liberal use of lounges, hallways, closets, and even elevators, wherever they could stretch out. The fourth floor submitted photos to the *Daily* showing four of the interim residents, called "crashers," sleeping in the hall. The fourth floor wanted "to thank Rochdale for the new carpeting."[4]

This was "Camp Happy-Hippy," as an ad in the *Daily* put it. "No Washing No Television No Rules No Regulations / Camp Happy-Hippy is equipped with only two beds, so only the first 400 applicants will be accepted / 'Guru on the premises.'"[5]

As if the nerves of the residents were a welcome mat, the crashers and crowds wore them out. Troubles began in the first month with "roving bands of drunks through the building. Rumour says that these guys are from a local frat…The police have been called in once already."[6] Crashers stole breakfasts and left messes. Often they were friends of the tenants in the ashrams, one resident complained, who were themselves irresponsible. Crashers wouldn't wash dishes, and they urinated in the halls. In one incident, six crashers were found at 4 a.m. sleeping in different storage closets with stolen dishes, cutlery, and food. "Some of them were very upset that anyone should 'dare' hassle them."[7] Dennis Lee and governing council member Paul Evitts issued a statement in search of a policy: "Some of these creeps who have no stake in Rochdale and use the building like their privy, we want pure and simply to dump. No principles involved."[8]

But, although the residents had become an Establishment by acquiring a building, the role didn't feel right. Who had the right to restrict entry? On what grounds? "None of us were screened when we arrived," said council member Jack Jones, "and it bothers our conscience to set up 'entrance requirements' for others."[9] The members of the Rochdale community in the first year, as chaotic and unformed as the community was, faced their first crisis of conscience. Crowd control needed cops, and no one knew quite how to take control while rejecting the principle of control.

Any time an effort was made to control entry, it met as much resistance from within as from without: "the cry of 'fascist' or 'paranoid' or 'square' is heard, and it paralyses all."[10] Door locks became the item that focused the issue. In November '68, a fifteenth-floor meeting decided that one resident was "a bastard for stealing the lock from the kitchen door (so somebody would tell him why it was there in the first place, he says)."[11]

The front door drew the most fire. Late in 1968, the *Daily* recorded that "it was stupid of Rick to lock the front door on his own authority (if he did) and it was incredibly insane of Bernie civil servant Bomers to watch the door being locked a full week or two before non-resident MEMBERS get keys."[12] Then, according to a "Counterblast by Joel" in the *Daily*, a governing council member removed the front door lock early in 1969 and broke it. By a less contentious version, "the lobby door lock...failed repeatedly and was ultimately abandoned."[13] Yet another version said that the front door lock had been stolen three times by January '69. By all versions, the front door was wide open. Aside from the screening problems, it was impossible to buy tenant's insurance. The owner of a car that had been broken into twice appealed to the council for repayment of the $1,000 loss. His insurance company had refused to pay.

The building itself amplified the problems. The rooms in the east wing didn't have proper locks to begin with, so transients tended to discourage paying tenants. As well, the lack of living room space in the east wing led to crashers claiming space in bedrooms. The

Ashrams, by design, invited public use with their lounges next to the elevators. In one case, twelve people in a "responsibility unit," intending to share a single Ashram, quickly became twenty-seven. Could a "people's" area like an Ashram lounge be legitimately locked?

Recurring thievery eroded another ideal. Especially in the first few months, many Rochdalians felt that material possessions should be shared by all members of the community. Coach House Press, located in an alleyway behind Rochdale and closely associated with the new college, succeeded in this enlightened sharing, according to Sarah Spinks. "The Press, though it had expensive printing equipment, opened its doors to many people at Rochdale who wanted to come and learn to print. In a materialist society it is a revelation and a joy to watch a press-man walk out the door late at night, look over his shoulder at you gingerly squeezing ink onto a letterpress, saying: 'Make sure the rollers aren't down when you leave.'"[14]

In this case, the presses themselves and fast, tangible results created discipline. Karma is easily grasped when it is offset. But in too many other cases, thieves just grasped. The *Daily* printed a plea that appealed to reason: "An oval, black and white 'Dylan' poster and a colored 'Endless Summer' poster have been stolen from the 12th floor lounge — so if you happen to see them about your 'friend's' abode, help him realize that he's too old to be in this building."[15] Another *Daily* circulated a helpful motto: "Don't steal anything you can't use."[16]

Many times, things not stolen couldn't be used because they had been vandalized. The free phones were already gone, but Bell Telephone threatened removal of the payphones as well because of the number of long distance calls on phony credit card numbers. The *Daily* made the affair faintly subversive by publishing instructions on how to make those phony calls — using credit card numbers of large corporations.

As the discussion about locks continued its non-academic course, the residents started to realize that something so simple as an open door could be radically unlike the surrounding society, and could shift unpredictably into something the society would judge illegal. "There is a problem with runaways," said a November '68 *Daily* — "they have already been here and so have the police and although these kids need a place to sleep, if we take responsibility for them we could wind up in some legal shit creek."[17] The writer, however, still wanted to be helpful. "We could unofficially form a runaway underground and keep these kids elsewhere if we judge their case worthy of our risk."

Others were not so kind. A fourth-floor apartment displayed a sign: "WARNING! This apartment is protected by a 40-megaton nuclear device which will be triggered by the entry, or attempted entry, of any unauthorized person, chicks included. So watch it."[18] Crashers could see, written on a wall, that "Rochdale Doesn't Like Weekend Slobs. Are You a Slob?"[19] The *Daily* reported that "the Rochdale Clean-up-the-Crashers Committee...arranged volunteer labor to scrape from the terrace any crashers found on the higher floors."[20]

And along with the bluffs came more serious attempts. Early in 1969, an emergency meeting of the governing council banned crashers except as guests of residents, and an "Official Rent-Paying" petition assembled 250 signatures and declared that crashers were trespassers. But of course, no amount of banning and declaring managed to lock an unlocked door.

Most seriously, the college worried about increasingly obvious drug-dealing and -taking. A room open to the public for film-showings and the second-floor washroom already had a reputation as good locations to buy and sell drugs. On a weekend in January, two Rochdale members had pulled guns and had taken money from two people who were in the midst of a $750 hash deal.

What was going on? A changeling had been put into what was meant to be a cradle of education, and the changeling showed every sign of growing. Many members of Rochdale College, as well as their visitors, meant to learn about other kinds of consciousness — or other kinds of kicks. At the very least, the course taken in this college would be marijuana. Although not everyone smoked pot, everyone defended the right to do so. In October '69, even two members of the governing council were charged near London, Ontario, with possession of hashish and marijuana.

The worry about drugs was more accurately a worry that uncontrolled drug activity might — like the runaways who slipped in with the crashers — draw the attention of the police. In the first month of the College, the *Daily* passed on advice given by a lawyer to a Rochdale audience: "Grass itself is required for evidence. Ashes alone aren't too good. Watch for undercover boys who buy from you and use it as beautiful evidence. If you know about searches and come on straight, non-belligerent, cops will fuzz-off. If you get action, find out about suit. It's the only thing that really works."[21] A bail fund began, and more warnings appeared in the *Daily*.

Some of the people crossing the threshold — Rochdalian, visitor, crasher — weren't satisfied with marijuana and hashish alone. In 1968, for example, speed was a new craze and Toronto was being called the speed capital of North America. Those taking speed became separated from the others inside by the strong effects of the drug, both the hyper-energy and the neuroses it promoted and the infections that resulted from the careless use of needles. With speed and other hard drugs came theft by users needing cash, and possible interference by motorcycle gangs who dealt in hard drugs.

A wide-open Rochdale College had two sides racing out of control at the same time. It somehow had to screen outsiders coming in and throw unwanted insiders out. At all times, the college couldn't be sure what was now morally and philosophically In and what could be justified as Out.

In the early months of Rochdale, attempts at security were confused and ineffective. The first plan was to set up a nightwatch with volunteers each taking a one-hour shift. The loose, co-operative approach had problems, however. When a motorcycle gang took over an upper-floor lounge in December, ate all the food and refused to budge, a meeting of residents couldn't reach a consensus. Someone took his own initiative and phoned the police. At this point, the bikers didn't have their own security against police — and left.

In December, security had become part of a larger plan by solid, disciplined leaders like Dennis Lee and Judy Merril, an older woman, a writer and editor of science fiction who had come to Rochdale from the States. Their plan included a Communications Center at the front door. "A group of 'determined people' led by J.M. and D.L. (who cannot be named) are manning the desk by the entrance on a voluntary basis at first. 'We need to greet people with a 'hello, what help do you need?"' said the Grandmother of the scheme.[22] The Communication Center would include a desk, files, telephone, and a volunteer member at all hours. The idea was introduced with an elaborate poll and balloting procedure, with all the twists and turns accounted for. The scheme was visualized in such detail that few Rochdalians faced the task of reading it. Like many of the campaigns by the serious leaders, it was "prepared" to death.

That month, a general meeting elected "God" as night watchman and gave him authority to deal with crashers as he saw fit. The new night watchman patrolled the halls, but the position changed hands at least twice in the first two months of 1969, and sometimes no one knew exactly who was patrolling what. A nightwatch, however, was an easy concept to grasp and required only competent, trustworthy people to do it — unlike one Chief Nightwatch who "left Rochdale and Toronto abruptly, with a large sum of other people's money, reportedly collected as advance payments for undelivered drugs."[23] After four people attacked Turtle, a former crasher-turned-resident-and-nightwatch, and broke his jaw, pressure for a fulltime, uniformed doorman increased. A doorman? The doorman's uniform, the joke was, would consist of "green satin pants, red cape, and a sword."

Less easy to grasp was the concept of control for those who had become residents. In the struggle to sort out unwanted insiders, the college had only one, imperfect weapon. That weapon was eviction — an act of will by an organization that often couldn't tie its own shoelaces and wasn't sure it believed in shoelaces anyway. "What was taken more seriously than anything else," says former council member Jim Garrard, "was the idea that someone might be unjustly evicted. No matter what anybody did, they had somebody supporting them on some level, philosophical or personal or something."

An early attempt at evicting dealers was thwarted by a sense of fair play. At the end of January '69, four unidentified residents learned that an outsider — code-named "Janus" — would join a patrol of the building. "The four of us talked to Bernie [General Manager Bernie Bomers] and he told us that this man was an investigator for a mining company downtown, and an acquaintance of Jack's; that he entered the building [and] had volunteered to go compile a list of dealers for Jack and Bernie, who intended to get the uncool dealers out of the building by asking them privately to leave." [24] The four insisted that no outside person do any such thing. "[We] went back to Rochdale, took the man's list (which made no human distinctions) away from him and set a deadline for his leaving...At the same time we told [the people on the list] and others that we would very much like to see: no hard drugs in the building, no rip-offs or burns, and no chemicals being pushed without first being analyzed and published, and no big dealing to outsiders." Ironically, the dealers who were the intended targets of the message stayed — and the marksman was put out.

The night following, on January 31, 1969, Rochdale tried its most direct intervention. It was a Friday night and the masses were beginning to arrive. General Manager Bernie Bomers explained in the next day's *Daily* that a front door lock would take weeks to arrive. Also, residents afraid that the intercom system could be used to listen to activities in their rooms had sabotaged the units, and thus the intercom couldn't help screen friend from freeloader. Someone else would have to do it. At ten o'clock that night, Bomers pulled the Communication Center desk across the front door and began a Rochdalian form of sacrilege: he questioned the people who wanted to come in. He was joined by nine residents, five from the governing council, and they barricaded the door until 3 a.m. During that time, 400 people entered and an estimated 15 were turned away.

This, the Barrier Incident, was a "self-righteous vigilante escapade," according to resident Mike Donaghy.[25] Another resident, Ken Mason, watched the visitors being screened and decided that "the whole scene seemed a repeat of the trip to 'clean-up' Yorkville, or Montreal, of all those hippies, the trip we all condemned in the 'outside world.'"[26] Mason sat on the desk and as quickly as people were turned away, he told them that the back door and the restaurant door were unlocked.

The Barrier was unauthorized and controversial, but its opponents need not have worried. Official steps had to be repeated and retracted repeatedly before it could be seen that nothing was being changed.

The next month, residents were still coming to the Rentals Department to complain about cleanliness and crashers, and Rentals' solution was both vigilante and democratic: "If your floor has cleanliness problems, do something about it! Too many crashers? Kick a few out! Appoint a head crasher, maybe, to regulate crasher traffic. But do something!!!"[27] By mid-month, Ian Griggs and his Cadet Corps began a twenty-four-hour crasher patrol, and by March, security was being called The Watch. Crasher reactions became even more unrepentant. A group of crashers met "to plan (not to discuss) how crashers can seize their rightful share of power in Rochdale." A "Bonified Crasher Card" — and Proof of Chutzpah card — was proposed with the wording: "I declare on the one hand my intention to beat any system Rochdale sets up for us or over us which we crashers consider unfair. On the other hand I declare my intent to respect Rochdale's need for economic survival and agree not to exploit others in any way or to be servile."[28]

Some residents tried to integrate the crashers into the community by setting up a Crasher Co-op. Members of the Co-op would be given Rochdale membership, guest resident status, and meal tickets in return for cash or labor. Their privileges would be suspended "if found sleeping in a public area."[29] The Proof of Chutzpah card above had been inspired by the more benign "crasher card" proposed for the Co-op. It would carry the following inscription: "I will attempt to maintain good relations with the formal residents of Rochdale. I recognize and respect Rochdale's imminent need to reduce crasher cost to nothing. I further agree not to make a mess for others to clean up, not to con people, and not to exploit people in any way."[30]

Resident Bruce Maxwell drew up a list of tips for cool crashers: "If you jimmy the locked door with a spoon, don't. Find a resident with a key and be his guest when you are in the kitchen...Don't sleep in public areas. Residents will know that you did even if they don't wake you up, which most of us won't...Residents mostly are crashers with money. Don't treat us like cops."[31]

The "upper classes of the crashers became integrated" in the Crasher Co-op, but the turnover was too high for it to be more than a noble idea.[32]

Meanwhile, the issue of eviction continued to excite breast- and brow-beating. In February, according to Alex MacDonald, "a General Meeting passed a law outsiding speed freaks and then adjourned to go to the thirteenth-floor hash room and beat up speed freaks." In the same month, Govcon voted 27–3 in favor of twenty-four-hour eviction notices instead of five-day ones. Again, in the first weeks of May '69, council conducted a "sweeping vigilante-style eviction" of forty speedfreaks and dealers.[33]

A three-member Evictions Board was set up to report to council and a Secret Security Group began to carry out evictions and bouncing, "breaking up gatherings in public places. There were 'actions' in the lobby every Friday night…The [second-floor] Lounge was locked. The seminar rooms were locked. The movies were stopped…Gary Segal was authorized to rent a safety deposit box to implement the arms control measure (How many guns are in the box, I wonder?)"[34]

All of the threats to security came together in one package when Rochdale faced the motorcycle gangs. In one small incident among many, in March '69, the Detroit Renegades had been hanging out for several days in The Same, a twenty-four-hour restaurant in Rochdale, and the Coffee House. On a Sunday, four of their members found themselves separated by a locked door from three baggies filled with white powder and some pills that they had stashed on the roof terrace. Several Rochdale officials not only refused to give them the key, but called the police. The bikers "hit out" with their fists, but that wasn't the only scuffle going on. At the elevators below, two residents were trying to stop the police from going up. The motorcycle gang disappeared, one resident was charged with assault, and both residents were taken by the police to 52 Division. Later, a Rochdale man "went out on the 17th floor terrace to walk his dog and found another bag of drugs, which was flushed with great ceremony down the toilet in full view of a number of respectable witnesses. We pause here for all you crankers to take a good deep breath."[35]

By May '69, a "Chicken-wire fence no-mans land" on the south side of the elevator lobby separated the public restaurant from the building — a futile but visible sign of Rochdale's skirmishes to find a border. Despite definite statements that "so and so" was accomplished, the definite actions disappeared in the indefinite movements of hundreds of young people following their own notions of what was in and out, who belonged and what belonged to whom. Like the crashers, the visitors, and the drugs, the bikers would return again and again.

But the bikers too would change — and be changed by — Rochdale, itself a changeling constantly changing. When Dennis Lee outlined a territory he called "liberal," he didn't reckon on the wider ranges of "free" and its wider powers. "Use that word 'free,'" Lee said in December '68, looking at the buzzword that was cutting his ideal down, "and it triggers off an extraordinary number of reactions in people's heads...I find people who don't live here wandering down the halls, banging on people's doors, wanting to know where the action is."[36] Where the action is — and freedom. "This cat who lived in a communal house in Buffalo said where he lived before freedom was a little kit who came up and licked you on the cheek and then ran away. In Rochdale, freedom was a tiger that jumped out at you and would maul you to death if you didn't learn how to grapple with it."[37]

PART TWO:

THE TYGER
BURNING BRIGHT

6

Pass/Fail

The changeling on Bloor Street inherited a changed kind of learning
that was not easily fitted into Dennis Lee's "liberal education." The
academy being established seemed to have more to do with encounter
groups and therapy than with seminars. "Although one should know
his material and respect it," went the wisdom, "he does not study the
subject matter for itself. Rather it is used as a central reference point,
creating a common language in which students can relate their experiences and thus find out more about each other."[1] It was predicted
that "[in the Seventies] more liberals will leave the university and set
up person-centered (as opposed to book-centered) post-secondary
schools with names like Gestalt, Explore, Growplace, Mellow Yellow,
Zonk, and Groove. Rochdale will be considered a brave but somewhat
[lame] forerunner."[2] One leader was challenged during a seminar
for "trying to convey information...but information is a put-on; it
doesn't exist by itself...What are you trying to communicate, Ted,
information, this intellectual game thing, or your commitment to
it?...You seem tense and hung up and want us to accept it...What
do you feel?"[3]

In its first year, Rochdale College continually tried to conduct
its original mission, the perfecting of a liberal education, but under

the scrutiny of encounter groups, a disinterested pursuit of knowledge became difficult; if a truck carried intellectual cargo, it met so many weighing stations that it seldom arrived. In addition, the mindgames of these therapy seminars found a graduate form — as the mindgames that drugs promoted. A person involved in a mindgame continually assessed the other people playing, estimating motives and assumptions, trying to outwit, strip bare, defend, defend the defending, defend the attacking. In its competitive form, winning such a game — "blowing a mind" — was equivalent to winning a hand in a cardgame. In its benevolent form, as a kind of non-academic education, a mindgame uncovered mental foundations for the sake of rebuilding upon them. In both forms, however, the mindgame was neither liberally disinterested nor academic.

As the academy mingled with the street, Rochdale tested numerous projects and — just as continually — discarded them. The projects were more para-academic than academic, and when they failed to open shortly after jumping into view, those falls too were called education.

In some cases, the projects failed by trying to probe the inexpressible by means that the new Rochdalians considered unpronounceable. As a resource person in October '68, Brewster Kneen offered a Center for the Study of Institutions and Theology. "The methodology of the Center's work is dialectical, that is, it is based on the assumption that social analysis radically engaged in must lead to existential questioning and a conscious understanding of the operative assumptions of the political, social, and economic consequences of personal faith."[4] Courses would include "Dialectics, Marxist and Biblical...Authority and Power, Biblical and Contemporary...Taxation...Futurology: How do we think about the future? This should include consideration of Eschatology and the Kingdom of Gor [God], cybernetics, political process, and social change." Imagine all that in the living room of the best party you've ever found.

In November '68, the Utopian Research Foundation announced plans to "organize a structured, systematic, physical, chemical, biological, cosmological, and technological investigation laboratory" with experiments in "light, sound, magnetic, and thought vibrations...aerodynamics...biological reaction to stimuli...perpetual motion...saucer vehicles...profitable inventions."[5] December '68 saw the arrival of the Barry Luger Institute for Silent Studies (B.L.I.S.S.): "nine p.m. until four a.m. or thereabouts...come and say *nothing*... Come with a book, or your mind for meditation. Leave your tongue outside. It will not be needed. Coffee will be served so that you'll have something to do with your mouth."[6]

At all times, Rochdale disdained traditional education. At one point, a seminar was held on education models and on the university as job-training; it called its topic "Edu-catering."[7] In place of meat and potatoes, Rochdale tried for more colorful meals. Seminars offered during one week in February '69 included a Magicians' Workshop, Primitive Religion, Yoga, Ceramics, Confucius, Sculpture, Revolution, Chess, Cooking, Jungian Psychology, and the weekly session of the Thomas More Institute, a French organization based in Montreal. In March, one week offered Flying Saucers, *Summerhill* (the film), a Touchie Feelie forum, History (of Atlantis), and the Serial Poem, while another week brought History of Jazz, Folk and Pop Songwriting, Judaism and Religious Existentialism, Laser Rap, and Social Journalism.

A floor plan issued in March '69 showed—in addition to useful landmarks such as the KWOP Shop (a co-operative store) and the "Bureaucracy" in "The LBJ Suite" (with secretary Linda, general manager Bernie, and registrar Jack)—locations for seminars by Victor Coleman (The Serial Poem) and Jim Garrard (drama workshop). In April '69, the Thomas More Institute was thanked "for letting us try our high school French and for treating us as equals."[8]

Reaction to these projects was mixed. One anonymous student testified that "my Ideas are tested through constant conversation with fellow Rochdalians who tell me when I'm full of shit and correct me."[9] On the other hand, a Ryerson journalism student criticized Rochdale education as "lousy—people decide what they want to study and then get a group together to form a seminar. They only study what they agree with, they never meet opposing views, and education degenerates into nothing more than the reinforcement of what they already think and believe."[10] Another resident agreed. "Unstructured situations with resource persons are not necessarily educational and are often boring. They inevitably degenerate to sensitivity sessions or group therapy."[11]

Some thirty seminars died in the first four months of the high-rise College, and fifteen survived into the fifth month. By March '69, it was clear that "the average life-expectancy for the formal seminar [is] 6–8 weeks. Average attendance for the more enduring ones: 6–8 persons. Workshops, projects, formal and informal tutorials throw up brief structures faster than the mind can boggle."[12]

The formal projects died of poverty if principle or apathy didn't get them first. A budget existed, to be sure. One budget drawn up in February '69 shows salaries of $832 a month to Ian MacKenzie, $500 a month to Dennis Lee, and $320 a month to R. Bennett. But much of the coordinating and fundraising depended on individuals who, like any mortals, were unequal to the task. When potter Bruce MacArthur wanted to set up a ceramics workshop, Rochdale offered him $500 to teach a course and $250 to help set up the workshop. "Unfortunately," said an account in the *Varsity*, "[the] lavish promises were based on a $10,000 budget, $5,000 of which was obtained by over-drawing a bank account, and $5,000 of which was to come from a non-existent fund-raising project."[13] MacArthur set up the workshop on his own, left it open around the clock, and paid for materials himself. However, "freaks and dabblers continually came in to 'play,' wrecked valuable equipment and left the place in constant need of cleaning." Locking the door and charging twenty-five cents per pound of clay helped control the dabbling, but in the second winter, MacArthur pulled his workshop out of Rochdale.

Another victim of poverty — though the pulling out took longer — was an organization that came to Rochdale fully formed. The Institute for Indian Studies had already operated for six years before it moved to the seventeenth floor of Rochdale in the fall of 1968. Leader Wilf Pelletier, according to Jim Garrard, was "a strong influence" on the early Rochdale; "a profound, or profound-seeming Indian in a community that was trying to live more in the way they imagined native people had previously lived." The *Globe* called Pelletier "one of Canada's major Indian philosophers." [14]

In the summer before the highrise opened, Wilf Pelletier received only two applications for the new premises. "Indians deal in reality," he explained. "They couldn't apply to a building that didn't exist." [15] Then, after the opening, the Indian Institute conducted a quiet kind of activism. It lobbied for native rights and, as a "folk school" to study and teach native languages, history, and cultures, it made contacts with the Pan-Indian movement in North and South America. With the help of Rochdale, it also provided a home for its students. By December, the Institute had twenty students and four resource persons, including Pelletier. At least three of its members were being assisted financially by the Institute. Members sold literature, received donations, and shared with other members. The Institute sent out invitations to an orientation session for "immigrants to North America since 1492," [16] and Pelletier explained Indigenous attitudes in interviews. "Poverty to an Indian is not lack of material wealth, but not sharing; not giving is poverty to Indians." "An Indian child is never rejected at any time...Even if a child is dirty, he is not rejected because he is dirty; he is handled — dirty or not. The dirt is rejected, not the child." [17]

The Institute, however, had bills to pay and, over a period of two years, Rochdale questioned whether it could afford to have the child, dirty or not. When the issue came to a climax, a governing council member argued for continuing support. In 1967, he said, the Indian Institute passed on a $2,500 grant to the Rochdale education fund. "This goes against an accumulated loss of about $3,000 to Rochdale over the last two years."[18] The council was not convinced. "Rochdale was being bled dry by them," says Jim Garrard, "because of some agreement signed prior to the opening of the building... we didn't benefit from having the Institute there because they were just too damned expensive given the amount of educational revenue available." As a one-time fundraiser, Garrard was particularly annoyed by the "fabulous contracts" that two of the Institute members had. "We found that it was in their contract to get six months severance pay!"

Rochdale reduced funding for the Indian Institute from a requested $1,240 to $400. Pelletier refused to take the smaller amount, protesting that the decision was made by people who knew nothing of the project. "I think the majority of people here basically believe in the theory of no structure but in practice it doesn't turn out that way. The way they handed out money for their education programs was just how government agencies have given out money in the past."[19]

And so another early leader of Rochdale pulled out (or was pushed), joining an exodus that was so overwhelmed by people both coming and going that the refugees couldn't be told apart from the movers. After four months in the full-scale realization of his dream, Dennis Lee complained that the "atmosphere at Rochdale [is]... dominated by those of us who are stagnating, or going zombie, or getting trapped in a self-hating round of petty squawking and 'forbidden' indulgences (what a bore *they* are!)... anything but mediocrity and compulsiveness is discouraged... A minority with fairly desperate emotional needs... ties us into a syndrome of crisis/letdown which frustrates all the slower and more organic processes of education."[20]

The street people and the academics distrusted each other so consistently that one resident developed a theory he called a "culture of poverty." By this theory, "to say 'I have the answer, here's what Rochdale needs,' is to say 'I am a benevolent rich man.'"[21] Thus, whenever the academics made suggestions, they promoted a culture that placed affluence over poverty. Unfortunately for leaders like Dennis Lee, a leader would disqualify himself by having leadership to give.

Disagreements between student and street led to charge and counter-charge. The unruly, non-student Rochdale members, said one student, "graft themselves onto this student residence as a sycophantic freak show."[22] On the other side, one governing council president maintained that "Rochdale people are paying their rent. It's the straight people who aren't paying. University of Toronto, Ryerson, and Ontario College of Art students think we owe them a place to stay."[23] By April '69, the anti-academics were winning. "[U of T students] have been slandered, jeered, avoided, ridiculed, gypped, and generally stepped upon," complained one such student in the *Daily*. "Now Rochdale has adopted a membership policy not-too-subtly geared toward the weeding-out of undesirable elements from U of T."[24]

One element from U of T — Dennis Lee — weeded himself out. Contrasting the community around him with his vision, he must have remembered the discomfort and suspicion that hadn't come fast enough and hard enough to take counter-measures. In May '67, before even the Rochdale Houses had begun, he had argued that the proposed Rochdale should include people with specific interests, people who were joining Rochdale for reasons other than community. "The emphasis has suddenly shifted in these talks from education (very widely conceived) to a kind of total community with educational aspects. Again, this disturbs me...that change would almost certainly involve the chosen few legislating it on behalf of the ignorant many...the whole thing smacks of armchair community."[25]

In the first winter of the highrise, Lee realized that Rochdale should try again with less ambition. He proposed that the number of fulltime members be decreased in 1969–70 to no more than 100, with the rest of the residents either studying elsewhere or working. This would "[cut] back drastically on the therapy/Yorkville-social-agency aspect of Rochdale."[26] A frequent critic at the public meetings in the College, pipe-smoking and stern, Lee "started to seem like a tiresome adult to most of the people" according to Jim Garrard.

A rift had developed between the chosen few and the changeling, the collective many who had other ideas for Rochdale. Lee's withdrawal from the College came in stages, and after one stage, Victor Coleman responded in May '69 with an "Apolitical Manifesto:" "The come-back of Dennis Lee signals a re-birth of public apologies. Everything must, in his terms, have its explanation. Just about every piece of publicity Rochdale has received has had some statement from Dennis in it. I sincerely doubt that we need such an apologist."[27]

Lee submitted his notice of resignation for May 31, 1969. Rochdale had become "an institution I can no longer live with."[28] Like others of the "groomed people who fled early on," Lee resigned "not by choice, but to preserve myself. I just couldn't spread myself as thin as the situation was forcing me to."[29] Ironically, in the nine months of his stay in the tower, Lee had found the problem was not one in which the chosen few were legislating an armchair community—but the opposite. No one, few or chosen, could legislate the community, and armchairs were as foreign to the "ignorant many" as tobacco pipes.

Also ironically, Lee left just before one of Rochdale's most successful—and educational—ventures. All the failing of formal education projects had another side: the passing-on of old projects stimulated the passing-around of new ones. That which was not busy dying, almost as Bob Dylan expressed it on educational stereo, was busy being born.

The Summer Festival of July '69 succeeded in blending the formal and informal in a way that seemed to vindicate Rochdale's approach. This most successful project relied heavily on the organizational abilities of Judith Merril, author of *Shadow on the Hearth, The Tomorrow People, Out of Bounds*, editor of anthologies, reviewer for *Fantasy and Science Fiction* magazine, grandmother — and Rochdale resident. In January, Merril had chaired a "Space Workshop," a group formed to decide who used which space in the building. When the workshop had gone down the chute like many Rochdale organizations, Merril turned her energies towards a project that became steadily more ambitious. Planning began with a two-day library-opening in mind, and expanded into a two-week Summer Festival, a celebration of the U.S. moon launch and landing.

Billed as an "Inner Space Odyssey," the Festival combined science fiction, drugs, art, and miscellany. A "Spaced-Out Library" opened with 10,000 titles; the Art Gallery advertised an "Art Exhibition, Total Environment, Surprise Room — bring your head"; a drug symposium featured a talk by "our resident biochemist-drug researcher"; the University of Toronto Astronomy Department sponsored a "See-Out," a moon watch with telescopes; Ed Apt's sculpture group did a "weld-up" of The Competition on the patio, and followed with the "unhatching of Brock Fricker's Giant Toad"; Richard Needham talked on education; Rochdale resource person Eliot Rose talked on "Witchcraft, Then and Now"; Bill King ran a pornography seminar limited to age eighteen and over; and Judy Merril moved through it all as resident science fiction expert. Adding to the choices, the Mariposa Folk Festival brought into Toronto at the same time big names such as Joan Baez, Ian and Sylvia, and Joni Mitchell.

The Summer Festival reached a high-water mark for Rochdale, and then, in the ad hoc fashion valued by Rochdale, the organizers shed their organization once again in search of the education that would be right for Rochdale College.

7

Govcon

The ideal of education had been mixed from the start with an ideal of co-operation, self-government for mutual benefit. The resident-owners had been provided with a charter that specified a governing council elected at annual general meetings, and included all the usual by-laws approved by parliamentary practice.

The first elected governing council, or Govcon, took shape during the pre-ordained November '68 General Meeting. But what shape was the shape of the new ideal? What symmetry would frame the Open, the free? The new idealists wanted, not a proven co-operative structure, but an experimental non-structure — self-rule by natural, anarchistic consensus, with leaders emerging on an ad hoc basis. Government would be horizontal, among equals, rather than vertical, the old form by which leaders are separated from the led as a higher, smaller class.

In this first General Meeting, "the chairman, who volunteered to be chairman, said he could not be a chairman in the conventional sense, that the council could not be called a council, that it could not (even though elected representatively) make decisions binding upon all members of the college."[1]

Then, in the first meeting of the newly elected council a few days later, more than the elected councillors attended — and everyone elected themselves to every executive position. "All 32 of the 12 places on that august body were filled...the only casualty was the nomination of the white cat who is at the moment the only official floor representative in the building. It was understood that the cat could not be elected as it was not present at the meeting."[2]

At the same time, the *Daily* printed an attack on General Manager Bernie Bomers, who has been described elsewhere as "a taciturn, 26-year-old cigar smoker with brown hair, long sideburns, and a puffy Victorian mustache."[3] The *Daily* charged that "Bomers is essentially a Bank Clerk because of how he wants to order his world. Anyone that upsets his order is upsetting him...The only way to make this system work is the complete separation of the independent parts so that at least they do not interfere destructively with each other...In short, the freaks are getting up the noses of the straight people and vice versa. Yet there is one other way that is dysfunctional for a while, but in the long run beneficial. This is to completely freak everybody out of their established habit and conceptual stances to such an extent that any way of putting them back together again would involve us as a whole community."[4]

A "Creed for Head Meetings" proposed a kind of parliamentary zen: "meetings are rivers / don't build dams / *Beware of Structure Freaks / Beware of Rules / Beware of 'At the Last Meeting We Decided' / Don't Go Back — There was No Last Meeting / Don't Go Forward — There Is Nothing.*"[5] "'Unstrictured' [sic] means no useless rules. You rule yourself, in your own way."[6]

Another move against structure in the meetings came from resident Mike Donaghy: "Rochdale is essentially family and should be kept informal wherever possible. Spontaneous conversation should be desired and the chairman should interject only to assist and not to stunt. The inflexibility of the closed-mouth hands-up speaking policy was shown when those who adhere to it decided to physically remove those who do not."[7] Paul Evitts agreed and wanted to have the open council meetings "operate by consensus. This means no votes."

No past, no rules, no votes — and no definitions. One meeting objected to planning for the 1969 Summer Festival. There should be less planning so that "the THING which we are creating... be not casually allowed to jell into something, to be labelled and hence defined, not even for the summer months, not even for the sake of saving our economic asses."[8]

All of this "no-ing" made Rochdale's internal politics unusually loose, so loose that council meetings from any period of Rochdale reveal the same timelessness. One of the last governing councils was "elected" from the names of anyone interested. "When all names were in, [two children] grabbed 13 names out of the hat... The meeting was adjourned because there was too much noise to continue and quorum was lost... dingaling..."[9] The *Daily* defended this example of democracy *in extremis*. As "equal worth" members, "any 13 of us working together have the capability of keeping the college going."[10]

Adding to the confusion, the official governing council was only one of a mixture of voices speaking on behalf of a changing mixture of groups. "The council governs," *Change* magazine decided, "only insofar as those who happen to learn of its legislation happen to agree with it."[11] Other voices would arise on temporary issues, and others would represent the communes, the *Daily*, the education council — or the dealers. The case of dealer Syd Stern illustrates the politics that paralleled the activities of Govcon.

"Huge numbers of us tried to throw [Syd] out for years," as Alex MacDonald, member of the Evictions Board, tells it. "It never worked. Evicting Syd was a political issue. The bureaucratic equivalent of impeaching Govcon was evicting Syd... When Syd came to the building, his first act was to attempt to overthrow the governing council. Syd was the elder statesman of the anti-establishment." Stern entered Rochdale politics during one of the attempts to stop drug dealing with outsiders. "Syd, in opposition to this treasonous policy, decided he was going to move into the second-floor lounge and go on a hunger strike until Govcon was impeached. Well, Govcon was never impeached and Syd never went on a hunger strike, but he also never moved out of the lounge. From June '71 up until the Christmas–New Year's season there was a party that just sort of continued with Syd presiding. It was very different from the previous dealing season. Syd made his friends, he made his connections, and he looked after kids. These goofs would come in and Syd would take care of them. It was a much more humanistic kind of thing. Syd was as much a part of the bureaucracy as I was, to the extent that he was a representative of a particular community. He was the principal spokesman for an otherwise inarticulate group of yoyos. But they had to be represented."

"From the day the building opened," says MacDonald, "nobody controlled it. There was no force that could arbitrarily make decisions that swept over the whole population. The place was a democracy; the original franchise was awarded to everybody who showed up; and the original population was very largely random." In 1969, only 100 out of 800 residents were College members. "For the vast majority of the people living in Rochdale, the council and its activities were of little or no interest," according to Kent Gooderham. [12] "Rochdale membership was not THE method of creating community."

Some residents wanted to revert to mainstream structure as a way of creating government that was effective as well as democratic, but structure needed some way of separating members from non-members, and then ranking the members. Thus, a battle continued between those who wanted council meetings and decisions open to all, including non-residents, and those who argued for closed meetings with elected representatives. Both factions were obstinate. The "missionary-type rebels" who wanted structure "are not expelled but their ideas are ignored." [13] Conversely, when "Jerry Rubin came to Rochdale and talked of a free society without laws, he was laughed at," according to *Image Nation,* since "Rochdale was opened without laws and suddenly it was discovered that laws, good laws, are always necessary." [14]

At one point, Govcon tried conducting two types of meeting, one open but with no vote, the other closed with only council members voting. Current chairman Byron Wall would interpret policy with General Manager Bernie Bomers. "That may seem arbitrary to some, but that's the way we are set up." [15] The tough tone accomplished no more than a dulcet one. One early council meeting lasted five hours and had a hundred people come and go. There was "a non-stop parade of 'points of order, Mr. Chairman,' and mini-debates over who had been recognized by the chairman as the next speaker — though it wasn't always clear who the chairman was." [16] No decisions were made, and those who protested indecisiveness did so indecisively. Jack Dimond, for example, announced his resignation, then said later that he wasn't really resigning, he was just expressing his frustration.

Sculptor Ed Apt described the council meetings as a washing machine. "Whenever the 'laundry' of Rochdale is to be done, stuff the machine, turn it on, and let it do its thing." [17] However, after one meeting was "invaded" by the public and opened to all for voting, council turned into "a washmachine standing still with its hatch wide open through which many hands reach in washing the laundry." During this meeting, said Apt, sitting on the floor became significant. "I'm not kidding you, the main thing was not what you said it was where you were sitting... Then came the real thing, the structure phobia in which we first stopped voting and next were told by the chairman that there is no such thing as council."

A sketchy government attracted a sketchy "civil service." The secretary to Govcon commented in a job description that "filing is vague at the moment but a mental record is kept as to what has been filed and what has not and why not." [18] Her job involved "complying with or objecting to the whims of 12 constantly changing councillors who each think they have just acquired the services of a personal, private secretary."

Constantly changing, yes. Rochdale suffered from a continuous turnover in both its leaders and their constituents. *Change* magazine reported that "the turnover has vitiated Rochdale in two ways, by downgrading its population [the average age and level of education was dropping] and by robbing it of an effective collective memory, thereby lowering the level of intellectual exchange that does occur and stretching out the period Rochdalers require to arrive at a consensus on major problems." [19]

"At regular intervals, every few months," says former resident Sharon Kingsland, "there would be a new group on council that felt you had to get rid of the old to get the new. Like the American political model, they would claim that their predecessors were no good at all. It was a touch exaggerated, but you could see that it was part of their growing up. How could you be angry with someone like little Scotty?" During 1969 alone, five governing councils passed through the offices and out the other side. "It was like living through a bloodless French revolution, with an endless number of regimes in charge." [20] One set of former leaders was denounced by the *Daily* as "the old Jones-Bradford-Garrard-Pelletier clique" against whom the Publications Office was launching "a major offensive." [21]

Resignations happened more often than elections and appointments, and all were frequent. Registrar Jack Dimond, for example, resigned at least twice. When he and fellow leaders Byron Wall and Paul Evitts resigned in March '69, who could tell who was serious? Byron Wall moved on, but Dimond and Evitts stayed to fight each other in the summer.

Government with no structure had many risks to run. One *Daily* reported that "last night's council degenerated into a cock-pit for flights of hostility. We say things when we're stoned or agitated that should either remain unsaid or, better yet, be published." [22] In a later

General Meeting, in addition to six cases of beer and three gallons of wine supplied by Rochdale, residents brought their own. "The excess proved unnecessary to oil the wheels of progress, instead it rather stopped them dead... Eighty percent of the audience sat comatose in the back of the room... various bad melodramas were enacted in the front of the room... unfortunately, the actors were playing themselves." [23] The meeting was rescheduled.

An intended cradle of democracy, Rochdale once again found the cradle robbed, and in the place of government, the perplexed parents found something that looked like theatre. The actors in this theatre seemed to switch between frustration that the play did too little work, and delight that they were no more theatrically absurd — and more aware of it — than the governments in the outside world. And if nothing was getting done, what of it? The work ethic is too much with us anyway; live for today.

"The council meetings were a lot of fun," says a former resident, "since there you got the bright people. No one had high expectations of achieving anything, so they made sure they enjoyed it." Meetings would be brightened by irreverent gags ("Does anyone know why policemen have bigger balls than firemen? They sell more tickets") and irrelevant motions ("that Lionel Douglas be allowed to look in the Province of Ontario for whatever he can find," defeated). [24] "Mike Donaghy was a particular star," one observer remembers. "He had a gift for monologues, stream of consciousness stuff but always to the point. He would come down from the back during Govcon meetings as different characters, say crouched over like an old man with his hand out, gazing prophetically into the distance and saying, 'The invasion of the moon is coming, and they have chosen Rochdale.' A little bit later, the same thing, the crouch, the hand out, but he didn't say a thing. Everyone laughed and applauded; it was the only time he had ever been silent. Mike was very wrapped up in an image of himself as Irish — golden tongue, black heart."

The risks to a meeting could come from any direction. During another General Meeting, serious discussion ended when "a chant of OM began in one part of the room, soon spread out, a reverberation of Moody Blues that pre-empted the legal boggle." [25] One floor meeting recorded in the *Daily* had similar interference. "We had a meeting on the 15th; no sooner was the matter of maintaining the ashram lounge brought than Guess Who starts with 'let's have an orgy...let's love...let's fuck...I love you all...you're all beautiful people.' The voice of a guy trying to keep to the subject was drowned out by Steppenwolf. I left." [26]

In addition, some council members liberally used the drugs that softened their constituents, according to resident psychiatrist Dr. Bryn Waern. "Marijuana was standard," and as she says, "marijuana does not promote efficient administration or focused processing of problems, but long, rambling, tangential dialogue and boring, inefficient meetings."

The victims of all this were the decisions that needed to be made. When Dennis Lee charged in May '69 that the council was incompetent, it was too early to see that all the councils would share the same problems. Lee complained that the council "takes months to come to non-decisions on matters that demand decisions in a week, administering purity tests to niggling details while the college falls to pieces around them...This council is capable of the Great Debate, and now of the Great Gesture, but when it comes to calm assessment of where we are and trudging, unglamorous man-hours of work to get somewhere else, it is a non-starter." [27]

Another resident protested that "I got the impression of a lot of people talking without having much to say, just talking for the sake of hearing themselves talk. So many people reinforcing their own ideas, sort of like a cheerleading section." [28] *Change* magazine reported that "Rochdale's governing councils have oscillated between stalemate and issuing unrealistic *diktats*." [29]

In reaction, a short-lived group named The Rochdale Bubble-gum Company announced a decision to install a bubblegum machine with "yes" and "no" gumballs. "One cent. Four decisions. Soon will become indispensable for decision making at Rochdale... All members issued fifty-one per cent of stock, EACH."[30] Sir Basil Nardley-Stoades, mock editor of the *Daily Planet,* had his own version of Govcon's problem: "After careful analysis of the content of the speeches of the Council meeting last night, brought to me by a team of perspiring idiot savants, it was discovered that this was a repeat of the last General Meeting, played backwards. This would lead me to suspect that we are becoming the victims of that most deadly of modern diseases — industrial espionage."[31]

Or, as council member Bill King expressed it for the *Daily*: "The answers to your questions are yes, no, yes, yes, no, no, and yes. But not necessarily in that order."[32]

8

Dismanagement

As Govcon fiddled, the problems of freedom kept burning brighter. This highrise shelter for self-government had a mess on its hands, but more importantly, it had a scapegoat. We are not truly independent, it could say. Rochdale College had been brought forth from its Campus Co-op parent, yes, but with a cord attached. The cord that bound, and bound poorly, was an external management.

After the building had been opened through the development work of Co-op College, Campus Co-op tried to protect its investment in Rochdale and its share of the student market — in an "increasingly ineffective manner," according to Howard Adelman — by means of yet another organization, the Toronto Student Management Corporation.[1] If you, the reader, have trouble sorting out Campus Co-op, CCRI (Co-op College), and TSMC (Toronto Student Management), so did the Rochdalians.

In early 1968, the Toronto Student Management Corporation took over administration of both Campus Co-op and Rochdale. Of the eight directors, four came from Rochdale — but Co-op College appointed members of Rochdale's board in order to give Campus Co-op control of Rochdale (it got complicated). Suspicion about the arrangement arose before the highrise even opened. TSMC was, for a start, not a co-op at all, but a limited company. A TSMC spokesman acknowledged the "considerable fear by those deeply associated with Rochdale College that Management will snuff out the freedom and experimental character" of the college, but he warned about the responsibilities of a $6 million building. "When Rochdale College accepts the Rochdale structure from the Developer, it is a liability and not an asset that is being received. If only one of the expense items...gets out of line, it could mean a critical financial position, which may or may not be recoverable."[2]

Apt words from an organization that had no highrise experience. The "Toronto Student Mismanagement Corporation," as it came to be known within the college, launched into the handling of rentals and maintenance as though Rochdale were a Campus Co-op house — and the system "almost immediately" broke down.

Problems were multiplied by an uneasy mix of co-op expectations and management. Not only was the new college residence difficult to manage, it was also to a large extent unco-operative. The population came and went too quickly, and the work ethic had reached a new low. The cleaning crew, for one, tried "a rather unsuccessful work arrangement where residents would do a job in return for a meal ticket. If the fellow who was cleaning the 14th floor happened to catch a lunch with a friend, the cleaning crew was minus one worker."[3]

Some of the chaos came from repeated failures to set up methods of membership. How could a co-op survive if the people in it couldn't be sure they were members, or if they were, what they should do as members? An enrolment policy of the Rochdale Houses stated that "we feel that objective criteria cannot be set for entrance into Rochdale. However, every member of Rochdale will be urged to meet immediately after notification of acceptance with one member of the admissions committee to discuss the implications of membership in Rochdale."[4]

In the highrise, the implications became fierce. The issue of who was Inside and who was Outside was troubling the front door, and disrupted the attempts at self-government. Now the terms of belonging itself needed to be clarified. Just how could the realization of a dream of co-operation become co-operative?

An Admissions Policy Workshop considered the problem in detail. The policy-makers were as high-powered as the stirred-around levels of power allowed, and included college chairman Byron Wall, plus governing council members Nelson Adams, Ray Bennett, and Judy Merril. The workshop felt that the "real basis of Rochdale is Membership, not Residentship."[5] They wanted "more distinctions between members and non-members, and less between resident and non-resident members."[6] Applicants would have to do something in addition to paying the twenty-five dollars that, at that point, bought a Rochdale membership. One proposal would have had applicants write an essay or submit a work in any medium. Judy Merril published a "Grannygrunt" in the *Daily Planet* calling for a rent requirement to be paid by all residents: two hours a week manning a Communications Center, a Hospitality and game room, and a library, all twenty-four-hour. By spring, the proposals had developed into a formula: ten dollars plus ten hours plus a combination of dollars and hours to a total of sixty-five. "The new fee is higher, but you can get in cheaper. What you can't do is get in without noticing."[7] All residents would have to become members.

The Admissions Workshop prepared a course catalog in March '69 despite two interruptions — one by Jack Dimond when he wanted to personally add a $200 tuition for non-students, and the other at Coach House Press in order to delete a phrase considered improper in a catalog ("the great mindfuck-mindfuck").[8] Now membership required seventy-five dollars or seventy-five hours, or any combination of the two, plus acceptance by a Membership Committee or by at least five Rochdale members. Nelson Adams, a twenty-six-year-old New Brunswicker, was given fifty-five dollars a week as a screener of new members.

All the policies proposed were highly detailed and theoretical. In the face of the brute problem of visitors and crashers, and the repeated no-shows by workers, those policies became so much knitting in the front lines. Even so, the attempts at defining and enforcing membership continued sporadically. In December '69 membership activities included "putting up Stop Spadina posters...manning the phone for Red, White, and Black [a self-help draft-dodger group]... sleeping with the Rental Manager." [9] Of the seventy-eight repliers to a 1971 survey, 13 percent were active in the Rochdale community, 35 percent were active in the educational programs, and 48 percent were Rochdale members. By 1972, the criteria for membership had become sixty-five hours or dollars in any combination. "Generally, any activity which is Rochdale-oriented rather than self-oriented counts as hours. Paid work doesn't count. Cleaning up after yourself doesn't count. Cleaning up after someone else counts." [10] In July '74, 174 people were claimed as Rochdale members, each owing sixty-five hours of work to the community.

The Rochdale spokesman did not say how many of those hours were worked as well as owed. Throughout its lifespan, many members assumed that Rochdale the Residence could take care of itself while they attended whatever Rochdale the College had become.

But however unclear the co-op side of Rochdale remained with the rank-and-file members, the souls who were appointed as management in the first year were clearly being overwhelmed by the unmanageable. The College had employed a General Manager at $10,000 a year, but how could he or anyone else manage? Breakdown itself was General. Rochdale later confirmed that "no accounting records, or records of any kind, were kept. Money disappeared." [11] According to another report prepared by Rochdale, one fundraiser overspent his $25,000 education budget by $6,000 and was unable to raise any funds at all. He was also expected to start an admissions system, but none survived during the first four months. That particular official was worn out by November. "I came here to hear what people were saying behind their words. Now I hear what they are saying behind their words and I get angry. I guess because I'm pretty tired most of the time."[12] He left behind confusions and accusations of being a "power freak".

The average age in the rental department was seventeen. One photograph shows the distractions faced by this inexperienced bureaucracy: pictured is a bare room with a blackboard displaying the phrases "room allocation," "rent collection," and "death to the mini." Sarah Spinks reported that "nearly everyone had negotiated an individual rental policy. And no record existed of all these exceptions. So when the rental manager left for a farm in B.C., the whole office was to be thrown into chaos."[13]

As the time neared for the first General Meeting of Rochdale members in November '68, efforts at organizing appeared throughout the building. The parking garage attempted "official permanent private-style parking spaces" with keys to the garage door and official simulated plastic parking permit stickers ("no parts to assemble").[14] Jack Dimond exhorted members about ID cards. One group felt "the dawn of a new era: organization has set in. The rental bureau to be established will be open on specified days between specified hours." In the excitement before the opening of this new play, "The General Meeting", all of these efforts ran about excitedly — but though the meeting opened, it never reached a final act.

Mismanagement and the absence of any management — which could be termed dismanagement — became most visible in the services Rochdale was expected to deliver. In one case, in order to arrange door-to-door postal service, Rochdale promoted a complex scheme designating east-wing "hotel" units using numbers and west-wing "apartments" using letters in their addresses. The identifying tags were painted on the doors with "absurd enormous packing-crate stencils."[15] But it was not to be. "Enter another man from the post-office, *the* man, so to speak, who is perhaps a little unhappy that we cleverly contrived to call ourselves an apartment-hotel, and *he* says: mail will be delivered to apartment addresses consisting of numbers only (no letters) and the numbers on the doors must be raised and attached with screws or something. And we couldn't cheer him up. No way." Rochdale had to settle for a mail-drop in the lobby.

In no other area was a breakdown in services more apparent than in the cafeteria. In that first year, rent could include all meals except Sunday dinner, and Kafka residents were required to buy the $45/month meal tickets. However, for the first two months of its existence the College provided 600 TV dinners a day because the cafeteria wasn't finished. Almost 41,000 TV dinners were consumed before the kitchens opened. Then, as part of the general shape-up tried in preparation for the General Meeting, meal tickets were introduced for the cafeteria. The cafeteria kitchen was expected to turn a $4,000 profit each month while supplying a restaurant and two dining halls. Instead, the food operation lost $2,000 a month and by the spring of '69, had overspent its budget by $13,000.

Fault for the loss had to be shared among poor freeloaders, poor design, and poor management. A resident asked in the *Daily*, "why should we run out of all too infrequent desserts before we run out of all too FREQUENT TV dinners?...eating an entire meal with only a soup spoon, however challenging, soon loses its thrill. Having to use a juice glass for coffee is not our idea of fun!"[16] The cafeteria often ran out of eggs, and the two days' worth of milk that would be delivered at one time was too much for the size of the refrigerator and had to be taken to each floor. Morale didn't improve when, by September '69, residents considered that "the restaurant and cafeteria had been franchised to an outfit that had little experience and produced the most sterile food imaginable, while down the street one of Toronto's newest and most imaginative restaurants, Meat & Potatoes, was started by former Rochdalers."[17]

Most of the blame landed on the freeloaders, however. Unpaid-for meals and meal ticket fraud ascribed to the transients caused chaos. "Rents are inclusive, so residents don't pay. Neither did the gate-crashers."[18] Various methods were tried to enforce the meal tickets. "The manager finally appointed a crasher as cafeteria custodian. A woman of about 65, she sat at the door, asking for proof of residence. As payment, she ate free. She was the most efficient screener the cafeteria ever had, but residents objected on the grounds that it was a contradiction of the freedom on which the college is based. They took a consensus and fired the old girl. She stuck around freeloading for a week, then vanished. No one ever knew her name." By another report, the "little old lady...kept [the free-loaders] out, but she made life hell for us after the first couple of days."[19]

Some of the chaos facing the cafeteria can be glimpsed in the instructions put out in the *Daily* by two door-women: "Playing meter-maid is no fun but an unfortunate necessity here. The punching tickets regime is for you who...bear the cost of food being eaten by assholes who don't care (10%, by the way)...if you are a poor penniless waif you can work for a meal...you don't lend your ticket to a bunch of people when you go to Montreal, either...aw, come on — you don't eat that much — if you want to feed a friend, maybe we can have a week for it, meanwhile, don't sneak around getting double helpings... YOU DONT EAT WITHOUT A TICKET no matter who you are...you put me in an uncomfortable and embarrassing position when you expect me to let you thru because you are my friend. REALLY."[20] Despite such instructions, it was reported that the chef himself gave out tickets to those who said they needed them.

The best case of dismanagement in Rochdale, however, was supported by, fought against, or added to by every resident, alien, member, acquaintance, and manager of the College. It became an ever-present issue, one that challenged the root assumptions of Rochdale's middle-class surroundings, that alternately angered the residents and assured them that they had been set apart from the bland.

The issue was garbage. Filth. Most colleges never have to wrestle with crashers — and most will never struggle with filth. For those members who liked to be set apart, the mark of garbage was worn as proudly as a badge.

As a lowlife still-life that lasted from the start of the college to its finish, the scene at 341 Bloor Street can be painted with stains from any of its seven years. Take, for example, a 1971 *Daily* which reported that the most recent of many health inspections by the city found "vomitus in fire exit stairwell," "dog excretia on walls and floor," "the hallway littered with organic food stuff and dog bones (who's been eating dogs?)," "excretia in the bathtub (5th ashram)," and the "odour of decaying foodstuff in ashram kitchen." [21]

Was this just a bad day? One of the former workers on maintenance describes the continuing story: "Rochdale had a smell all its own. You avoided the stairwells, especially on the upper floors, or if you had to use them, you took a deep breath and dove. You know how we disposed of the garbage? Peyton and I dragged it from the garbage rooms, shovelled it into one of the public elevators co-opted for the purpose, took it to the bottom, and shovelled it out. A guy at the bottom would take it from there, but sometimes he didn't for several days so we'd just shove the whole mess away from the door. It was ghastly. The elevators would stink of foul disinfectant and garbage, or of pure garbage. Every time we finished, it was routine to check ourselves for fleas and lice and take a shower."

For a social and educational experiment, dirt of this magnitude adds grit to what could have been froth. From the days of the Rochdale Houses, Dennis Lee knew that ideals would be challenged in this way — though he had no inkling to what extent. "Freedom and openness," he said, "start to change their complexion when you're sitting in the middle of some crummy little room and you're free to clean it up or smell the previous occupant's socks for the next eight months." [22]

The topic of dirt received so much detailed attention that it qualifies as one of Rochdale's more permanent education programs. For the briefest moment, immediately after the opening of the highrise, pure and simple idealism was tried. "Let us always clean halls together smiling in the laughing dust of garbage-hauling parties." [23] All too soon, the "laughing dust" started laughing at the parties.

The mess began even before the College began. "We have notified the construction people," said an early *Daily*, "that we are sick and tired of carrying out the rubbish left by the sub-trades." [24] In a Report from Hades (the basement), Orpheus listed the "garbage, sand, lumber, heating pipe insulation, bottles, cardboard boxes and an amazingly wide assortment of other crap" left by the building contractors. [25] Rochdalians started to add to the garbage. Though the *Daily* called the pilers of the garbage "thoughtless," people on the upper floors had reasonable objections to carrying their garbage by hand to the ground floor. The garbage chute, like so much of the building, was not yet in service.

As the managers tried different arrangements of maintenance crews and volunteer labor, individual residents were expected to pitch in. A first attempt to coax came when a "Waxman" bin for garbage was placed outside at the back. "Waxman is large and red and friendly and guards your comings and goings at the back. But Waxman is very hungry and may get irritable (you would too if people left your food on the floor). But never fear! Our eviction evasion committee has discovered that he really grooves on leftovers a la cardboard or green plastic. Waxman is on our side. Boo fire inspector." [26] But even when the garbage chute became usable, many residents never made it past the "lobby stash," small storage rooms on each floor already jammed with garbage.

"The 210 Cleaners ask... do you really have to scuttle down the hall with your garbage clutched under your arm like a football full of heroin, dodging the white knight, dumping it into the lobby stash before you're caught in full embarrassment of public garbage contact?"[27]

The maintenance people tried promotions. They announced in the *Daily* "THE FIRST ROCHDALE HOME SHOW AT SOME TIME WITHOUT WARNING IN THE FUTURE. CLEANEST HOMES IN THE VARIOUS CATEGORIES RECEIVE A LIFETIME SUPPLY OF DETTOL OR CASH EQUIVALENT."[28] They tried humor: "Coming soon to an ashcan lounge near you, all the thrills and splendor of a shiny floor."[29]

They tried anger. The *Daily* published an open letter from a maintenance worker: "Yesterday on my day off I spent 15 hours working on the fucking elevators. Some asshole had left a firehose running in the basement, and five feet of water had accumulated in the bottom of the shafts. There was so much garbage in the shaft, the sump pump jammed. The shaft had been cleaned 3 weeks ago. Five feet of water floating with cigarette butts and paper cups from the cafeteria (how the hell do you guys squeeze stuff like that through the cracks?). The cleanup operation cost us (Rochdale) $115 for an auxiliary pump, plus elevator repairman hours for inspection and re-greasing so the cars don't corrode all to hell...I won't go on too much about shitspilling, window busting, wallscribbling, toiletcramming, but shit, let maintenance get on with cleaning and maintaining the place, not cleaning up after yer fucking messes. Remember, whatever goes down gotta come up."[30] Then they tried an ultimatum. To the "Dear People," Sunshine Maintenance announced that, "to save us, and you, the embarrassment of having [the health inspector] see dirty Ashrams and hallways, we will turn off the main electrical control panels of those entire wings he would not appreciate seeing."[31] However, the threat to leave them off until the wings were clean convinced no one. Cleaning itself needed light, if not sunshine.

Workers with "MAIN TEN ANTS" had to work like ants, and the toll on the psyche was hard to calculate. "Do you have a conception of how constant dogshit duty might affect a mind?" asked Peyton Brien. "I've cleaned up in excess of 120 heaps from the stairwells during the last eight weeks...It doesn't simply disappear after the two of you walk away."[32] Maintenance workers resembled front-line troops, here today and replaced tomorrow. One of the early heroes, namely someone surviving long enough to be recorded by name, was Tom Saask, who wrote after the first year: "When I in Sunshine Maintenance left (to turn alchemy, our frustration a vacuum, change, blessed be), it was partly to get out of the system of never being allowed to touch the people without the building."[33]

In 1970, the *Daily* announced that "the peace building, hippy haven, and Bloor Street monolith can now hang out its shingle as THE sanitary landfill site for Toronto."[34] Resource people were available for "cram courses in 'Stairwell Garbage Drop' and 'Urine Assimilation in Rugs,'" and a physical examination would be required for "Catshit Heave."

Rochdale took out a contract with an exterminator for weekly treatments against "bed bugs, roaches (cock-), and mice."[35] A year later, psychiatrist Lionel Solursh just had to ask in a survey: "who among you had a shower or bath daily?" A full 53.9 percent of the seventy-eight respondents did. Another 40.8 percent had a cleaning a few times a week. That leaves an unmentioned 5.3 percent in the dirt.[36]

One *Daily* calmly described a hall rug on the fifth floor that, "after soaking up dog shit and urine for lo these many years...was already a hazard to health and aesthetic sensibilities before the plumbing in the washroom gave way and left it submerged in dirty water for an extended period of time."[37] Bizarre complaints came from Maintenance: "we have found," they said, "chicken bones, bottle caps, pieces of wood, combs, and half a kitten in toilets in this building."[38]

The crasher problem had a new twist; in addition to the hundreds of humans, there were hundreds of pets. Some prescient person in the first month of Rochdale had written: *"Pets, Appliances, and Children:*

No restrictions have been made on any of these things. God help us." [39] Of the three, pets had by far the most impact. By January '69, a resident reported that the "red carpets stink from cat piss" and that dog and cat waste was decomposing the padding under the carpets. [40]

The uncleanliness caused by pets continued unchecked until 1972 when new policies were adopted. At the peak of the "pet fad", 30 percent of the residents had pets that were: 60 percent cats, 35 percent dogs, and 5 percent "turtles (large ones), snakes, guinea pigs, and indeterminate." [41] Other pets included trout, tadpoles, pigs, monkeys, and rabbits. The College heard but didn't act on a solution for 35 percent of the problem — the construction of a dog toilet attached to the building.

Not only did Rochdalians have pet dogs, they had exotic dogs and a room that could only be described as a crude kennel. When the Toronto Humane Society warned that they would raid Rochdale to find unlicensed dogs, the *Daily* advised that "you people with wolves had better describe them as 'part Shepherd to avoid even worse hassles." [42] Outside the room where a tenant raised Siberian huskies, the corridor rug was covered with long, greyish dog hair. "He kept a fairly clean room... except for the dog hair in the air. They took him to the hospital for exploratory examination. And they found a ball of dog hair in his intestines." [43]

The outside world couldn't stomach what they saw and, worse, what they heard about. One of the health inspectors who had to deal with Rochdale was "obviously bewildered by why things don't happen as quickly as he imagines they might." [44] After police had searched one room during the summer of 1970, Rochdale exhibited the room to a reporter/photographer as evidence of damage caused by the search. The police insisted the room had been in disarray before they arrived. "The floors were filthy. A strong odor prevailed, attributable to several cats present in the apartment, and their urine and droppings were scattered about the apartment. A box used by the cats for this purpose was filled to overflowing. Dirty dishes and pots and pans were on the kitchen table, stove, and counter. Soiled articles of clothing were scattered throughout on beds, chairs, and floors. No damage whatever was caused during the search."[45] At its worst, Rochdale decor could be called Early Aftermath.

Rochdale itself must be a disease, ran the consensus. "White blood cell pig cops attack us," as the *Daily* expressed it when police raids began.[46] Towards the end of Rochdale's septic lifespan, some definitions began to alter, and the continuing plaint by maintenance used a word previously reserved for the outside: "I am tired of the bullshit of cleaning up after the pigs."[47]

If the dirt wasn't attractive, it did draw with certainty the borders of Image Nation. For poet Victor Coleman, "the surface of Rochdale is rich. The guts are guts; here they even look like guts. All those clean-living North Americans are pretty disillusioned with our freedom: it smells."[48] "The dogshit in the halls was a pain in the ass," says Alex MacDonald, "but it was part of the rent to live in an environment that had interesting, exciting people in it who were doing things, into politics, into art, into music, whatever it was. You could accept that as a part of the price you pay and people would bring up their kids in that environment and that was okay."

9

Independence

To the Rochdalian in the middle of a mess that was part-exciting, most-aggravating, neither the external management nor the internal fiddling of Govcon promised much. By the spring of the first year, it seemed that everything was being tried a little bit at a time. Why not try out-and-out insurrection? Why not bypass the stuffy bylaws of Rochdale College Incorporated and have a good time as well? Out there in the straight world, the straights had other models that hadn't been touched. With a grin, Rochdale chose an Old World model — and set up a monarchy.

This turn of events had been foreshadowed in the first months of Rochdale by Registrar Jack Dimond declaring himself dictator. At various times thereafter, he was lightly referred to as King Jack or the philosopher king. The real crown, however, would fall to, not a Jack, but a Jim.

A literate and courtly historian portrayed the months leading to the ascension of King James I of Rochdale. Those months were "the terrible times of Chaos, Apathy, Panic, Indifference, and Repression (CAPER)" that masked the operation of a Scheme. What may have seemed to be confusion and mismanagement was not that at all, concluded the historian, but "the first successful revolution of a Power Structure against itself." Through the careful use of inefficiency, the Scheme prepared for the coming Sovereignty, and required an era of Evictions, Resignations, Removals, and Retirements (ERRAR) that came to a peak in March. "Perhaps the most successful, and certainly the subtlest, discrete action in the Confusion Campaign of those final weeks was the Maintenance Down masterminded by one P. Turner (variously described as an American Draft Resister and a Biafran Pilot), who introduced a lovable but diseased Brazilian monkey into the Merry Commune where all but one of the surviving maintenance staff resided, with the result that the entire department was incapacitated by Dinghy Fever at the height of the immediate pre-coronation action. Without this highly effective manoeuvre, it is uncertain whether the larger lineaments of the Scheme could have operated effectively."[1] It is not clear from the account what threat Merry Maintenance would have posed for the incoming King. Perhaps cleanliness might have created godliness for the outgoing regime.

According to council minutes, it was Jim Garrard of Theatre Passe Muraille who proposed: "set Rochdale up as a monarchy... Jack will be put in stocks for not raising enough money... We can get foreign aid... We need a bomb... We must have beheadings..."[2] Paul then proposed that Jim should be the absolute king, and Richard added that Paul must be queen.

The King-to-be had paid his dues. Months before, in November, he had begun the necessary initiation by running for a lower office. "From the eerie heights of the 18th floor it was learned today that Jim Garrard, bon vivant, lech, and resident director of the Rochdale Theatre Project, will run for a seat on the Governing Council... His campaign manager is his father, a 70-year-old retired railroader from Oshawa. Smiling radiantly, he stood before his living room window, posturing to the crowd gathered on the Bloor Street terrace below, feeling their warmth and support, listening to their choked cries of

'Garrard, Garrard,' watching beaming parents hold their little ones up for a closer look."[3] Formal invitation cards were prepared for a Speech from the Throne by Garrard on April 2, 1969. James I's acceptance speech took place on the Bloor Street patio and ministers were named for Finance, Mythology, Health and Welfare, and Security. A Court Jester was appointed, as well as Captain of the King's Guard, Maintenance Head, and Rental Agent/Spiritual Advisor.

In Rochdale, whoever played the better pipes called the tune. Given the fresh and coherent idea of a monarchy, how could the citizenry refuse? "Council accepted the monarchy as a good way to govern," says Garrard. "They became, voluntarily, dukes and earls or whatever. They weren't really puppets. We had breakfast meetings and Wu [the cafeteria cook] would cater them. His idea was we'll do this up properly; we'll ship up the very best of food and good wines. It never came to that. Instead of council meetings, we'd have get-togethers. It was legitimized because a monarchy can operate that way — behind closed doors. You have a select group who were probably elected anyway and if necessary, you'd use an edict, but a clever monarch doesn't make into an edict something that's indefensible, that's going to take the power away from him."

For a while, the monarchy supplied a kind of government, then the idea began to face a competitor. The troupes of Govcon and the external management were warming up a talent show. Unlike the monarchy, these politics had an added thrust: since they originated in the charter of the College and in other legal arrangements such as contracts, they were legitimate. The show would be a showdown, and the issue would be independence.

And in one of the few periods of coherence and willpower shown by a Rochdale government, a council rose to the occasion. Disputes had been escalating between Rochdale, as loosely represented by its governing council, and its external management, embodied in the Toronto Student Management Corporation (TSMC). In one instance,

Rochdale expressed horror at TSMC's plan to mail 5,000 posters invit-
ing college people everywhere to come to Rochdale in the summer.
The intention, of course, was to help the finances with summer
occupancy, but Rochdale was already wiser. More bodies didn't
necessarily mean more money.

Along with external disputes came civil ones. Not only was the
Toronto Student Management Corporation a scapegoat for the mess
that dismanagement made, but the ineffective Govcons of the first
year seemed to be feeding the goat. "The biggest experimental college
in North America slumped into civil war about money and administration."[4] A citizens' meeting passed a vote of non-confidence in the
governing council in April. Though the proceedings were amiable,
council refused to recognize the non-confidence vote. Then a series
of bulletins entitled MaySay appeared in May '69 to raise issues for
a general meeting. The movement reconsidered Rochdale's com-
mitments to the Indian Institute on the seventeenth floor, and to
founders Ian MacKenzie and Dennis Lee.

More importantly, MaySay had its sights on the contract with
TSMC. The contract would come up for renewal at the end of June. At
stake was the whole set-up of Rochdale, and the movement decided
that "the financial advantages of the Toronto Student Management
Corporation arrangements with Campus Co-op are outweighed by
the confusion and anxiety this arrangement causes."[5]

As in any large-scale real estate development, the highrise had
been built with a number of distinct cooks for one soup — including
in this case two development companies, Rochdale Council, the
City as expressed by municipal bylaws, and the architects. Now in
the running of the college, it seemed that the remaining cooks were
too distinct. In a study entitled *Rochdale College: A Managerial and
Corporate Paradox with Educational Overtones*, Rochdale recorded
its complaint: "We must speak to a corporate man with two heads,
two memories, and two sets of emotions."[6]

As "Rochdale's liberation front," MaySay charged that the external managers regarded Rochdale and its parent, Campus Co-op, as "one body and manipulate finances and administrators as such."[7] Rochdale's assets would be used to pay Campus Co-op's normal summer deficit, they warned. The other half of the two-headed corporate man, Campus Co-op, was just as suspicious of Rochdale. The parent co-op feared that Rochdale would offer lower rates in the summer and cut into co-op revenues.

A management that was already divided became a good target for the other division that was troubling Rochdale, namely, the street youths versus the students. Dennis Lee's desire for more university students didn't just get ignored; the movement to oust the external administration identified aloof students as part of the problem. Rochdalian leaders blamed Campus Co-op for "the large percentage [of] non-participants in this building which is fucking us about."[8]

Campus Co-op became the "primary target of disparagement" by Rochdale when Rochdale's administrators "became identified...with those who wished to limit the authority of the students," according to Adelman in *The Beds of Academe*.[9] Here, Adelman is making no distinction between "student" and "resident." As new residents joined Rochdale, ignorance of Rochdale's history increased and so suspicion of both Campus Co-op and Co-op College increased. Former student-power people found themselves in positions that limited power, and reacted to their unease "by indulging student authority, permitting it to outspace capacity and abrogating their own positions. Instead of increasing the experience on which the intellectual and creative authority of the local group could rest, attempts at avoiding suspicion were made by...surrendering authority over areas where the new group put on pressure."[10]

When the attacks came, the joyful capitalists headed by Howard Adelman had already left — or were on their way. "The men instrumental in the project," said Sarah Spinks, "were guilty of the same naivete that the hippier types were. They thought they could do a job and then leave, without making sure that there were others in the building who would carry on." [11]

Adelman himself lost interest in projects once they were underway — an entirely natural reaction for a man in charge of a development company. "What he wanted to do," says Alex MacDonald, "was build buildings, not stay around and manage them. He wandered off and built more of them; he built them all over the province." Co-worker John Jordan travelled the whole summer before the opening of the highrise setting up other projects, again according to the mandate of his company. Other figures, expected to "fill the building and establish a system," filled the building and left.

Since the original authorities failed to develop the qualifications of those to whom they surrendered authority, Adelman wrote (including the University of Toronto as an original authority), they must take the blame for the process they began. [12] The under-qualified who gained power were afraid of losing it, and sought to protect it by expanding rather than perfecting areas already under control. The more they succeeded, the more the formal authority became separated from experienced users of authority.

Rochdale wanted a separation, and by June '69, Campus Co-op was just as eager to go. The Co-op president explained in a letter to the *Globe:* "We feel that parents, whose sons and daughters are members of Campus Co-op, may be unduly alarmed by this identification of the Co-op with Rochdale...At Campus Co-op, we wish only to provide low-cost housing owned and operated by students in a co-operative manner. We prefer, therefore, to remain upright in, if not out of, the public eye." [13]

Rochdale found a leader in John Bradford, editor of the *Rochdale Bulletin* in 1967, former president of the graduate student body at the University of Toronto, and "Cromwell" to the monarchy of James I. As Alex MacDonald tells it, Bradford and his associates, candidates for a new council, had been reevaluating both TSMC and the current, contested council. "Just back off for a sec," said Bradford and Lionel Douglas, "'we want to meditate.' Like it was assumed that it would be a rubber stamp re-approval. This was the first big impeach Council drive, the one that actually succeeded. Before just blanket-renewing the contract, Rochdale wanted to look at the books and [the external management] was not at all excited by this prospect. There was a fair amount of espionage and stumbling about and breaking into offices at night, flashlights and looking at numbers."

Just before the Toronto Student Management contract came up for renewal, Rochdale made its move. The previous governing council was impeached and the new one headed by Bradford took over. It was June 10, 1969, one day before the lingering construction of the building officially ended.

The Bradford council occupied an unused Ashram from which it could co-ordinate citizen's committees and for seven days and nights, prepared a "Nude Eel" for Rochdale. People resigned, people reshuffled. Numerous staff changes were decided upon with a confidence that extended to posting a Comptroller to a two-year contract. The report from Council was itemized and efficient as never before (or after). According to the somewhat revisionist *Rochdale Catalogue* of 1972, the new leadership replaced what had been the "Shadow Council," began a security force, banned hard drugs, evicted the first forty speed freaks and dealers, and set up systems for rental, accounting, and maintenance. Howard Adelman reported that the "new resolute council" evicted seventy and replaced "casual hippie labor with professional cleaners."[14] Faced with the continuing mess in the food services, the Bradford council reorganized the cafeteria and brought its losses down from $12,000 to $1,250 a month. Then Council made meal tickets optional for Kafka residents and let them use the Ashram kitchens.

On June 30, Independence Day, the contract with its external managers lapsed and Rochdale let it go.

The dispute with the parent organizations worsened as the summer progressed. Glenn Greer of Co-op College wrote a demand for parking rental marked "Pay up or Die." "The balance of $36 will be recognized as a credit to Rochdale on transfer of the building. Rochdale at present owes Co-op College approximately $35,000." [15] Rochdale counter-charged that Co-op College had borrowed $50,000 from Rochdale in January and $10,000 more in March. In July, Rochdale withheld its mortgage payments to CCRI until the alleged loan would be repaid.

The crasher problem declined temporarily when Rochdale's population thinned out for the summer. The issue even became calm enough for Rochdale to welcome visitors officially again. "You could see them coming," says Jim Garrard, "with their big knapsacks on their backs and they'd be from literally all over the world. That was during the great hitchhiking phenomenon. Youth has never been more mobile than they were during that particular summer; you couldn't drive your car down the 401 without passing 150 hitchhikers. Today you wouldn't pass a dozen."

A council member reported that "the police were asking us to use our resources to alleviate the problem of wall-to-wall kids expected at the Toronto Pop Festival...We arranged for a church to put up as many as possible and John and Steve spent the night watching over it. We rented rooms for $2 a night and broke even in terms of expense and trouble — there were a number of ripoffs that weekend and garbage was strewn in the halls by newcomers who never learned where the garbage chutes were. Most of the kids came expecting to pay $5 per night and we could have made $3,000 by having them lay it on us." [16] During July as well, the highrise hosted the science fiction audiences of the Rochdale Summer Festival.

Meanwhile, on the political front, the purging continued. Paul Evitts took a central role in the ousting of former coordinator, registrar, and council member Jack Dimond. "The clash of personalities and the problem of history" prevented useful talking, said Evitts.[17] "In my typically fascist way," Evitts said, "I recently attempted to keep Jack Dimond, our venerable ex-registrar, from occupying the 18th floor Zeus suite...Jack's living here would not be in the best interests of the College."[18] Jim Garrard says that Dimond was "older and a genuine scholar and humanitarian, a real wise man," but even so, Dimond and Campus Co-op were looked on as "the enemy." Why? "Well [laugh], he was a Jesuit...He didn't live in the building in those days, that was the big complaint about Jack."

Dimond was fired in August and in September '69, Evitts threatened to "bailiff-lock suite 211 and seize its contents."[19] Co-operative College co-operated, and vacated its office in suite 211 in mid-month.

Rochdale had successfully ousted its external administration and, according to Adelman, had satisfied its "irrational suspicion and fear" by independence.[20] Doing so, however, displeased the bigger bosses, the holders of the federal government mortgage. By the rules, the developer should have retained control for five years, and the Canada Mortgage and Housing Corporation "regretted" the turnover of the building to Rochdale College.[21] Already, in one year, Rochdale had won both independence and a curiously remote official disapproval.

10

The Money Mess

The governing council headed by John Bradford scrambled to save Rochdale. As Alex MacDonald tells it, "a very small number of people did a staggering amount of work to take a multimillion-dollar project which had no accounting system, and no reservation system, and no... they had to develop the physical logistical systems to run a big apartment complex after the damn thing had already been opened for six months." But the more they looked into the scattered and inadequate books they had inherited, the more they blanched. While the average Rochdalian may have thought the enemy would become the policeman or the middle-class prude, the real enemy was beginning to look like an accountant. For a number of reasons, the College was already at — and beyond — the point of disaster. The mess in the hallways had its equivalent in the finances of the College, and the reasons for the mess began at the very start.

When the government amended the National Housing Act in 1964 and allowed the Canada Mortgage and Housing Corporation to lend government money to co-operatives, Rochdale became eligible for government money via a 90 percent mortgage at 6.9 percent interest, when normal rates were 9.25 percent. The $4.8 million mortgage was to be amortized over fifty years with payments to CMHC beginning

March 1, 1969, at $26,000 a month. So this was the first financial target, before operating, renovation, and educational expenses: each month, $26,000 plus payments to three other creditors. All to be met by an institution running without subsidies...

Rochdale protested that even universities with fifty years of experience and "huge grants" can't operate residence halls without a deficit. "The building," says Alex MacDonald, "was financially a turkey from before it was a hole in the ground." One Rochdalian wrote a poem about the mortgage called "Albatross 520-U-3," in which the mortgage is the "Great hump-backed whale of Mammon ... And a neck/ceases."[1] Certainly no help could be forthcoming from its parent organization, Campus Co-op, even if goodwill had not been destroyed. Campus Co-op had its own financial business to attend to.

The first budget had been drawn up while the highrise was still being constructed — and counted on a 3 percent vacancy rate. It couldn't foresee the transient population that would flood Rochdale, nor did it consider the gap that would come each summer as students left. "The Rochdale management," with the advantage of hindsight, "argued that the mortgage structure was unreasonable in light of the Ontario decision to throw out the tri-semester system, thus depriving the colleges of three months of income."[2] Going into the new building in the fall of 1968, Rochdale did carry a surplus — a minuscule one. The amount was estimated, as close as the bookkeeping would allow, at $1,165. The college also had a period of grace. As the *Daily Planet* reported, there was an agreement with CMHC whereby no payments would be due in the first year if there was an operational loss.[3] Operational loss there was. Four months after opening, rent collection had fallen $40,000 behind, vacancies cost another $40,000, and the food operations had lost $17,000.

Many Rochdalians viewed their corporate debt as a bill of rights and a weapon to be used against straight society. "The rents were a continuing debate," says a former resident, "and one strong faction would argue, 'screw the rents, that's one of the reasons we're here; they'll just go to CMHC.'" When this resident lived with a friend in Rochdale for six months, neither paid rent—nor were they asked for any.

Rochdale argued that 1 percent of the mortgage, "by established practice," was due from CMHC for setting up a rentals administration, and because CMHC didn't pay that 1 percent, rental collection became chaotic. But 1 percent or none, "it wasn't until the fall of 1969 that the Accounting Department took seriously the idea that people should pay rent," says MacDonald. "Ken East from Accounting started going from door to door at all hours of the day and night and he'd say, 'give me some money or get out right now.' People actually got thrown out for non-payment of rent, which was a revolutionary change."

Very few saw the repayment of a loan as their own affair. During a talk attended by Syd Stern, MacDonald was saying: "there were these great big guys with calluses all over their hands and sweat and stuff like that and they spend all afternoon turning fucking cement mixers and pouring concrete and they really, really insist at the end of the day that they get paid, so we went to CMHC. A lot of people in Rochdale thought CMHC was the enemy when in fact — this was just like a dope deal — CMHC fronted us five million dollars." Stern interrupted: "What we had to work to give them back was just the interest on the money, Alex. What's wrong with not paying a shylock?"

Then, too, Rochdale tended to spend as if it were bigger than it was. Council member Lionel Douglas published a warning in the *Daily*: "Ladies and Gentlemen, Thieves, Prevaricators and other Assorted Slugs: One principle which must be understood and accepted and adhered to *strictly*, is that a budget must be undertaken to which the management must adapt itself rather than applying a budget to the existing situation. This budget must be a reflection of existing income rather than expected expenses. There has been a great deal of attention given to the fact that we are a 'big business' and can therefore operate extravagantly and expansively giving subsidies to deserving parties and so on. Well, it just ain't so friends; we are a relatively simple, yes simple, organization with a fatally self-destructive penchant for taking on the airs and mannerisms of a bourgeoning prosperous corporate entity." [4]

By this point, all of the mess was covered with a fog of mismanagement, and accounts were kept so poorly that no one could find the pins to pin the blame. A later report by an external auditor threw up its flat little hands: "we are unable to express an opinion as to whether or not these financial statements present fairly the financial position of the Company." [5] But was the money mess the fault of managers who didn't manage — or decisions that erected the financial structure a lot less firmly than the concrete one? Some explanations seemed too easy: the "ill-considered financial structure, when pointed out as unviable, was merely dismissed as mismanagement." [6]

One element of that structure could not be more vital to both the identity of Rochdale and its finances. It was, it insisted, a college. However, despite the educational ideals of such people as Dennis Lee, some other founders saw status as a college with a practical eye. "Rochdale was originally called a college," says MacDonald, "not because it had anything to do with free education, but because they figured they could avoid paying municipal property taxes." The *Rochdale Catalogue* for 1972 agreed: the founders were "approached," it said, to run an educational program within the residence, with the property in Rochdale's name in order "to gain the tax status" of an educational institution. [7] According to MacDonald, trying to qualify for tax deductions affected the organization of Rochdale since Rochdale had to own its own building. This helped change the original plan to have Rochdale one part of Campus Co-op.

Early in 1967, the financial structure began erecting its steel girders in clay. Although the charter for status as an educational institution was still being negotiated, the planners over-optimistically counted tax breaks before they broke. "The tax benefits realized from obtaining such status will furnish the College with a significant part of its operating income after September '68," said the planning report. "Rochdale Council has earmarked the municipal tax exemption of $90,000 for education."[8] It was also possible that $28,000 could be saved for each of the first ten years "if the rebate for taxes on building materials were applied at once to the redemption of debentures." This federal rebate applied to educational buildings only, and like the municipal tax exemption, depended on a status not yet granted.

Besides those two sources, Rochdale would have no income other than rents, fees, and fundraising. It would be "the only university in Canada that is wholly dependent on private and foundation support, beyond its own internal revenue," the planning report enthused. Government support would be refused to avoid the "policy strings attached," since Rochdale was "aspiring to the kind of excellence which can only be bought with private support." Of the $190,000 projected for educational expenses in the first year, only $17,000 would come from fees. Even with the exemption and rebate, $55,000 would have to appear from fundraising.

The setbacks began. The two sides of Rochdale's identity, college and residence, neither fish nor fowl, cancelled each other out in the eyes of the authorities. Because the residence tried to include educational aims, Adelman said, some of the development costs were refused by CMHC, which was not entitled by law to support educational aims.[9] This setback had not happened before to Adelman, since his previous projects had been for housing purposes only. Then, because the college had residential aims, the Metro Assessment Commission inspected Rochdale in September '68 and decided it was not a "seminary of learning," but a student residence.

Not a College! Municipal taxes, including the education tax, were duly levied. Those taxes came to $134,000 and were paid — under duress. One educational institution was being forced to pay for the operation of others. The College filed suit with the Supreme Court of Ontario to stop the taxes, but the first stages of the trial disappeared into the thick calendar book of the court.

Rochdale fared no better with the tax rebate on building materials, a matter of $200,000. The Department of National Revenue refused the application. Then, with both the exemption and the rebate gone, an audit in the summer of 1969 deleted an additional $200,000 in furniture bills from the capital costs submitted as part of the original mortgage. According to Adelman, these denials continued a series of irresponsibilities on the part of the government and the university that denied Rochdale College an "equitable start" with free land, exemption from municipal taxes, and building grants for a dining hall and educational areas. [10]

Rochdale inherited the ill-starred tax question, but that was not all. Suspicions began to arise that the debt it had to face should not have been so high; indeed, a number of student residences built under the same legislation all shared the same ill-star. By July '73, it was apparent that six large co-ops mortgaged under Part 6a of the National Housing Act were all facing financing problems that could be explained only partly by summer vacancies. As reported in the *Globe,* the Opposition attacked the federal government in the House of Commons for agreeing in principle to yet another co-operative residence when previous co-ops were in difficulty. [11] Besides Rochdale, Pestalozzi College in Ottawa was in arrears on a $6.2 million mortgage, as was Neill-Wycik in Toronto. Tartu College, across the street from Rochdale, had to be bailed out by a private organization.

The University of Toronto student newspaper had published an account of the financial troubles that sympathized with Rochdale and had spoken of "a staggering debt, an inflated mortgage." [12] Now one of Rochdale's own took up the offensive. In pamphlets titled "The Housing Pyramid," "A Story of the Bastardization of Co-op," and "The Student Housing Mess," Alvin Wood accused the developers of

Rochdale of financial wrongdoing. Al Wood had wanted to manage Rochdale after coordinating the Waterloo Co-op from 1966 to 1970. His offer was refused in 1971, and so, "due to delays which have never been satisfactorily explained, I found myself without a career." [13] Al Wood angry is Al Wood in capitals. "WHY IS ROCHDALE BEING BLAMED ON IRRESPONSIBLE YOUTH CULTURE???" he asked in his analysis. In several pages of diatribe, Wood made charges that tried to turn the blame around.

In September '74, a *Globe* story reported on the complicated interlocking of directorships for the developers, architects, and contractors involved in the troubled co-op residences, as recorded in a confidential federal government report. [14] The same story investigated the assembly of the land itself for a sister co-op, Neill-Wycik College in Toronto.

Land for Rochdale cost $1 million. According to one critic, it was worth less than $300,000. [15] So what were the founders saying? Howard Adelman published a rebuttal to a controversial *Varsity* article in which he said the land costs were $760,000 without interest, carrying charges, and legal fees. [16] He acknowledged that Revenue had a land profit of $200,000 and a building profit of $200,000, both of which, however, were offered as a second mortgage. The developer, he pointed out, could not possibly make excessive profit when the profit was not realized in cash but reinvested at low rates and, as it turned out, at high risk. Jack Dimond added, "I wonder if Revenue Properties feels today that they have squeezed the taxpayer after having been talked into investing their entire profit in a second mortgage on a property which isn't even meeting its first mortgage commitments." [17]

All the long-term financial impossibilities were being discovered — or suspected — by the governing council under John Bradford during the summer and fall of 1969. After six months of scramble, by November, Rochdale seemed demoralized. Judy Merril complained that many creative people could not function because of the wearing effect of the place. Cafeteria losses reputedly had fallen to $250 a month, but despite all efforts, the cafeteria surrendered and closed down. Uncleanliness was cited. As well, the twenty-four-hour restaurant on the ground level, The Same, cut back on its hours. The Communications Center at the front door was not manned. The Free Store had folded. The Chapel on the second floor was "not in use much." The regular *Daily* had ceased because council had passed no budget at all and a dispute had developed over paying for the mimeograph and stencil maker. A new paper appeared: the *Naked Grape*, sometimes spelled *Gripe*.

But most disturbing of all, the period of grace on Rochdale's corporate debt was ending. Mortgage payments to CMHC, a $26,000 tab, would be coming due month by month, and with the continuing lack of dependable rent income and the messy handling of the little money that showed, the payments would be most surely missed. As the first mortgage payment passed into default in November, Albatross 520-U-3 began to smell.

The Bradford Council considered the options: negotiate a new mortgage. Start an offensive for funds. Collect enough rents ("impossible"). Or sell the building. Sell the building...Important figures said yes. President John Bradford, Paul Evitts, Bill King, and Lionel Douglas said yes. "The battle was going to be lost," says MacDonald, "that was clear as early as the summer of '69 when Rochdale College took over management. Bradford and [his council] got a look at the books and they went OH, NO. Their response was to try and sell it before they lost it." Bill King complained that the external students had stopped paying rent in the last months of the school year. Since grades could not be withheld as in a normal school, and since he believed that 60 percent in Rochdale wanted a student residence, he proposed that Rochdale "retreat and retrench" in a smaller building.[18] "The only intelligent thing to do," says MacDonald, "was to sell the building, take the money, and go do something else."

The council had collected only $20,000 of $54,000 in rents due in October, plus another $12,000 in late payments — and that was the last chance. Council recommended to the residents that they sell. There were two offers, it said, that would yield a $2 million profit, one from a private firm and the other from a public agency. One offer to buy came from Ab Campbell, who would soon be chairman of Toronto's Metro Council. He wanted Rochdale for a nursing home. A group including Wilf Pelletier, John Bradford, Ian MacKenzie, and Jack Jones travelled to Ottawa to talk to senior officials, but the other offer remained secret.

The resident owners had had enough of leader John Bradford. The recommendation of his council, says MacDonald, "had absolutely zero appeal to the rest of the building." Opinion makers such as Jim Garrard, Bob Naismith, and Ralph Osborne said no, and the rest said, "well piss on that, no no, wrong idea." Resident Steve Grant charged in the *Naked Grape* that John Bradford had committed "foolish actions on national TV news" to reinforce doubt about Rochdale and help encourage its sale. Furthermore, the regular *Daily* was partisan, Grant said, and had refused to publish his piece — as Jack Jones of the *Daily* replied, "If I only knew what council's view was, I'd be glad to suppress anti-council stuff." [19]

"Council salaries have not decreased during the whole crisis," Grant continued, "while the members have lost things like the library, telephones, and bedding service for want of money." Grant took seriously the rumor that the police would be asked to "prevent disturbances" at the general meeting that would decide the sale. The same *Naked Grape* printed the sour grapes of Stephan Van Beek, a vice-president who had been removed from office by a secret vote. Council meetings, said Van Beek, consisted of "confabulations with poisonous weak liars." [20] He told Rochdale members that "being screwed up the ass in blissful and well-deserved ignorance — as you are — leads not to beatitude and enlightenment but to reliance on too much truss."

The general meeting and the time to sell passed on, and so did
the Bradford Council. Kent Gooderham did not mourn its passing.
The beginning of the Bradford reign in June, he said, had ended "a
particularly creative and exciting period in Rochdale's history."²¹ With
the new council, "almost all seminars and all happenings ceased. The
music left the halls. So too did the dog shit." But by November, the
residents "threw out 'big daddy' after he had put their home back into
working order but threatened to take it from them...Projects began
to blossom. The library, the 'schop', the art gallery, the *Daily*, all of
which had been dormant for months reappeared one after another."

11

Hipheaven

While the dim finances of Rochdale College gathered like a thunderhead, drug-dealers and -takers were having a picnic. Drugs were being moved and consumed in basketloads, wholesale and retail; they were tasted and pushed, dropped and copped, the spread on the picnic blanket usually hidden under covers, but sometimes laid right out in the open. Indeed, at one level of Rochdale life, there was no money mess at all. At that ground level, some of Rochdale had an ample income.

A mess of money fills the stories of Rochdale dealing. In one example, a box of cocaine — and the look on the face of its owner when it was dumped by accident out a window and into the snow — was worth $20,000. The market at Rochdale became so lucrative that one dealer moving out of Rochdale sold his address to another dealer for $1,000. The tellers of another story pointed to a wood and leather chair in the ninth-floor lounge: "a $20 million to $30 million [drug] business was done in this chair through the years. Eventually, nearly 75 percent of the [drug trafficker's] money was used to bring relatives from behind the Iron Curtain — Hungary — and he set them up in business in Canada."[1] According to another source, "one of the biggest drug dealers there, a Hungarian, purportedly took out of the building $200,000 when he was evicted."[2]

The dealers offered a wide selection. One resident told a newspaper columnist that "somebody knocks on my door at least once a day selling drugs. They peddle grass, hash, acid, mescaline, psilocybin, MDA, and coke. [Cocaine] is supposed to be banned here, but they have it."[3] In a 1971 survey, 12 percent of the respondents said they never smoked cannabis, while 31 percent smoked daily, another 31 percent weekly, and 26 percent monthly or less. For the psychedelics, 4 percent used them weekly, but 53 percent used them not at all.[4] An overwhelming 97 percent never touched speed, but 1.8 percent used heroin daily, 5.3 percent used it monthly, and 4 percent less often. The majority of users had started before age sixteen and before they had moved to Rochdale. Of the 3.2 percent who said they were dealing while in Rochdale, more than half had been dealing in at least the three months before becoming a resident.

Rochdale developed a drug culture on two levels: internal use that centered on small-scale, friendly distribution of soft drugs, especially marijuana — and large-scale commerce with buyers and sellers who had little connection with the community. Once inside Rochdale, the large-scale dealers were protected by the size of the building and by a warning system. These dealers made full use of the building. One of the Rochdale cleaners says that the dealers "started using Stash Rooms rented by an ad hoc group of dealers so that none of them would have stuff in his room. Those rooms would be changed every so often and used only by the big dealers." Room registrations at one point included at least twelve false names "assigned to rooms for the purpose of storing property."[5]

"Everyone dealt a little," says the former maintenance man, "selling to their friends, but I would guess there were less than twelve big ones in the building...I went into the dealers' lounge once just as part of the cleaning...They had between one and two dozen green garbage bags of marijuana lined up against the wall, tens of thousands of dollars' worth." One cleaner at least "got all his dope from the garbage chute. They were just careless about it. The place was full of the stuff."

How did such large quantities enter and leave the building? Individual buyers had many tricks, including loading up dummy beer cartons, but the main shipments seem to have entered via the basement garage. Sid Smith, a later property manager from outside the Rochdale community, had opportunities to learn some of the methods. "Restaurant people," he explains, "would come in with a van loaded with groceries, health food, and the dope would be inside. And the police did find $50,000 worth in a car in the basement." The drugs were brought up from the garage by the kitchen's dumbwaiter. "Then people who were supposed to be bona fide students would move in with it stashed in their mattresses," says Smith. "The dealers would approach good students and say, 'Look, you move into Rochdale; I'll give you $300; you give me the key and the receipt'. This would bypass the screening which I had set up for new tenants." Another method of bypassing screening gives new meaning to the term "drug bust": "the hash came in one-pound balls in the girls' bras. It was funny, too, because the girls never wore bras; but they did when a shipment came in."[6]

One dealer testified that he wasn't caught sooner because "the police never stopped anybody going into Rochdale, they always checked people coming out."[7] That placed pressure on the export half of the drug business and penalties could be severe. The story circulated about "some dude" busted with 300 hits of acid while travelling from Rochdale to Ohio. He received a twenty- to forty-year sentence.[8]

"It was common practice," reported the *Globe* in December '71, "for male traffickers to hire girls at Rochdale to run drugs to various places in Canada ... the system is known as 'the Dope Run' and girls usually were paid $50 for each trip to Newfoundland."[9] Hashish bought in Toronto for $100 an ounce sold for three times as much in Newfoundland. Police in St. John's had missed drug couriers previously because they had checked only males. This time, two girls had been charged and one carried drugs worth $11,500, including a pound of marijuana.

Whatever could not be taken out had simply to wait for customers to come in. Demand by young people, often from the suburbs, was strong. A dealer testified that "there would be lineups outside my room on Friday and Saturday nights...about 15 to 20 people at a time."[10] Rochdale residents had ample reason to feel crushed. Not only did they face crashers who wanted to "steal sleeps" and thieve food, but they had to cope with the crowds of an all-night drugstore.

With dependable lines of supply and demand, and with private premises, dealers were able to refine their business as never before. "The dealers were highly organized," says Police Officer Dean Audley, a policeman who lived for a time inside Rochdale, "even more military than we were. I was shown the accounts of one dealer and I tell you, Clarkson Gordon never had books kept as well as that."

"I would say there were four major dealers [during one period]," says Property Manager Sid Smith. "They had their own territories in different parts of the building. A guy who wanted to buy a large quantity would give Rochdale Security a colored card which would tell them which one of the four he wanted to see." Competition for the territories was strong and not always honorable, according to Audley. "They would say of some dealer, 'Oh he's a cool guy,' and I would tell them he'd sell you out for twenty-five cents. Sometimes they turned other dealers in to get their territory."

Another observer identified four types of dealers in Hipheaven: "Middlers and small dealers who deal to survive," residents who have larger operations under cover of a "community-oriented enterprise that provides employment," those who come to Rochdale to make specific amounts, and dealers who live outside and maintain rooms "because they can't stand the noise generated by the other dealers' customers."[11] Alex MacDonald confirms that "there were people who lived in High Park (a Toronto district several miles away) who rented six or eight rooms, and who employed people to sit and deal in them. They would come now and then and pick up the money."

After the end of the College, Sid Smith — a romantic at heart — gave a tour of the roof to reporters. "Over there is the executive sandbox," he told them. "They used to sit up here on a summer night — with no clothes on and smoking up — and make some of the big deals."[12] According to a security guard during the same tour, Room 322 was a hash-oil room. "The oil kept blocking the pipes and the plumber either had to take them out periodically or unplug them. I told them to leave the pipe here; it might have been worth a million dollars." Smith confirms that "on the third floor, there was a Hungarian employed by another Hungarian, manufacturing the stuff. After we got him out, we had to practically disassemble the plumbing. There was a small fortune in the drains."

"They were very clever," says Smith. "I went to one apartment which was empty, though there was rent being paid. Absolutely nothing in there, but in the corner was a small cupboard with three drawers. I opened one... and immediately shut it. There must have been $50,000 or $60,000 in cash, in twenties, hundreds, tens, fifties, all in bundles. I went downstairs and got the security guard to come up with me, and after no more than seven minutes, I opened the cupboard and there was nothing in there. On the front door were trip-wires that set off an alarm down the hall and the guy must have come and got his money."

Of course, the first thing a dealer protected, even before his stash and his territory, was his name. One trafficker, in court after being caught with sixty-two pounds of marijuana, said he had borrowed $9,000 from "Mr. Big" and bought the marijuana at $175 a pound from a Rochdale resident who imported from Mexico. The man claimed he "could not remember" Mr. Big's name.[13] However, at least two of the dealers at Rochdale College raised their heads high enough that they can be identified — one by admissions in court, the other by candor in the face of an interview.

After a ton of hashish in sixteen crates was intercepted at the Toronto International Airport, the RCMP charged twenty-six-year-old Robert Rowbotham with conspiracy to traffic in drugs. Officers testified at his trial in Brampton in 1977 that $73,000 had been found in a baby's crib on his Beeton, Ontario, farm. Four co-conspirators had already pleaded guilty, and the principal had received a seven-year sentence — but Rowbotham decided to defend himself. "Bob the Goof" testified on his behalf. A deserter from the U.S. army and a next-door neighbor, Bob the Goof maintained that "Rowbotham distributed marijuana throughout the building and throughout the city, but he wasn't into any other kinds of drugs."[14] A non-violent vegetarian, Rowbotham was opposed to "man-made drugs" like LSD and had served on the eviction committee that enforced a soft-drugs-only rule. He was innocent of the hashish charge because he dealt exclusively with marijuana. Rowbotham himself testified that he stayed with marijuana because it came into Canada more consistently than hashish, allowing him to build up a regular clientele. He told the court "how his supplier would bring in 500 pounds of marijuana at a time from California and they would store it in the underground garage at Rochdale College in Toronto. 'We are talking about tons and tons and tons.'"[15]

The other dealer with a name — and tons and tons of candor — was Syd Stern. "Rochdale was the best place in the world to live," says Stern. "I was probably one of the few people who realized how safe Rochdale was for pot. Oh God, they had to go to 500 apartments to find you." Stern was forty-eight years old when he was busted in August '71 and "charged with a little of everything."[16] "Syd lived in the second-floor lounge, in a corner," says one eyewitness. "He slept there, and at some point he moved in a fridge and a table. He's the one who bought my last quarter pound. I was getting $340 a quarter pound, less ten for _____ and ten to Rochdale Security for keeping an eye out. I had given the hash and went to see Stern to collect as I was told, at 7:00 in the lounge. I said, 'I understand you have some money for me.' 'That may be,' he answered. 'I'm on the level,' I added and he looked me straight in the eye. The lounge was busy. We were surrounded by people — and two of his women. 'I believe you,' he said and pulled out a great big wad and peeled off $320. To a complete stranger!"

Another side to the man, however, is indicated by a security report filed in the last year of the College. According to the report, Syd Stern met face to face the security guard who gave evidence towards his conviction for trespass. Stern called him "profane and abusive names as well as a liar... and then threatened [him] that... he would bite [his] nose off and spit it back at him." [17]

Dealer organization reached its peak with Big Al's sixth-floor Fortress in the summer of 1970. According to Alex MacDonald, "the response to domestication [in Rochdale] was to imitate what the residents were doing — which was to form a commune. Dealers rented the sixth-floor east wing for what was to be the most spastic, orgasmic two months of excess that this city has ever seen. Every room in the corridor except one was dealing major quantities of dope flat out."

The *Globe* reported that "guard dogs prowled the halls, bikers manned the doors, and if you did business there, you did it through a slit in an iron door. Unlike other Rochdale dealers who dealt mainly in marijuana and hashish, it was at Big Al's Fortress that the heavier items hit the menu — heroin, speed, and chemicals with initials like the degrees their users would never take." [18] *Tab International*, a shrieking little gossip sheet from England, made no secret of its opinion: "The police, as well as the press and some of the general public, knew that on the SIXTH floor of Rochdale, an armed camp

of gun-toting dope pushers held forth, with a stock that police knew
was supplying the ill-famed Mosport Rock Festival. The 'inmates' of
Rochdale call the cops PIGS. It makes an enquiring reporter wonder
if they should be called 'CHICKEN' instead."[19]

The locked door that separated the sixth-floor dealers' fortress
from the rest of Rochdale needed an apology. "Pat" explained to
Rochdalians that "some of us on the sixth floor have discovered we
have a common self-interest and special problems in dealing with
people, both as individuals and as large, well-organized outside
groups."[20]

Dealing? Large, well-organized outside groups? Here the language
throws up an unusually thin mask. Is this, perhaps, the Mafia? In the
Daily for May 20, 1970, there is a cryptic portrait of the president of
the "Hedgerow Fuckers Association Inc." — "tight-lipped, his financial
eyes snapping, his financial finger crackling" — who says that "the
first operation's been a great success — great success — Bloor is ours
from Huron to St. George. We've made a new appointment — a top
executive from the Italian Community — great connections with the
Press and construction boys — great connections."[21]

With a topic as sensitive as this, parody may be the closest we
will come to truth. As for the "Hedgerow Fuckers Association," the
real thing seems innocent enough. In May '70, they attempted a
garden along the Bloor Street front using bedding plants, onions,
lettuce, and roses. The project raised funds as an "outdoor sexlab,"
promising a hedge of lilacs, roses, and honeysuckle "great to hide
behind and under."[22]

12

To Serve and Protect

Meanwhile, down at the front door, Rochdale was preparing itself for an enemy. It was clear that the problem of screening undesirables must soon include that most undesirable element — the police.

Even before the highrise opened, some intended Rochdale to be a sanctuary. One Rochdale official said in February '68 that "Rochdale as an institution is just a shell. It provides a place for people to live, tries to keep them from getting busted too fast."[1] The *Daily* assured its readers that "police without a proper warrant or special reason, such as a bank-robber chase, can be forcibly barred at the front door."[2] The readers of the *Daily* had reason to be assured. According to one survey, a third of the seventy-eight respondents had at least one conviction, 40 percent of those for trafficking, 15 percent for possession, the other 40 percent miscellaneous. However, only 7 percent had a greater number of convictions after coming to Rochdale while 93 percent had fewer. This reduction could be explained by either fewer offences or "relative immunity."[3]

How many people on the run made use of that immunity? No one can say. The better the haven worked, the less we have a record of it. The highrise was intrinsically protected, given its size and the small number of entrances, but still the defenses of the concrete castle needed work. Despite some initial confusion, the resident-owners helped each other set up Fortress Rochdale, Hiphaven.

In the first four months of the College, the fire alarms rang more than 100 times. This was due to faulty hook-ups and vandalism, but a suggestion was planted in the ringing ears of the residents — and led to the perfecting of a distant early warning system. The police who would face this system complained that "the fire alarm in Rochdale will ring each time the police enter and especially so when a drug investigation is underway. In fact, a staff member is quite frank in stating this is a method used to alert tenants that the police are present. The elevators suddenly quit operating when the police enter. The alarm affords the tenants time to hide or dispose of their drugs in one way or another."[4] The *Star* quoted Inspector John Wilson, head of the Morality Bureau: when police enter Rochdale, he said, "1,000 toilets flush simultaneously."[5] The success of Rochdale as a haven is evident in Wilson's frustration: "I don't buy putting criminals in one building. I would far rather see that type of person...in a three-story building so the job of law enforcement would be that much more possible."[6]

The key to that success, the new "lock" on the front door, was a private police force of a size and nature unheard of in this country before or since. With crowds of outsiders, with unruly and sometimes dangerous unlawful activity, Rochdale needed cops — but everyone agreed the cops they needed couldn't be the outside police, the "pigs." To make the matter critical, Rochdale repeatedly suffered the visits of motorcycle gangs such as Satan's Choice, the Vagabonds, the Black Diamond Riders, and the Paradise — or Para-Dice — Riders. After one disagreement with Rochdale people, the Paradise Riders threatened to return and destroy. Rochdale took the threat seriously enough to post watchers at the entrance with beer bottles filled with gasoline. Another time, "Grumpy" and "Jono" of the same gang were accused of stealing 200 tabs of LSD from a fourteenth-floor room.

"When the bikers got in [Rochdale]," says Sid Smith, "that's when it went downhill. They used to raise hell. They'd go up to the top floors in the elevators with their motorbikes and they'd race down the backstairs on their bikes. They'd drink beers on each floor and the first down was the winner."

Rochdale solved its security problem by giving it over to someone else. Bothered by bikers? — enlist some of the bikers to throw out the rest. The "someone else" moved in and became resident members of Rochdale College. They identified themselves as a group, as if they were a commune or a cult. They became "Rochdale Security." As with many Rochdale groups, the membership was ever-changing and often ambiguous. In the account to follow, "Rochdale Security" will be linked with illegal activities, but it must be understood that the actions of any individual within Rochdale Security may have had nothing at all to do with the activities popularly ascribed to the group, and "Rochdale Security" of one time could have nothing in common with "Rochdale Security" of another time.

"Incredible as it seems, the people who were chosen when a security force was the quickest answer were the type of people laying on the violence."[7] "The bikers gravitated towards situations that suited them," says former resident Sharon Kingsland, "so they handled security. They had an office at the front and chicks on their knee as they checked people in and out the door. If something happened, they could go and menace. It was necessary to fire all of them once in a while, whenever they started getting uppity. Mostly they slacked off."

The absorbing of bikers into a security force was not always smooth. Rivalries between gangs complicated the move, and bikers were easily offended. In May '70, Govcon posted a $100 reward for some bikers who beat up two wives of Rochdale Security men. One was six months pregnant at the time. The other reported that she herself had been beaten repeatedly during one week, once with a glass milk jug over her head, and once she had been "grabbed by arms, one hand clamped over her mouth (severely bit), dragged down fire-staircase; head banged against steel guard-rail (cut on scalp). The two heroes forced her arms open and cranked 3 hypo-fulls of unknown substance into her, banged her around and split."[8]

One new Rochdale recruit was "Chico," a "wiry native of San Luis Obispo, as he has it." Chico "acted as close liaison with the Choice, Vags, and Paradise Riders (letting them use his 15th Ashram double-room as headquarters for their multifarious missions to the interior) but also claimed success in reducing the number and size of rip-offs or robberies, as they are termed by landed gentry."[9] But successes at liaison were fragile, even for Chico, and the *Daily* documents the following power play with excerpts from a security log. On April 2, Chico persuaded Satan's Choice to leave the building with a man, "K," who was being held prisoner in one of Rochdale's empty rooms until he could come up with $202 that he owed the bikers. Chico warned the front door man to keep a sharp eye out for cops. The next night, two policemen answered a call from the eleventh floor. Chico told them he could take care of the situation. The police left and Chico noted, "will try to investigate who called the cops." Shortly after, charges by a young woman that she was raped by Chico in his room — which he denied "ON MY MOTHER'S GRAVE" and "ON THE COLOURS I USED TO WEAR" — led to protests in Rochdale and his resignation from Rochdale Security. Rochdale's front desk would continue to be monitored by "Gypsy" (of the Satan's Choice) and "New Yorker."

At the same time that Chico was resigning, the Vagabonds heard that Rochdale was planning not to allow them in the building any longer. "Junkie," the vice-president, came to Chico's room and made an agreement that the Vagabonds would not hassle the residents if they were not hassled in return. The bikers had been misinformed that Chico had made the rule. Then, as Chico said, at a meeting with Rochdale "it was brought out that I was personally responsible for keeping the building from being partially destroyed tonight by the Vagabonds."

"During the meeting," said Chico, "although unknown to me, there were two guns being trained on my person from a room opposite mine, waiting for word from a certain person."[10] Chico informed Govcon that his life had been threatened by the Vagabonds because he had lost his job and thereby jeopardized the bikers' use of the building. In a four-hour meeting, Govcon rehired him as "biker liaison officer."

"Security fluctuated very dramatically depending on the needs of any given time," says Alex MacDonald. "The principal requirement to be on security in '69 was to be large, and to have a congenital fondness for beating up speed freaks. Intellect, integrity, tact — none of these things were thought of as important because in February and March, your average speed freak was not into getting thrown into the street. It's cold out there."

In many of its versions, Rochdale Security loved a raw image. One resident described them as "those degenerated Nazis at the front door, very intimidating. I remember one security tough. He had a dog and a scarred face. 'Where are you going?,' that was the question." They wore at one point a uniform — fascist blackshirts with a white "Rochdale Security" patch on the chest. A poster in the summer of 1970 showed five in a posed portrait with rifles and cartridge belts. Behind them on a wall hung a swastika and storm trooper insignia. The poster was entitled "To Serve and Protect."

For this squad of young toughs, fantasy mingled happily with facts. In July '70, the *Daily* printed a "Field Report" from the "1st Rochdale Security Regiment": "July 1970 Maneuvers. Commanding — Colonel...(Fritz)...Sargent at Arms, Oberleutnant Zip (second name unprintable), other assorted champions of justice. The first-floor lobby was successfully occupied and the regiment proceeded to show the flag in the rest of the building, thus exorcising narcs, pigs, and other assorted unholy creatures of the night. Despite the failure of the 2nd Rochdale Panzer Brigade, the operation was termed a success." [11]

The facts, when they came, were tough enough. One of the first nightwatchmen listed his qualifications in the *Daily*: "I am a U.S. army deserter. I am qualified as expert on the M-14, 7.62 caliber rifle, the M-16 automatic rifle, the .45 caliber automatic pistol, the M-50, 7.65 caliber machine gun (which has effectively replaced the B.A.R. in combat), the M-50 machine gun first used in WW II and still used in Viet Nam. I am trained to kill with my hands and feet employing various elements of karate, Special Forces tactics, etc. I am trained in the art of bayonet fighting." [12] Imagine the effect of this list on the peace- and education-lovers! Would the Nam move right in and spoil the neighborhood? After his display of strength, the nightwatchman assured *Daily* readers that "I have never employed any of this training to the purpose for which it was intended, killing men. I prefer not to."

In the Rochdale community, where rank was a free-for-all, Rochdale Security had undeniable status. "The status is so high that half a dozen people wear black shirts and work on security for nothing." [13] (In October '70 at least, the status must have been lower — security officers were paid $80 a week.) To get that status, Security members had to perform several jobs well. One constant job was quality control. "Many of the kids who came in for dope were ripped off," says Police Officer Dean Audley. "The dealers were more capitalist than any of us would be. They would sell Javex or Comet. If it was white powder you wanted, it was white powder you got. Of course, the kids who were burned didn't go back to complain in case they were filled in. I used to stop some and say, 'Let me see your oregano.' I'm sure the stocks of the local oregano company went up 100 percent." The "Space Duck" comic strip in the *Daily Planet* gave good advice: "Wanna have a good time? All you have to remember is the first one is always free. (Another day, another dealer.)" [14] The advice came from "(Burn-Artiste) Parsley Flakes."

The outsiders and novices had to watch for themselves, but the insiders wanted protection from rip-offs and impurities that could cause serious damage. Fifty people attended a seminar on drugs in February '69 and an expert led the discussion. In answer to the problem of drugs mixed with strychnine or Drano, the expert suggested finding a rich person's supplier. "Their dealers are a little more concerned about losing a customer than the [Yorkville] village freaks are and consequently the 'social' use of dope...has brought forth a really fine array of smoke and hallucinogens. The meeting came to an end on a downer, with people vainly trying to think of a rich friend." [15] In April '69, Report 1 in the *Daily* warned that LSD of the varieties Light Blue, Orange Tab, and White Tab were all incompletely synthesized, while Pink Tab at $7 a hit was "very good LSD; no strychnine, no STP." The MDA at $3.50 was neither MDA nor meth, but "a burn." The $5 Meth hits, however, were fairly clean. "One sample sold as crystal was actually MDA (the person who took this ended up in the hospital)."

Some of the warnings originated from Rochdale's own Free Clinic, which had "a service for getting dope and other drugs analyzed to ascertain their true composition, and from time to time issued warnings to the hip community to avoid this or that type of acid tab or cap as a burn." [16] Florence's Parlour, one of the versions of the clinic, advised needle-users that "Gamma Globulin *does not* work for serum hep [hepatitis]; so, if you're that worried about serum — STOP CRANKING...or sterilize your works." [17] Always, someone could be counted on not to take the advice. Mother Fletcher of the clinic talked of the "yellow stoned-looking eyes" of hepatitis. "I can't remember a time in the last 3 years that someone here didn't have it." [18] A related organization, Trailer, published information on arrest and drug dangers; the information was made available in Rochdale.

In addition, Rochdale took steps to guarantee purity at the source. "I support," said one resident in the *Daily*, "any efforts to grow our own grass, manufacture our own quality acid, and stamp out speed and the Mafia." [19] The efforts mentioned were already in progress. *Maclean's* magazine reported that "all LSD that comes into Rochdale can be — and usually is — analysed at what one official described as student-run acid-test laboratories." [20] A catalog of projects underway in November '72 mentioned that a "Science Lab" on the sixth floor experimented in "the manufacture of chemicals from waste materials and Canadian raw materials, and in recycling methods. Emphasis is on creating domestic sources of chemicals which at present must be imported to Canada." [21] This was probably the same project that a *Daily* reported on earlier. The "Rochdale Science Center" on the sixth floor, it said, was now "able to produce a large number of fine chemicals, and if any of you have connections in the chemical trade, he can offer them a good deal and also pay a handsome commission." [22] "He can offer…"? No, this is not bad grammar, but the Rochdale love of gigantism. The Rochdale Science Center, apparently, was a "he."

Keeping track of bad dope and enforcing fair dealing became much easier when Rochdale Security reached its prime. In this role, Rochdale Security was a shadow version of a Better Business Bureau and had the enforcement powers — and moral imperative — of a Vice Squad. In one example, warnings in the *Daily* included one about bad grass that was brown or black with no seeds or twigs. "If you get burnt, dealers will return your money. If you can't get your $ back, see [the security head], and he will get it for you." [23]

Another constant job for Rochdale Security was screening people at the door and keeping out undesirables, both the unknown, suspicious ones and those who had been previously evicted. "Security had a fair amount of leverage," says Alex MacDonald. "Anybody who was a complete right asshole could get thrown out. Having political clout meant being able to defend yourself from Security. Security would throw out anybody they didn't like. That was the first level of screening, but they didn't have any authority, they just did it. If you didn't have the jam or the smarts or the connections to realize that they were not in fact entitled to do that, you deserved to be thrown out."

Screening in a self-professed democracy gave problems an average biker had difficulty in handling. One Rochdale resident protested in April '69 that "I have watched for five nights while *every* decisive action taken by 'security' has been hassled to death by member-residents. Chico (and Jeff before him) have been asked both to act and to give an ongoing ethics seminar while acting... Residents and councillors must be prepared to say openly (i.e. in front of the persons in question) who they want out and why. The residents must also expect to physically assist security in the ejection of whoever it might be who needs ejection." [24]

Rochdale Security's riskiest task, however, was to stand between the police and the drug dealers. Until the summer of 1970, "an informal agreement existed between the college and city police," which marked the peaceful stage of that task. [25] Warrants would be shown to Rochdale Security, who would escort officers inside and open doors with the master key.

But the police and the Rochdale community alike saw clearly that Rochdale Security had something going on. At the time of the Bradford council election in June '69, "speedfreaks seemed to be protected by a security head who may have been dealing himself," said a governing council member in a draft of a speech. [26] "The problem with bikes and speed was very tense. Our security head seemed to be protecting a small group who were friends, customers, or too powerful to deal with. He was caught between pressure to evict speedfreaks and fear for his life if he evicted them all." Govcon tried to ease the pressure on the security head by participating in the evictions. "This led to numerous threats including someone pulling a knife on [a council member] just outside the building." The security head left in the middle of the night.

A former resident's story confirms the connection between Rochdale Security and the dealers: "At Christmas, I had taken a plane to England and mailed back some dope in shortcake tins. I wanted some money to buy a sailing boat. As soon as they arrived, I talked to _____. It was Nepalese hash, VERY good stuff. I waited in _____'s room while four or five dealers came in over a space of two or three hours. The amount of cash was impressive. Each of them must have been carrying — carrying — several thousands of dollars. Of course I walked out later with $3,300. And it was impressive how good Rochdale Security was. The fire alarm went off while I was with _____ so we stuffed the dope in our pockets and stood in the hall. That was the usual thing during a raid, everyone went into the halls to make it difficult. The security guy came up and told us it was okay, the alarm was false. He'd known exactly where we were. Of course, he got $80 for the job."

In another incident, police caught one resident with dope in his car and two officers went with him to search his room on the sixteenth floor. Rochdale Security intervened and delayed them by asking for a warrant. By the time the officers reached the room, they could find only vitamins. The room "amazingly enough, was just 'cleaned' by maintenance." [27] On another occasion, a security person put duty before caution and rang the fire alarm in view of the police who were entering on a raid. That landed him in court on a charge of obstruction.

Meanwhile, the members of Rochdale Security came and went as restively as the rest of the residents. By the summer of 1970, the new edition of Rochdale Security had style and character as well as intimidation. One Security member called himself a "sometime sculptor." He made one piece "mostly out of fits and droppers, security's gleanings from the less together among us. It's in an art show now." [28] Then there was "Zipp." Zipp drew *Acid-Man*, a comic strip which first appeared in Vancouver's *Georgia Straight* in September

'67. The villain was "Ego Cop — Society's ultimate weapon for the preservation of hate, greed, sadism, brutality, outdated Victorian laws, and the rest of the simple joys the older generation worked so hard to establish." [29] "Zipp was short and quiet," says Sharon Kingsland, "though he projected a tough guy image." Zipp had another occupation as well as Security: he acted as Rochdale's Bishop, conducting religious meetings and performing weddings.

Soon, late in the summer of 1970, Zipp would be seen on the front pages of Toronto newspapers trying to conduct a different kind of meeting. All of the city would see him in his black shirt and black glasses, on his motorcycle, trying to calm an upset crowd. When Rochdalians faced the interlopers they had long expected — an unhappy public represented by unhappier police — both the defenders and the attackers of Fortress Rochdale would be unpredictable and possibly violent.

"Army" of Rochdale Security, at the front desk.

"Trooper Drooper" of Rochdale Security, at the street-level lobby.

A 1971 Govcon meeting in the second-floor lounge. Figures include Jimmy Newell (far left), Pamela Berton (hand raised), Jay Boldizsar (foreground in white), and Mary Ann Carswell (lying, facing camera).

The dayshift at Rochdale College: people who were on staff in various capacities in the summer of 1973.

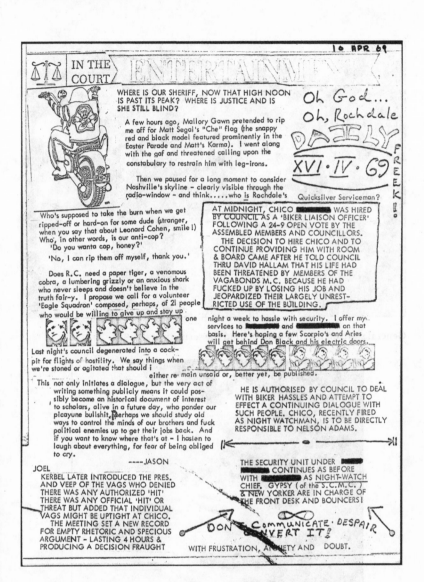

One page of the *Daily*, April 1969. (Photo courtesy of Thomas Fisher Rare Book Library)

General store on the first floor behind the security desk, 1972.

Michael Regnart making pottery in the second-floor pottery studio.

The Rochdollar, good for co-operative service. Reverse of a Rochdollar.
(Photos courtesy of Aulene Maki and Mark Buckiewicz)

Weaving from Tom Ward's sixth-floor weaving studio.

The Unknown Student, a bronze sculpture by Rochdale's Sculpture Shop, unveiled in April 1969, and turned around to face the street by the renovating company. (Photo by the author)

Rochdale security posing in the basement parking level, summer of 1971.

Rochdale Security with guard dogs in the basement parking level, summer of 1971.

The "last incarnation" of Rochdale Security, Christmas 1973.

PART THREE:

THE EIGHTEEN-STORY HIGH

13

High Society

Now we leave the whitewater stream of events and enter the larger lake — the waters that Rochdalians swam in day to day. This part of the story will explore the activities that were continual and timeless, activities that had little direct effect on the survival of Fortress Rochdale College, but which together made Rochdale a symbol for a lifestyle. If a sense of postponed, interrupted disaster hangs over this part, that sense reproduces the feeling in the residents. What was happening was too good/too unusual/too bad, to last.

At the very least, Rochdalians wanted to join "one big happy family," and in pursuit of that richer social life, Rochdalians used two watchwords — love and freedom. Those two came together variously. On the one hand, a resident like Pamela Berton could eulogize, after three years of living in Rochdale, "the joy of concocting a communal stew for 30 of her neighbours, the satisfaction of a floor well-scrubbed by 15 people, the excitement and mess as an entire floor congregates to decorate a Christmas tree with cranberries, popcorn strings, and silver cigarette wrappers, or the peace of evenings spent drinking tea in the lounge as everyone shares a newspaper."[1]

On the other hand, the effect could be one of hypocrisy. "The place proved to me the idiocy of the counterculture," says one former resident. "It was considered de rigueur to speak on the elevators, since nobody did on the straight ones. In fact, it was every bit as taboo not to speak as it was to speak in any other elevator. So you'd wind up having inane conversations...Really, I had very little social contact. But still, a feeling grew that was, well, relaxing. Anything went. You felt you were in some sort of fortress and since everyone did what they liked, you could too."

"Miriam" told the *Telegram* that "there isn't any fear here. Only being caught by the law. But the trouble is, there isn't any love. People in here are trying so hard to be groovy, they're afraid to be humans. Being groovy? Well, you know, they're never shocked. They don't ever give a straight answer. They speak in abstracts. Most of them are so stoned all the time they speak in abstracts anyway."[2]

Rochdale put social freedom on display during its parties. In 1968, residents marked the Fall Equinox (with solar eclipse) with a "ritual celebration" on the roof. "The Virgin yields to the Lion. Singing dancing. Come with friends and musical instruments. Survival cookies will be passed out."[3] The following month, the Utopian Research Institute sponsored a Halloween Party and suggested that people come dressed as "a hermaphrodite from Gemini, a child of the moon, a civilization from the sun, the lost tribe of Israel, an Indian from Venus, a sex empress from Scorpio, a pair of thighs, a skeleton, a new age baby, a pair of feet..."[4]

In one "happening" in an ashram at 2:30 a.m., the happeners added light to their show by burning a garbage bag from a ceiling fixture. As a vinyl Donovan sang his "Season of the Witch," smoke filled the ashram. In another case of sensory freedom, a "People's Gallery" on the street level held a two-week black light show with "Blackie's (she's a she) day-glo robe, Friar Tuck's psychedelic Tie-Dyes, and Frank Fury's 'dream machine,'" an electric hash-pipe.[5] During the two weeks, Friar Tuck presided over four weddings. The *Daily* reported that the "Black Lite Show finally came off...with body

painting. The people drank acid kool-aid and moved in the dark with
leaping flames on their bodies. Vibrating breasts and snakely arms
mingled in the crowd."[6] This, like an event advertised for an Open
House, was "a Not-so-Square Dance."

Then too, Rochdale reserved the monarchy it had set up under
James I—like Great Britain itself—for ceremonial occasions. Starting
in 1971, the Morgravia-Boulognia Embassy Ball was held with pomp
annually on Maerspeche Day. This special day in December marked
the time when, one member of a floor group being accused of tyr-
anny, the group decided everyone was royal. "Maerspeche," short for
"long-winded speeches," began with the marriage of King Gustav of
Morgravia and Queen Irma of Boulognia on December 4, as recorded
in Mike Randell's history of the Duchy.[7] The Ball in 1972 attracted
"some of the brighter lights of Rochdale society, as well as most of
the shadows."[8] Invitations to the ball later came "By Order of The
Ambassador H.C. Joseph P. Wertz: You Are Requested To Appear
At The Fifth Annual Embassy Ball of the Embassy of Morgravia-
Boulognia To His Majesty's Government King James I of Rochdale
On The Occasion of Maerspeche Day, December 4, 1975...Medals
Will Be Worn." The program included "The Anthem...Ach Der Gutte
Faderland...Mitte der Gutte Vine und Bierre...Gotte Sie Dronke
und Soa Amme I...Drinke sie Punch und Zmoack sie Doap."[9]

All events in the highrise, royal, special, and daily, were accented
heavily with music. "You have to realize the *sound* in there, the bedlam,"
says a former resident. "The sirens, the dogs barking, the music, all
coupled with a state of mind moving between mania and depression.
Televisions were always on, but often with the sound turned off and
replaced with rock and roll. Music was all-important in Rochdale."

At one point, a Rochdale party—which tended to be public due
to the noise level—went civic as well. This was the "Rochfestival"
planned for May '71. Rochdale would sponsor a City Hall gig in which
"a 150-foot magenta peace symbol" would be erected "on top of city

hall." The brochure announced that "the fountain will be full of electric kool-aid and Mayor Dennison is expected to give Rochdale the keys to the city." Five hundred kazoos were ordered and the whole party would be used to celebrate the opening of the Yonge Street mall. "The city is going to try their hardest to make this a dull event because they never really wanted to close the street in the first place. We will make Yonge Street come alive... Imagination is the most powerful weapon we have against a system that is sorely lacking in it." [10]

Unfortunately, the plan was sorely full of it, and only a reduced version reached the Yonge Street mall. One hundred yo-yo's, donated just before the parade, added color and motion to the sonic effects of the kazoos. The Rochdale Rockettes, a "crack-drill chorus line," entertained, and Toronto Alderman Bill Archer addressed the crowd. "When I was in school," he said, "I never let my lectures get in the way of my education." [11] Fifteen Rochdale diplomas were given out in a convocation ceremony. In all, Rochdale spent $5,000 on the smiles.

If Yonge Street was dull to a Rochdalian, the highrise on Bloor Street was dullest. Rochdale College couldn't be beautiful and well-endowed — but it could be different. Every other highrise numbered its floors; Rochdale used letters, all displayed on the buttons in the elevator. (By that reckoning, this is Chapter M.) Floor "S" attracted red graffiti announcing "sincerity" and "serenity".

In another flight from the Dull, Rochdale planned to build a dome on the second-floor terrace, but the plan was different enough to create a "running feud" with city officials: "The City has decided it is an 'enclosure' and wants us to dig another sub-basement out to provide more parking space for the people it shelters." Govcon suggested that the dome be re-classified as a sculpture. Someone else suggested that "it be mounted on four hundred casters bought from Canadian Tire and classified as a vehicle." [12]

The *Daily* refers to a swimming pool on the fifteenth floor; this may not be a put-on, considering the flair for changes shown by

Rochdale interior decorators. The fifteenth-floor residents planned to ask the YMCA for a subsidy and to approach the sixteenth floor "with respect to cutting a hole for a diving board in the ceiling."[13] The filter pump they bought for $35 "came in a bushel basket and we can't figure it out." They did, however, find a lifeguard. Even figures in sober Co-operative College Residence Incorporated caught the spirit of the place. When it was discovered in June '69 that the building had a possible eight degree tilt towards Bloor Street, coordinator John Jordan remarked on it in a letter. "Rochdale," he said, "was experiencing a counter-gravitational vertical thrust which had added 29 inches to its height. Since this figure cannot be explained in terms of the co-efficient of expansion of the structural elements, we were reduced to postulating that the building must be experiencing a high."[14] As the inscription over the eighth-floor elevator announced: "Gee, Toto, I don't think we're in Kansas any more."

For their bold use of the roof, Rochdalians deserve at least a footnote in an architecture text. In good weather, the roof became the most popular lounge. Rituals and celebrations were held there on religious or natural occasions, such as an Easter Morning Sunrise Celebration that blended East (Hare Krishnas) and West. Solstices and equinoxes were observed. On some warm summer nights, films were shown, and on hot summer days, a cooler supplied beer.

But mostly, the roof provided sunbathers with "Rochdale's tar beach." Near the end of Rochdale, the Beaver family, a commune on the fifteenth floor, proposed the buying of two to six tons of sand to convert the beach from tar to sand in time for the "Sun of 75." A sand beach would "facilitate the nudists, the touch/sight therapy groups, the bartending classes (which were among the best attended in the past, anyway), and the gardening experiments."[15]

Like a Caribbean resort, the private beach was surrounded by a chain-link fence. "One striking physical feature of the building," the police reported, "is the eight-foot wire fence on the north portion of the roof," erected to stop the dropping of objects from the roof, "equipped with three strands of barb wire sloping in." [16] One photograph in the Rochdale archives preserves the "Night of the Eclipse 75" celebration. Shown is a crowd with two men and a woman naked, bottles of beer, a clarinet, and behind them all, the fence at the edge.

By the final year, besides the barbed-wire fence, there were gardens in the wooden decking where tomato plants, sunflowers, corn, and marijuana tried to grow. Bathtubs from the suites below served for mixing soil, and where there is horticulture, there is fertilizer. "I hope no one objects to the swimming pool being used for the lovely compost that's coming out of that space," said one unnamed publication. The seventeenth-floor ashram planned to put grass around the pool, and residents drove the college "bus" out to the country for "more wormy dirt and old, old shit." The Boogie Bus took eight residents to Holland Marsh "to liberate from the hands of the false government 1/2 to 1 *ton* of rich wormy soil, smuggle it back home, pack the elevators, put it all on the roof and celebrate at the 'if this is Wednesday, this must be Rochdale's party.'" [17] After the end of Rochdale, reporters were shown the "holes in the ceilings where water from the penthouse vegetable gardens — and from tenants' water beds — poured down. 'On hot nights they slept up there (on the roof) on water beds and, when they were finished, they just dumped out the water. It had to go somewhere.'" [18]

This was freedom, one of the watchwords. Property and material things could not compare to spirit and a good time. But what of the other watchword, love? Love and freedom together, of course, spells free love. One resident proclaimed that "we must live together and take the pornography out of sex. Go out and find someone to ball; if you can't, come home and ball yourself. Masturbation is your revolutionary duty." [19]

Casual sex became a part of the image Rochdale promoted, despite some disclaimers. "I doubt whether there's more promiscuity here than elsewhere," said a twenty-year-old woman resident. "People who live in Rochdale do it in beds, and people who live in ordinary university residences or with their parents do it in cars. Beds are more comfortable."[20] In response to rumors of group sex, another resident answered that "we couldn't possibly do that in bed...it would degenerate into a pillow fight."[21]

The reports of free love and casual sex were, however, persistent. According to Kent Gooderham, "serial marriages, group marriages, and legal marriages are all acceptable. The last being the most unusual."[22] *Maclean's* publicized the sign found on a fifteenth-floor apartment: "I LOVE LOVE / (Except between 6 and 9 p.m., when I'm studying, and Wednesdays and Fridays, when I'm ironing or doing my hair)."[23] In one issue of the *Daily Planet*, a dispenser for The Pill was used as a pseudo-Eastern cosmological symbol.

"In some cases," says later property manager Sid Smith, "young girls were in Rochdale, freaked out, and the lesser lights [minions of the dealers] were told to get rid of them. They'd call a cab, pay the cab driver off, and he'd go and leave her on the steps of St. Joseph's Hospital and take off. There was a lot of sex going on, and prostitution." The *Daily* felt it was necessary to publish a warning. "*Security Says:* 13, 14, 15 year old chicks are illegal, balling them is a statutory rape charge, could be good for life. p.s. cons don't dig rapists."[24] Rochdale Clinic, Rochdale's own health service, did its best to educate. In a pamphlet, resident Ann Pohl warned that "gonorrhea can lay dormant in a chick for long enough for the infection to do dreadful horrid damage to her baby-making facilities. So always tell the chick!"[25] Later, the Clinic announced that "rubbers are now free."[26]

Rochdale played up its image of free love. An ad for a showing of *Deep Throat* said "Admission $10. Cum naked FREE."[27] Similarly, Pipe Productions (Rochdale's home-brewed beer) promised "Dionysian Celebrations" on hot weekends on the roof, with "sometimes music, sometimes cold beverage, sometimes hot squirming naked bodies."[28]

In November '68, the *Daily* announced that *"The Wet Bod First Official Co-ed Bathing Society* meets at Ken and Jude's place …come prepared…(one of the Harrad Experiment Seminar activities)." [29]

Nudism easily found disciples, especially in summer. "A lot of them went around the building completely naked," says Sid Smith. "It was nothing in the summer months to find in an elevator two or three girls and a couple of guys coming down naked to the store, getting a coke, and going back up to the roof." One *Rochdale Catalogue* listed Sun Worship as a course: "Sunning is an ancient pastime practiced by all orders of life, especially plants. People are encouraged to enjoy techniques such as basking, sunning, solar absorption seminars, tanning and sunburn. Clothing is tolerated." [30] Former resident Sharon Kingsland remembers that "in the summer there were always nude people on the sundeck. Some would come up fully clothed and ogle the women, but nobody really minded. We had an old alcoholic who came up often. No one bothered him because he was so pathetic."

The casual attitude went further. Jack the Bear, who had a tent on the roof, acted as a tour guide and was "the hit of our open house." [31] At an ashram bathroom, Jack said to the assembled members of the public, "'And here is the bathroom. It has three sinks, a bathtub, a shower, and two toilets in fine working order. In fact I'm going to use this one right now.' And he did." One free spirit, the Rochdale exhibitionist, became legendary. "Bob was the first streaker," says Sid Smith. "He used to run out into the street or cycle around the area completely naked, and guide traffic until he saw a police car and then he'd run into the building." When an external critic tried to stir up public indignation with reports of the nudity in the College, resident Reg Hartt wrote a letter to him: "Come Judgment Day, we shall all stand naked before God. We at Rochdale, will be prepared. Also, we'll have nice body tans. How about you?" [32]

All these progressive attitudes about the human body faltered when the roles of man and woman became an issue. Kent Gooderham concluded that "Rochdale is a man's world and many women play a role quite accurately described by the term Chick."[33] To Sharon Kingsland, the sexism in Rochdale "reflected the working-class attitudes of the people who came there." Examples of male chauvinism went unchallenged. At one point, monitors on each floor were paid $30 a month and were called "Floor Daddies."[34] Even when the monitors included females as well as males, the common language expected authority to come from Daddy. In another example, two new communes appealed for "females": "are the females waiting for the males to build a good living situation, and then move in? with our conditioning, creating community is hard enough without boarding school-like sex frustrations."[35] And in a list of activities good for Rochdale membership hours, one bureaucrat included "smiling (if girl, at my discretion)."[36]

A resident reported that "frequently out of the ceiling air vent in the bathroom I hear desperate female cries accompanied by the sound of a woman being kicked around the room."[37] However, the same resident used the occasion to complain, not about brutality, but about being left out: "While men tend to fuck just for the fun of it, for some of the women it is essentially a political statement, as we saw in What Do You Care Who Your Friends Fuck? Once these ladies find a guy who is more or less acceptable, both ideologically and physically, they cling to him like a shipwrecked sailor hanging on to a floating log. Sexual mobility in this enlightened community is considerably less than in the average downtown typing pool."

Which brings us to the "What Do You Care Who Your Friends Fuck?" debate, as recorded by "Miguel Machismo." A young woman had taken enough lovers to incite a vigilante group against her. "Given 24 hours to leave town by some very heavy broads, Mary showed more balls than any men by confronting her tormentors in front of the biggest ad hoc meeting in Rochdale's history," went the detailed account in the *Daily*.[38] "The spokeswoman for the vigilantes, someone called Suki, appeared at just the right moment. 'She has only been in the building 3 months and already she is screwing our men!' she said while casting threatening glances at neophyte Mary. 'She's been going from man to man,' she cautioned. 'Big Sister is watching you!' said Dirty Dan, while Nikita Littler pounded the table with his shoe... At this point order broke down and a fair bit of factionalism arose. It brought to mind an old Economics Lecture in which we learned about mercantilism... and its opposite, free trade, and finally Keynesian economics, whereby more and more people agree to share a bigger and bigger pie... One thing is certain: that the 'pie' being divided is Rochdale manhood."

Against the odds, feminism made a beginning inside the College. A Women's Involvement Program with twelve women produced videotapes on women's issues with a grant from the federal Local Initiatives Program, and a "Rochdale women's cadre" was formed in response to the drug-trafficking problems. At that time, resident Bruce Maxwell argued that "for Rochdale to grow we must elect women, natural visionaries to our council."[39] Indeed, the official activities of the College always depended on equal participation. The problem of sexism lay with the main body of residents, the ones unaffected by the minority of leaders.

If the roles of gender were not challenged, the roles of family were. The "one big happy family" of Rochdale included communes — experimental and sometimes volatile attempts at merging family with community — as well as cults with religious familial ties, and normal, nuclear families. Yet even the nuclear family with children became altered in the fusion pile that was Rochdale. "In 1972," says Alex MacDonald, "there were thirty or forty kids living in the building, most of whom had been born there." Or, as an anonymous cabbie put it, in Rochdale "you had a lot of babes with babies." Care for these children became a concern of more than the nuclear parents, and was shared as a continuing group project. In the first month of the College, daycare was being advertised in the *Daily*: "Mothers of preschool children: We the undersigned undertake to provide day care(fully) Noonly." [40] Afterwards, "one of the 4th floor Zeus suites was the Rochdale Nursery School until the law-abiding Provincial Government said you couldn't have a nursery on the 4th floor." [41] Kent Gooderham's youngest child attended Rochdale Kindergarten and "learned how to get ice cream from the restaurant by paying imaginary money." [42]

Acorn, a daycare center, began on the sixth floor in September '71 and continued through to the end. Acorn provided a free, co-operative space for kids and adults, and as late as Rochdale's final year, it was being used nine hours a day, five days a week, by twelve to fifteen people. During the summers, Rochdale funded a swimming pool on the roof for the children.

In the matter of birth, Rochdale insisted on holding its own. A *Daily* for November '68 announced the first resident not entering by the front door: "LOVE and a pinch in the unborn belly of the first/ ROCHDALIANI/O, the joy!!!/A fat little kid, bouncing about our humble home/(Like the first baby born on a rocket ship)/IS BEEG EVENT!!!!/ MUST BE CELEBRATIONS!!!!" [43] The event required some education for the young population of Rochdale. "Pat" published "a gentle note to all those who would click their tongues: a pregnant woman is not a special breed of invalid who must remain weakly by her bedside, even when she is three days overdue. She is a regular person who likes fresh air and walking and even has errands to do. The baby will not drop from her belly on a moment's notice, surprising an elevator full of people or stopping traffic in the street. Nature has provided plenty of time (sometimes over 12 hours) for mother to find a safe warm clean comfortable place for her young to come forth in." [44]

One birth documented by the *Globe* happened in May '74. Jack and Susan Brashear didn't believe in having babies in hospitals "because the mother is all zonked on drugs and the first thing the nurses do is take the baby, also drugged, away during a vital period when it should be right there relating to her... Jack says if you look at it, people started noticing communications problems and generation gaps about 20 years ago, or about the same time mothers got really keen on having babies in hospitals."[45] So they had their third baby in Rochdale. "They stayed up the other night and a friend came by to help with the delivery. Susan said it was 'really intense,' there in the room. 'It wasn't a breeze.' They woke little [eight-year-old] Mary up to watch and Mary got pretty excited when she saw the head come out. Susan said it was nice later, when she and Mary lay in bed hugging the new baby."

Another birth comes to us in an account by Jim Garrard, who was moving out of Rochdale. "I turned the key to my room over to a 15 year old girl who was pregnant, who was hanging around our ashram. A very nice girl with a hateful family. We always had a difficult time with runaways and with underage kids, to know what to do with them. Generally they weren't kicked out or sent home. They were allowed to hang around if they had a sponsor. This girl had her baby in my room after I left. No medical presence there. Somebody came down and was playing the violin outside the door of the room, in the lobby. She says she could hear the violin while she was giving birth to the baby, but nobody else in the room heard it. There was a recording of the birth — it was the kind of thing they did — and you could hear the violin going on, played as a serenade for her."

Babies and children in a place as chaotic as Rochdale had its risks. A former resident wrote that his "most persistently horrifying recollection involves a young child who could not yet form the words 'please' or 'thank you' (or 'father,' since he had none) but who knew how to say, *'Give me a toke.'*"[46] The *Daily* itself announced that, after a girl was born in the Rochdale Free Clinic, "this kid should have a head start on everybody since she was born stoned on psillocybin."[47] Poet Victor Coleman complained in the *Daily* that "I share the same space with three small children, ages 2, 4, and 5 ½ ... Somehow I like them to be free to go wherever they want to go ... The other day, before Christmas, my 5 ½-year-old daughter, Maryrose, came up to me and handed me a pill she had just picked up in the elevator hall on the tenth floor where we live. Happy New Year — who do we thank, now, that she was 5 1/2, not 2, to find such a pill?" [48]

While traditional families were testing a more decentralized communal life, more ambitious experiments in collective living were underway. "Our great social achievement," says Alex MacDonald, "was the development of the commune as a way of living in a high-rise building." The L-shaped Ashram units on each floor were ideal for communes, with their six bedrooms all opening onto common living, kitchen, and washroom space.

The communes came together and fell apart in a bewildering assortment. One of them, the Utopian Research Institute, began communing by October '68 and in the manner of Utopias, chose the floor that in many apartments doesn't exist — the thirteenth. Plans for the Institute included a meditation temple, a public coffee house, a musical instrument-making workshop, yoga, "a naked Ashram," entry restricted by locks and doorbells, and a twenty-four-hour educational program. For meals, "people will be seated on the floor on their pillows with a knee-high table made out of a stand with a cafeteria tray on top." [49] The intent was to teach "omniequilibrium."

Any commune being set up had to establish its identity and borders, and often relied on locks to keep out non-members. One such group formed in late spring' 69 on the sixteenth-floor east wing. "Just as Rochdale did when it opened," commune member "Orpheus" reported, "we got some creeps and vegetables. These are almost invariably people who didn't live here last winter. They don't understand the locking doors..." [50] In September '69, the ninth floor proposed a year lease. The floor would collect all rents, clean the premises, and keep the books. At that time, an eighth-floor commune had eleven

members under coordinator Stuart Roche. A fifteenth-floor commune that started up in spring '70 became "the single most powerful
political group in the building," according to Alex MacDonald. Like
several other communes, it added a voice in favor of controlling the
drug dealers. By 1972, communes had taken over the fifteenth floor,
then the seventeenth; the fifteenth-floor commune had expanded to
the sixteenth, the twelfth, and the sixth.

The most enduring and the most well-known commune, however,
began in 1969 on the fourteenth floor. In July, twenty people decided
to restrict entry to the floor with the help of four doors. Body-painting
parties raised funds for locks to "control the flow of undesirables." [51]
By August, the floor had thirty-five members out of a maximum
capacity of forty-five, of which fifteen were students. As in the rest
of the College, the students didn't mix well and eventually left. Still
inspired by the visit of John Lennon and Yoko Ono to Toronto the
previous summer, the non-student half formed the "Rochdale Peace
Center" in time for Christmas.

The new Peace Center had ambition. A two-page handout promot-
ing a peace benefit in March '70 announced that "All We are Saying is
Give Peace a Chance": "War is Over: If you want it / Rochdale: Peace
Center / Toronto: The Peace City / Canada: The Peace-Maker." [52] The
commune sponsored a benefit at the St. Lawrence Centre that same
month. "Rochdale's special brand of desultory listlessness permeated
the centre flavored with incense," reported the *Globe*. [53] "Inside the
concert hall, the sparse crowd listened to Leather, Mother Tucker's
Yellow Duck, the Perth County Conspiracy, and the Hare Krishna
people." Also in March, the Peace Center organized a music festival
in the University of Toronto's Convocation Hall. "The show began
in high spirits, with devotees of the Rama Krishna temple...leading
a Hare Krishna chant. Flower children joined hands and danced in
chains through the audience. The lights were on in the hall, and so
three or so barechested sinewy boys and several nymphets fled up

and down the aisles in ecstatic abandon. Long threads were passed through the audience, held carefully in hundreds of fingers, making their way around the hall."[54] Long delays and bad sound mixes followed. "It was a hard night on the audience's self-control," said the controlled *Globe* reporter, "but if there is hope for Peace Nation, self-control may be one of the directions in which it lies."

The fourteenth-floor commune entered the pages of *Miss Chatelaine* as the "nth floor commune ... which, if you remember the New Math symbolism of n (unknown quantity), is an interesting coincidence ... They live in a rabbit warren of rooms off a darkened hall; the door is kept locked."[55] The forty communards were united in wanting to convert the rest of the floors to their kind of commune. "What makes the fourteenth floor distinctive is a little difficult to discern, especially since, as the smoke keeps rising, the syntax keeps degenerating ... 'We have a society based on trust,' [says one commune member], 'where you don't have to lock [inside] doors. If every floor in the building were like this one, it would be so much easier to keep things under control.'"

The odds for converting the whole building were not good. At one council election, the commune leader won less than 6 percent of the votes for president and none of the others were elected for lesser positions. The commune had "accepted the role of conscience for the rest of the College," according to Kent Gooderham, and as Rochdale's "sacred cow," it was at the same time respected and resented.[56] The fourteenth-floor commune fridges, it was said, were the only ones in which food could be found the next day, but at least one member wanted out due to "untenable working conditions and lack of personal privacy."[57] He had been forced by a collective decision to house two crashers in his room for two weeks. A "concerned resident" reported to the *Daily* that one leader was evicted and almost charged with maiming when he poured solvent-based paint over someone's head. He said the leader had won a return to Rochdale by "veiled threats."[58] All was not going peacefully for the Peace Center, nor did it manage to escape the kind of mess that the College itself was in. A year after its formation, the Center had accumulated debts of $10,000, including $600 for printing and $1,000 for the St. Lawrence event, with no angel in sight.

The religious cults, on the other hand, escaped the *angst* that these more ad hoc groups had to deal with. The communes had to work to create organization and identity while the cults were already established or took their identity from their faith. And the cults, with their sense of mission, were solvent. "When Rochdale needed money," says Property Manager Sid Smith, "they consented to have the Hare Krishna people move in because they could pay a lot for their apartments, $700 or $800 a month in all...Rochdale finally asked them to leave because they used to go up on the roof and chant at daybreak." Another religious group, called 3HO, began at Rochdale. The three H's stood for Happy, Healthy, and Holy. They practiced yoga; wore white pants, tops, and turbans; and ate no meat. Like the Krishnas, they prospered and, after Rochdale, grew into a fifty-member commune downtown.

The most significant cult for Rochdale began on the third floor. A *Rochdale Catalogue* listed the "Jesus-Forever Family" as "a Christian commune, active in religious affairs in and around Toronto...There is a meeting room and a chapel. Fee: complete involvement."[59] According to Alex MacDonald, "the Jesus Freaks had one of the most stable communes in the building. They were the only cultural entity that ever came to Rochdale, squared off, and came out ahead. [Students who were not Jesus Freaks] would move in and would be crewcut, hard-working, do-their-homework-every-day students in September. By November they had dropped out and had gotten into politics and drugs and sex and all that shit. The Hare Krishna moved in and moved out almost immediately because they kept losing members. But the Jesus Freaks had a cultural identity."

Having an identity, however, did not mean the identity was popular. Love was being mixed with words that did not sound like Freedom. It didn't even sound like Love. Bill King wrote that "one nite the Jesus Freaks from the 3rd floor brought in some revivalists to play us some tunes and testify about how they were all junkies until they found the Lord. I think you gotta be a junkie or a speed freak to get into Jesus Freak School. Anyhow they sung us some songs and spoke of the Lord and we sung back Amen (marijuana) Amen (marijuana) Amen. Some people argued theology with them and they argued back. You believe in hell, man? What kind of a dude would create a place like that?" [60]

14

Under the Rock

As Rochdale the Drug Store moved its merchandise, Rochdale the College stabilized into a school that a school marm would have difficulty recognizing. The first step was already well advanced — the rejection of academic and disinterested learning. University of Toronto professor Elliot Rose styled education in Rochdale as "survival training in [an] up-from-anarchy situation,"[1] while resident Jack Jones pointed to the advantages of Rochdale as "an educational junkyard, an un-learning situation."[2] The *Daily Planet* praised "the slow striptease of our concepts, it is even this which builds us."[3]

Rochdale's idea of education had become elementary. As resident Pat Shafer put it, "I do not have to be sitting out on cold winterized Bloor to know when I have flunked, and I can have happy security fantasies of...the pleasantly stoned warmth of any Ashram lounge to know what passing means."[4] In some circles, passing now meant passing the joint, and "the working definition of intellectual honesty was a 29-gram ounce of marijuana as opposed to 26."[5]

Rochdale's claims to education make most sense when they refer to social experiment. Rochdale argued with the authorities that it was "a social scientific experiment which has already learned more about education than OISE [the Ontario Institute for Studies in Education]."[6] Unlike traditional studies, there was no merit in solitude: "Learn? Locked in a room alone? Good God!"[7] One unnamed resident expressed the challenge: "If you're a middle-class kid looking for your new Utopia, you come to Rochdale and really face yourself. You get food stolen off you by kids just like yourself who have an ethic of non-property. You start locking your door and never going into a communal area because it's such a pig-sty... You try and get a film shown in the Lounge, but some cat is 'doing his thing' with the TV turned up full blast. You know you start to get very mean and straight about these kids... The message isn't any longer to shake up people's property and spatial concepts... Instead you find yourself locking up the goddamned doors, evicting speed freaks in the dead of night, and telling the kids they ought to go to work. Big Momma!"[8]

Rochdale president Peter Turner, one of the College's best spokesmen, explained in the *Globe Magazine:* "Each individual or group entering Rochdale, in a sense, forms the image one is presented with when coming to Rochdale... There are those who come primarily for the 'freedom.' To the outside observer, freedom to these people means 'license.'" This lasts until they are confronted and tamed by the residents. The maturing of "slovenly, ill-considerate" new residents under those conditions, said Turner, was Rochdale's most relevant level of education.

"Rochdale was where somebody's problem had come to roost," Turner continued. "What IS hiding here? Well for one thing...some of your children." "In Rochdale, the runaway is one of the most accepted and recognized problems with which our institution is concerned." As president, Turner often received calls from worried parents. He would reassure them that "if their son or daughter is a juvenile the chances are that our security will apprehend them and the parents will receive a call. If they have reported the missing child to the police, this chance is almost certain, for the police aid our security with lists and descriptions." As a shelter and a source of rehabilitation for young people, Rochdale was coping with a larger social problem. "This project is no longer simply an experiment awaiting judgment. It is a full-fledged institution, and it is successful."

"Active members of the college," said another council member, Lionel Douglas, "are the baby-sitters to...the 14- to 18-year-old kids who flow through the building constantly, especially the screwed-up ones...We are trying to learn and at the same time teach these kids... the idea of 'enough'. In other words, a true and functional sense of proportion." [9]

Before he left, co-founder Dennis Lee saw the same thing happening, but without viewing the process as, itself, education. He watched newcomers to Rochdale first "go through a period of euphoria at this ideal world they've dreamed about, a sort of saturnalia. Then they become disillusioned when they see that the people in Rochdale are just as venal and just as dirty and just as nice and as nasty as in the straight world. Some of them leave, then, and some of them go through a second saturnalia to ease the disappointment." [10]

While this social cuisinart continued to chop and blend illusions, youth, and fantasies, activities that could be called educational — more strictly — searched for relevant form. After the successful Summer Festival of July '69, the same organizers tried a "Living Communications Committee" with sculptor Ed Apt as Chairman and Judy Merril as Secretary, to speak for "a conglomerate of some sixty artists and students working in a variety of media across the broad spectrum of the arts." [11] No distinctions were made among the categories; crafts, fields of knowledge, and the arts were all, interchangeably, educational. The Living Communications Committee announced plans, wrote a ten-page brief, prepared for grant requests to the Ontario Arts Council — and disintegrated.

Because the governing council seemed uninterested in coordinating projects, "entrepreneur and proprietor" (and improbability)

Sir Basil Nardley-Stoades launched an "Education Council" in mid-December '69. It too disappeared. Finally, a council took hold and began to exist alongside Govcon. Known as Edcon, it had its "fiscal genesis" in January '71 and by June, still had its deficit at a manageable $80. Alex MacDonald describes the arrival of the new council as "the meteoric rise of Edcon and legitimate projects." According to the Catalogue for 1972, Edcon was "ultra-democratic" with "no Chairman, President, Secretary, or King." [12] Membership was kept at twelve to "facilitate" a quorum. Later, Edcon declared "that the Education Council is in itself an educational project." [13]

Govcon and Edcon sometimes combined into Govedcon or Assortedcon, and when a tenant association began later, the three sometimes spoke out as the "triclinium." Edcon conducted its business with the same loose hand as Govcon. Minutes for one meeting of Edcon show that "Ernest von Bezold suggested concentrated telepathic group ESP to help Syd Stern and Nickie Morrison recover from their respective illnesses. A minute was taken to do so." [14] A motion that Dave Carey "be given all of Bloor Street, from Bathurst Street west, as resource space" was carried unanimously.

It was Edcon's job to decide which proposals deserved space in Rochdale. From February '72 to November '72, it recorded fundraising income of $11,571 and expenses of $9,921 that included grants to the Rochdale Library ($1,691), Rochdale Radio ($2,643), Theatre Passe Muraille ($3,600), the purchasing of "Brainwave Equipment" ($1,314), and fundraising costs ($3,270). The brainwave equipment had been ordered for a "Consciousness Development Research Group." Experiments had started with "trance induction with repeating word tape-loops," and a dual brainwave biofeedback apparatus — elsewhere called an alphaphone brainwave analyzer — would become the next step. [15] The catalog for fall 1972 had forty heroic pages. The crafts listed included silk-screening, weaving in a studio with eight looms, batik, and candle-making. A tool complex was available on a commission basis for welding, wood turning, hardwood joinery, and bookbinding.

Nor was Edcon short-lived. Rochdale held an Open House in May '74, and claimed over 600 visitors in two days. At that time, Edcon published a catalog of over fifty projects then underway. The projects included the Publications Office, movies by Reg Hartt, the Library (with 8,000 volumes), craft workshops, Radio Rochdale, the Toad Lane Tenants Association, the Ladies Auxiliary of Rochdale ("a studio and refuge for women"), the Ptomaine General Store ("tobacco, soda pop, vegetables, canned, packaged and frozen foods, cleaning items, hash pipes, etc.") and Animal Farm (a twelfth-floor pet service run by Richard Barnes).[16] The umbrella stayed up and intact while the projects underneath constantly came and went. In one instance, Edcon decided to be candid with some official visitors. They took them to the worst ashram in the building, but when they opened the door, someone in the previous weeks had beaten them to it. The worst ashram had been transformed into a complete sound studio.

Of the lasting projects, one of the strongest was the Library. Shortly after the highrise opened, a "Union Catalog" had 750 titles. This catalog simply listed the owner of a particular book and the lender had to make his own arrangements with the owner. In March '69, the governing council approved a Library Committee, which then operated from a room on the second floor helped by donations from the science fiction collection of Judy Merril and a $300 bequest for the purchase of books and magazines. Under the influence of Merril and the Summer Festival's focus on science fiction, the library could make claims by June '69 that it had "the world's best and most extensive publicly available [science fiction] collection."[17]

By May '70, the Library had become "The Planted Pot Room." There, "you can loll about on mattresses smelling the plants, drink tea, coffee, and cocoa you make yourself, or warm up with a glass of port and some earthly delight from our well-stocked porno section."[18] In November '72, the collection contained eight thousand volumes, strong in psychology, philosophy, and science fiction. The library had a large room and suffered no library cards or sign-out book. "I tell them," librarian Charlotte von Bezold said, "I hope they remember to bring the book back, but if they don't, bring back some other book."[19] The total number, she said, stayed about level. Even so, it was necessary at one point to print a reminder in the *Daily*: "If you are one of those aspiring librarians who have set up branch libraries of books with our stamp on them, why not negotiate a reconsolidation with the main branch?"[20]

With Edcon, anything that could be described as a project became education — and why not? In the rough weather resulting from the mix of anarchy and confusion, any project had already learned a lot if it was able to dig a space under the rock and survive. Rochdale, itself the grand Project, became a college by being — for the smaller projects that took shelter — a residence.

But Rochdale as a shelter and as a support extended further than the reaches of Edcon. Whenever it could, Rochdale reached outward from the highrise, lending its name and personnel, and sometimes spending its money. "Rochdale is decentralizing," said resident Sarah Spinks in November '69.[21] "To old houses on Beverley Street, in American exile-land, Toronto's new ethnic community. To farms in Killaloe where they build geodesic domes among the rolling hills of the Ontario Shield. To an old garage on Dupont Street and a big parish hall in downtown Toronto. Rochdale, Phase II, Decentralizing Communes, appears to be progressing well." A General Meeting in 1971 introduced plans for a new Phoenix "(pronounced Phoney)" College,[22] and as late as 1974, Rochdale considered proposing affiliation with the University of Toronto and with the Students Administrative Council there. When affiliated, the Shelter Capsule (a geodesic dome project) would align with the Faculty of Architecture, Rochdale

Video and Rochdale Radio with the U of T Media Services, and the Alternate Press with the Computer Center. "We should be able to offer fresh insights and approaches to the stagnant monster. With perseverance, we should be able to get control."[23]

Other projects expanded with the help of Rochdale, first by sheltering within and then by decentralizing. These included Theatre Passe Muraille, as we will see later, and a project that is quite possibly the Best of Rochdale College. Faced with the dues that had to be paid for living in the front lines of experiment, faced with health problems that standard medical facilities were unable to service, the Rochdale community developed its own version of a college health service: the Rochdale Free Clinic.

The clinic began in response to the crasher problem. "The informal 'freak squads' which have operated here out of necessity, have handled many potentially dangerous situations deftly and sensitively,"[24] but a more formal arrangement was needed. Early in 1969, Govcon was approached for a grant. The proposal came from eighteen-year-old Aunty Flo (Ann Pohl), who would be assisted in the organizing of a clinic by the Behavioral Science Department of the U of T Faculty of Medicine, "who were wondering about the state of health of the freak community."[25] Aunty Flo — short for Florence Nightingale — was "a child really with a snub nose and skinny legs and a very elegant blue patch on the seat of her faded jeans."[26]

Govcon agreed to help with $1,000 and "Aunty Flo's Parlor" · opened officially on the fifth floor in March. From the first, the staff was overwhelmed by "appallingly damaged kids."[27] The clinic staff had six persons, two per shift, and concerned itself with testing and referring, streetwork, housecalls "mainly in the building (important during flu epidemics), making soups and stews."[28] The staff had minimal medical qualifications, but were able to operate as an advice and referral service, or as one of the doctors from St. Michael's Hospital who made regular visits said it, as "grass roots social medicine."[29]

The first three months were supported by Rochdale, then a summer grant from the Opportunities For Youth (OFY) program took over. With this small public subsidy, the Rochdale Free Clinic served over 6,000 kids in its first year — 5,000 of them non-residents. In contrast, Rochdale claimed that the Alcohol and Drug Addiction Foundation in Toronto, with a $9 million budget, served only a third of that.

During the next winter, the clinic faded. At this point, it was housed in a Gnostic apartment. "It gave out little more than aspirin and bandaids," says former clinic worker Sharon Kingsland, "but it was a place you could go to. It was run by a young speed freak who didn't do a very good job. Then one of the council members applied for an OFY grant and got it, so for the summer of '70, we had six Rochdale people and six medical students, in shifts of two, on the first floor where the cafeteria had been. A doctor came once a week." Again in 1971, a $13,000 grant enabled a three-month summer clinic that expanded into the former People's Gallery on the street-level and stayed open twenty-four hours a day.

By the spring of 1972, the clinic operated around the clock from a fifth floor Zeus apartment. Now funded by a $31,000 Local Initiatives Program grant, it was coordinated by Paki Djervad, a twenty-six-year-old mother of two from Denmark. One of three doctors came for four hours a day, five days a week, and a nurse attended eighteen hours in twenty-four. Also on staff was Gwendolyn Gaylord, a guinea pig. People who were too high on drugs to relate to human beings would be given the small animal to hold.

The clinic aided more than 20,000 people that year. Calls and patients frequently came from the neighborhood or the suburbs. In one example, a suburban woman "playing house mother for a teenaged pajama party has taken Clear Light, a potent form of LSD. Now she is worried about what she may do."[30] The nurse took a taxi to the house to help. "People come to us with things they're ashamed to take to their family doctors," said Djervad. "Like VD. Or a good Catholic woman who won't face her Catholic doctor for birth control pills. Or the mother of a 15-year-old speeder." The clinic paid its way by health insurance benefits, scrounging, and government grants. Drug companies co-operated by donating necessary medicines.

Another coordinator, Mother Fletcher, moved the Free Clinic out of Rochdale in the fall of 1973. Of four or five versions of the Free Clinic during Rochdale, this was the second to move elsewhere and the only one to operate two locations, with the second located on Yonge Street (the Hassle-Free Clinic). In one and a half years, the clinic had given 17,000 treatments and had 2,500 patients on file. The 1974 Edcon Catalog listed the Hassle-Free Clinic on Yonge as a Rochdale project, and explained the external address as a refusal by the Local Initiatives Program to renew the clinic's funding if it remained in Rochdale. The catalogue also saved face by proposing a second reason — that "their services and talents were not as required in the building." [31]

For another major project of Rochdale College, an external address was the whole point. This was the Rochdale Farm, part of a Back to the Land movement that was turning the heads of many young urbanites at that time. In June '69, Bruce Maxwell wrote to twenty-five Township Clerks asking for land which could be had for no more than $300. "Several of my friends and I at Rochdale College are looking to buy ten to a hundred acres of hilly bush that no one else wants much to set up a retreat center which will operate year-round. We have made a pre-fabricated mobile weatherproof house out of aluminum pipe and clear flexible tinted plastic which costs only $50. It is forty feet wide and needs to be attached to a floor which we will have to build. It is an extraordinary house heated by solar heat and insulated by an air space between two layers of plastic. Architecturally it is the strongest structure known to man — a geodesic dome like the American pavilion at Expo. The retreat center is educational in purpose. Full time staff will keep the houses (we plan to build several out of sight of each other) in order, tend the garden, the bees, the cows, the chickens, and whatever else needs tending. People will come out to the center for a minimum of 2 week stays." [32]

Despite some objectors ("To head for Killaloe with a geodesic womb only begs the question" [33]) a rural campus gradually took shape. Govcon in September '70 agreed to co-sign for a loan for a farm to help people on speed, and a general meeting in February '72 approved purchase of land for $12,250. Then, like a generation of middle-class citizens before them, Rochdale needed to "get to the cottage." Rochdale purchased the Boogie Bus, a '51 Studebaker with aluminum body, its inside fitted as a camper with bunk beds and optimistically rated by the *Daily* at twenty-eight passengers. On one occasion, the bus broke down while carrying fourteen people to Killaloe. It was "like spending the weekend in a real friendly Rochdale elevator." [34]

The Golden Lake Campus lay "roughly 200 miles north of 341 Bloor Street West." In November '72, construction was underway on a two-and-a-half-story "zome," as a factory for pre-fabricated domes. Emphasis, however, was on "Paleolithic Technology," such as "wood chopping, hauling water, and care and use of the simple Outhouse." [35] The 350-acre farm had to be reached by an "awful" road. Once there, people built "places" beside the existing house. Over a hundred years old, the house came equipped with summer and winter kitchens. It had been used by hunters, and the neighboring farmers must have felt no change of owners could be a change for the worse. Local lore said that over a hundred dogs owned by hunters had been shot and killed by farmers in the previous two years — while chasing cows. The Golden Lake campus had bees, three veggie gardens, opportunities for swamp-cleaning, a barn, a 2x4 zome with aluminum skin ("like a giant golf ball, needing a scale size model of Eisenhower towering over it with a golf club" [36]), an A-frame, a two-hole outhouse with plastic picture window, a well with fecal coliform bacteria, no phone or electricity, and shopping five miles away near the Bow and Arrow bar.

And so more projects graduated from Rochdale. We have moved far from the dictionary definition of education, just as far as the new entry that Rochdale was writing for "college." With education so loosely defined, it would be possible to see any body — and anybody — that acknowledges a debt to Rochdale as legitimate offspring of the college. To investigate Rochdale's performance as a college more traditionally, we have to look at its achievements in an area it always admired. We have to look at the arts.

15

Arts Daily

In one of the more visible cases of Rochdale giving support and shelter, the recipient was Theatre Passe Muraille. The theatre group had been in Toronto since the beginning of summer 1968, and several of its personnel moved into the new college.

A theatre that goes "through walls," Passe Muraille conducted experimental, event theatre with radical kinds of audience/player contact. "From the moment you enter the little theatre," one production began, "you are already immersed in the characters. They are all about. They lie on the stairs as you go to your seat. They interview you on your pets. They throw you animal crackers and roam about the floors making animal sounds. A tape-recorder is playing in the background and occasionally among the animal sounds you may hear your voice commenting on something you've just said. A light piece of music comes to an end and the play begins."[1] The *Toronto Star* reported that the audience "may be questioned or quietly poked fun at, shouted at or scathingly insulted. Their pockets may be rifled, their opinions ravished, and at last, smothered by a torrent of shrieks, suffocating from a barrage of bad smells, they may be confronted by a wall of bayonet-wielding black actors, carted bodily off to join some weird dance or even asked to undress."[2]

Passe Muraille committed itself to "wiping out the idea of theatre as an innocuous and respectable spectator sport." [3] The "events" it provoked often started with feelings and not with a script. More importantly, theatre was not to be confined to "a theatre." Anywhere was theatre enough, and everyone an actor. The point was philosophic as well as entertaining, and made little distinction between the role-playing of normal activity, and the role-playing of a play. As theatre-in-the-daily-round, the action stimulated by Passe Muraille invaded Rochdale's rooms, halls, and lobbies, and contributed to a style of getting things done. We have already seen the ascension of King James I of Rochdale, both mock and serious — by Jim Garrard, a main figure in Passe Muraille. And if Passe Muraille did not use Govcon as a theatre for their performances, Govcon itself performed as if it were a theatre. Even the elevators became boards for fretting and strutting. Concerts and discussions, as well as improvisational drama, all managed at some point to use those tiny stages that magically opened up on random audiences. Some of these were the "Ashroom Lounge and Otis Seminars."

For a while, Rochdale tried to accommodate plays as well as players, and built a theatre in the sub-basement with egg cartons for acoustic tiling. Passe Muraille's first production after moving into Rochdale was a run of *Tom Paine* in this theatre — until after three days of overcrowding, the fire marshal closed it down. A building with no private auditorium couldn't hope for a public one.

So performances moved to the Central Library Theatre while Rochdale still provided funds, some material, and living-quarters. Passe Muraille productions in the year 1968–69 included *Tom Paine, Futz, The Smashing of the Television Set,* and *The Blind Trip to High Park*. The most notable of these was *Futz* by Rochelle Owen, the story of farmer Cy Futz's love for his pig, Amanda. The play not only dabbled in bestiality, but a mother also bared her breasts to her son. As *Change* magazine reported, "before morality officers arrested the producer, director, and complete cast — a first for Ontario — the play received fine reviews."[4] For the *Futz* obscenity trial, "many (though, for them, not enough) of the cream of the entertainment world in Toronto are testifying on their behalf."[5] In a parting shot, Jim Garrard promised a completely expurgated production of *Futz* to "give Toronto the kind of theatre it deserves."[6]

By May '70, the level of aid from Rochdale was falling. The Theatre was being given a room and $100 a month, but Jim Garrard had been taken off the rolls. By this time, the performances had been moved to Trinity Square, but no more rent for that space could be provided by Rochdale. A Govcon member explained that Passe Muraille had been "a large financial drain on Rochdale" and had to be "sharply cut back."[7] Like the other projects, Rochdale couldn't afford to support both itself and its alumni. Passe Muraille as an organization had graduated from Rochdale, but it left behind its style.

The appetite for theatre extended readily to films. Rochdale catered to its film buffs with a series of fly-by-night cinemas in the lounges, usually showing old Hollywood movies. In the first year, the audiences found Fat Daddy's Cinema Permanente Narcotique. One leaflet read: "remember: a movie a week keeps the pink in your cheek...Fat Daddy's Pink-in-the-Cheek Plan: Proven Results/See You at the Narcotic Cinema."[8] By February '72, the lounge had become The Spartan Cinema ("For the best seat in the house, bring a cushion").[9] The fee for "Movies at the Rock" in November '72 was one dollar, "but onions and bread have been received; also a couple of tomatoes and a squash."[10] Reg Hartt became a major impresario for the celluloid theatre. For his showings in the lounge, a screen was painted on the wall, but what was missing in sophistication was added in effects. For Hitchcock's *The Birds,* Hartt brought a number of pigeons and sparrows and let them loose in the theatre. This led to thrills, of course, and "a very hearty supper for some people."[11]

Not content to merely consume, Rochdale tried to produce. The largest film project attempted was *The Assassination Generation,* a feature scripted by two Rochdale members, Jack Christie and Michael Hirsh. Begun in May '68, it had chronic funding problems that were only partly solved by the setting up of De Fat Daddy Cinema. "The film is incorporated as a public company," the *Daily* informed the residents, "and the college already owns a number of shares and will be receiving more in the future. Money forthcoming from the film will go to the education fund." [12]

The script for *The Assassination Generation* was scatological, nihilist, sexist, and abused by the belief that shock is art. In an excerpt published in *Image Nation* in June '69, a main character, George, is running for president and God is his manager. As George relaxes in a bathtub "in hashish seventh heaven" surrounded by "nudie cuties," God narrates that "yes, George was an orphan. Yah, he was nothing when I created him...nothing...Intercut George in tub with pig. The pig pisses and George offers pig drink of tub water after drinking himself. The pig says: 'I wouldn't drink that piss, are you crazy?' George squirts pig in face with seltzer water bottle...Cut to Ludlow Fonce, assassin [of George], who picks up phone while boogying his old lady in his hammock hanging from the eighteenth floor of his apartment building." [13] Howard Adelman reported that Rochdale's first film was "a contender for a top prize of the Canadian Film Development Corporation." [14] The title was not mentioned, and *The Assassination Generation* disappeared.

Rochdale hosted film organizations of various descriptions. The Beaver Film Co-op received $5,000 from Co-op College in Rochdale's first year, and the November '72 catalog listed another film-makers' co-operative with 125 members and a monthly newsletter, as well as *Cinema Canada,* a magazine with an office on the second floor, and a distribution center with 200 prints of Canadian films, "the largest commercial distribution company for Canadian film," and largest print collection outside of the National Film Board. [15] Once again,

Rochdale was providing a home for organizations started elsewhere. The Canadian Filmmakers Distribution Center had been putting out catalogs for a year and a half before moving into Rochdale in the fall of 1968.

Musically, Rochdale enjoyed and made the sounds of its time, but didn't launch or save any careers. One early figure, Michel Roy from New York, wanted to organize a medieval music group for "avant-garde 2nd and 20th Century" music.[16] A short-lived Music Department tried to persuade Rochdale to buy a harpsichord at "two grand," since "there are hundreds of fat cats out there just dying to lay their bread on groovy ventures like our Baroque group."[17] A few months later, the *Daily* carried an ad for an improvisational music workshop: "Bring spoons, lids, keys, electric tangello, FISH, dildoes, cod-pieces, and your axe."[18] None of this playing seemed serious or professional. The most ambitious music project became a sound studio in the basement developed by Hot Melons Rock 'n' Roll Revue and run by Rudy Hierck. In operation by November '72, it lasted at least until spring of 1974.

Rochdale did, however, transmit its own selection of music. In the first year, Mike Goldstein of the Electronics Workshop in the basement began organizing Rochdale Radio, and by January '69, the private station was announced as almost complete. "To make Rochdale Radio work," says Sid Smith, "when they put it in, they couldn't afford the wire, so they took the whole of the intercom system and pulled it out, right from the top, and used it." In 1972, Rochdale Radio broadcast on FM cable for eighteen hours a day with $2600 worth of equipment, and had 453 albums from which to choose.

As for visual art, Rochdale wanted other avenues than the art establishment provided. "Let's have a new kind of art show," one resident wrote in the *Daily*, "living happenings that are in negation to those that support the conditioned way of living! I myself happened to see the process when [Robert] Jacks, with some of his friends, carried the paintings from Rochdale. And in some way they were more relevant to me then than they were in the Pollock Art Gallery, they were more real in the elevators or in the lobby than they were hanging in white walls in perfect 'law and order.'"[19] Rochdale tried its own street-level art gallery, the People's Gallery. In March '70, it presented a show entitled "Children of Rochdale: An Exhibition of Their Art…Kool Aide and cookies will be served."[20] The next month, Govcon tried to close the People's Gallery for the summer and rent it as a boutique, but supporters occupied it twenty-four hours a day and held a rally with the People's Revolutionary Band. The gallery was permitted to stay.

Along with unusual avenues, Rochdale favored unusual media. "One girl's mother used to come from Los Angeles once a month," as Property Manager Sid Smith tells the story, "driving a big Cadillac. She would bring boxes of food for this girl. She was always high on drugs, this girl. One day she came to me and said, 'This is for you.' It was the weirdest thing you ever saw. She'd cut her finger and painted, on canvas, a Roman gladiator in her own blood."

Perhaps because the building itself was stone-ugly, the walls invited expression as colourful as possible. "Soon after the college opened, crude graffiti in Magic Marker ink appeared on stairway walls," *Maclean's* reported. "Said one council member: 'We held meetings about it constantly. Some people were fed up with four-letter words and bits of anatomy all over the walls. But others thought it was a valid, spontaneous art form, so no one could decide what to do.' In February, in another outburst of spontaneity, a group of tenants went around washing walls, which was rather arbitrary of them."[21] A divided attitude continued. A year later, wall-writers faced a "$25 fine for defacing Rochdale property" while being offered, at the same time, a "prize for the best graffiti."[22]

The well-written, painterly wall became another distinguishing mark for Rochdale. "The graffiti were excellent," says a former resident. "And the gaudy colors in the hallways — vermilion, purple, some beautifully decorated. No subdued earth colors for Rochdale!" One spot advertised: "For sale: a newt's eye, never been used." More ambitious than most wall-work was an announcement in a *Daily* from someone who wanted "to paint a seventeen-story marijuana leaf in such a way that it would be visible only from the second-floor patio." [23]

The property manager who took possession of Rochdale at the end, Sid Smith, indicates the extent of the changes in decor over the seven years of the College, including later, severe vandalism: "The contractors I called in estimated a little over $2 million to put the building back to its original condition. The walls were all painted, some beautiful psychedelic stuff, fabulous the way they were done." And if the canvas was too small, they stretched it. In one case, someone in the fourteenth-floor communal lounge needed more space — and knocked out a wall. The walls that remained became scratchpad and bulletin board as well as artist's canvas, including, by one description recorded by the police, signs "giving prices of drugs and where to get them — first name only... Instructions on how to take L.S.D.... Reward posters for 'pig detective' involved in a shooting incident." [24]

The showpiece of the college became the lobby mural on the ground floor. The main part of the mural was painted by Laurie Peters, a girl who "compulsively painted on walls." [25] According to one of the later security guards, "[Peters] studied in Mexico — and all the faces are of tenants here. At night the wall seemed to move, the people jump out, life-like." [26] The guard said they tested visitors to Rochdale using the paintings. If they were not able to point out their host, "we threw them out."

A "Sculpture Shop" began in the first months of Rochdale. In Bulletin 1 for the shop, founder Ed Apt appealed to the romantic past: "Clay and plaster are ancient techniques, definitely left over from the days when people used to be substantial, strong, and patient and when materials and tools were basic, primitive, and time was galore." [27] Even so, at the start the shop had a "casualty:" "our model-to-be decided to leave us, after failing to fight off her inhibitions about being naked in public. A successor is wanted. She ought to be 'sculpturesque,' at least for this current project." [28] The first major project would be "a big piece mutually built by everyone," and after six ballots, the sculptors chose a design called "The Unknown Student."

Supplies were tight at first. Uncle Ed reported to the *Daily* that "presently we are waiting for replies of manufacturers from whom we are trying to bum stuff again. They better be generous because our money is down to a disturbing 38 cents." [29] The manufacturers came through and the work was done in the hearse garage of the old Thompson funeral parlour nearby. Unveiled on Good Friday, 1969, this sculpture that still crouches on the sidewalk next to Bloor Street has outlasted all the known students of Rochdale.

The Unknown Student was named, so the story goes, "by some miserable student sitting in the Rochdale cafeteria," [30] and was designed by Dale Heinzerling, one of the Sculpture Shop members. Rochdale's contribution to the public monuments of Toronto has been summarized as "a blob." The *Telegram* was a little kinder: "Visitors have noted how the sculpture — a beefy humanoid body sitting yoga style with its head tucked down — characterizes Rochdale. It exudes innocence simultaneously with strength, is large and a trifle mysterious." [31] In the words of Apt, the sculpture with its head navel-ward — or more accurately, crotch-ward — "faces in the right direction." [32]

Suppliers rallied in time for the Student, but the luck would not be repeated. In March '70, Jerry Ofo of the Sculpture Shop designed a sculpture of eight jumping men as "a freestanding arch of a man in an as-if stopped-motion photograph of the act of making the great leap forward." [33] The jumping men never landed.

Rochdale flirted with a literary scene, but nothing serious: there were no resulting children. Jean Genet visited with a group of Black

Panthers, Allen Ginsberg recited poetry under a plastic geodesic dome in a hallway, and the League of Canadian Poets held their inaugural meeting in the building. During that meeting, Frank Scott had to read from *Robert's Rules of Order* because of the uproar. John Robert Colombo left early and considered that the League had gotten off to a bad start.

Dennis Lee and Judy Merril were the best-known authors associated with the College, but none of their works invite the term "Rochdalian." A single creative work was published as a Rochdale statement, namely, *The Book of Flophouse Poetry: An Anthology of Ceilings,* in September '71. Victor Coleman introduced the poets by saying "most of them wouldn't know a 'good' poem if it came all over them; but what redeems these words is the action that preceded them, or the action that will, undoubtedly, follow."[34] Bill King planned a collection called "18 Stories," with each story titled by the floors of the College: SB, B, 1, 2, C, D, E, to S. The sixth-floor story would talk about the dealing commune as the "bust that never happened"; the seventh floor would be "The American Dream"; the twelfth would be the "March for Morality."[35] The collection never materialized.

Non-fiction items were also few or indirect. The Alternative Press Center, begun in 1969 as the Radical Research Center in Minnesota, operated in Rochdale in the fall of 1972 with four full-time workers. Their index listed 150 periodicals of the counterculture, and appeared quarterly. In addition, the *Canadian Whole Earth Almanac* issued for at least two years from Rochdale quarters. The Artisan's and Craftsman's Association produced a "Survival Companion for Craftsmen," *Handmade,* which was "conceived and born in the 15th floor commune" (editor, Aulene Maki). Itself beautifully crafted, the 270 pages of this book were hand-scripted and laced with illustrations. The most notable publication, however, was Peter Turner's *There Can Be No Light Without Shadow,* put out in March '71 while he was president of Govcon. The 432-page, $30 book defended Rochdale

College and included photocopies of articles and letters. Bound in a casual format, it contributed some solid analysis to the debate over Rochdale and then, lacking enough orders for a second run, went out of print by October '72.

Most of the writing at Rochdale came in the internal publications, the newspapers and specials that, under a variety of names, were the *Daily*. Like con-artists, the papers kept changing their names, formats, and staffs. The *Bulletin*, the *Tuesdaily*, the *Undaily*, the *New Daily*, the *Daily Planet*, the *Twodaily*, *Infra-Rochdale*, *MaySay*, the *Naked Grape*, the *Hourly Madness-Ghetto News*, *Da-Daily*, *Toad's Breath*—all passed on the news and opinions in sheets that were often remarkably well produced, thanks to Rochdale's association with Coach House Press, a first class-printing house located in an alleyway just behind the highrise and staffed in part by Rochdale residents.

The innovative graphics in these publications deserved a wider audience. Howard Adelman concluded in his postscript on Rochdale that "some of the finest graphics in North America are produced by the College printing presses." [36] Much of that printing, including posters and novelty items, was done in Coach House. More printing was done within the building by a Publications Office and by resident silkscreeners. Little of the printing led to profit of any size. Indeed, "Peter [Turner] went over $2,000 in personal debt to set up the silkscreen shop," a council member argued in support of council subsidies for Turner. "When he asked for over $1,000 to keep it going this winter, the council gave him $140 to buy a heater for an unheated building...Peter's total silkscreen income since he became president has been $6." [37]

The graphics delighted in cultural repartee. The Coach House archives, for example, include production materials for a mock cigarette-pack labelled "Nickle Bag" — with a five-cent Canadian beaver coin on an orange-net pattern and the slogan, "A puff of KIF in the morning will make you as Strong As 100 Camels in the Courtyard." [38]

A poster in the same archives shows two tombstones headed by "RIP" and "OFF."

Under most of its forms, the internal newspaper approached its job democratically. "You need only stop by for a minute," the *Daily* told the residents, "& write out anything you want to be published — or present it in any form. We can print anything. If you have access to a typewriter, type out any copy in a 3 ½-inch column on any kind of white paper — illustrate it if you like — and it will be printed exactly as is." [39] This was not just an invitation, but a demand. In one case, the *Daily* objected to phoned-in instructions to repeat an ad and add a phone number: "WHO DO YOU THINK RUNS THE DAILY? This is the sort of shit that pisses us off. Can't the guy come to the *Daily* office in the third floor Ashram and type it himself? YOU WANT IT IN — PUT IT IN YOURSELF." [40]

In an open letter to Prime Minister Trudeau, a resident explained the *Daily* approach as an important development at Rochdale. "ANY resident in the building," he said, "is free to write whatever he wants in the *Rochdale Daily* as long as there is room for the article. No one can deny him this right." [41]

With freedom of content and multiple sources, the resulting pages were often complex, more like a bulletin board with tacked-on notices than a conventional newspaper. Typographic errors became a way of life ("the Acotr, pronounced actor..."). The staff explained the mess: "the reason for [the *Daily*'s] inconsistency and fragmentation has been but a reflection of the uncertainty pervading Rochdale. We are not on a campaign to establish certainty. That must come through us, from you." [42]

The internal newspaper began its tradition in September '67, in the pre-highrise days, as the *Rochdale College Bulletin*. Soon called *Anything But Son of Rochdale*, it recorded in its name the words of one John Thurston upon hearing that the newsletter would be called *Son of Rochdale*. *Anything But Son of Rochdale* quickly turned bizarre. In issue "1:69," the layout disordered the information, pieces appeared upside down or in mirror image, and graphics intermeshed. A cubist front cover printed a head with the advice, "part slightly to the left," and the back cover took the Rochdale rhetoric ("Rochdale College... hopes to provide an environment in which students can freely explor — ") and exploded the letters into a wild pattern. What couldn't be twisted visually, editor Paul Evitts teased verbally: "After she died, I worked out a plan of how Vincent could appear on the streets without letting anyone know of his other head" — and that was all he wrote. [43]

The issue caused controversy. Nelson Adams, a graduate student of Greek who would later join Govcon, wrote from New Brunswick for information and complained that he received *Anything But. Exit!*, the successor appearing with fluorescent red letters in January '68, said *Anything But* was "Toronto's own eyesore," but editor Michel Roy couldn't resist his own experimental lines: "X-it?... X:it?... x-itw... Ecccsit... Echktzit?... Eck,zit... egg-zit... eggshit... eg.cit...?" [44]

The early *Dailies* couldn't even advertise simply. As announced by a border reading "paid advertisement," Rochdale's restaurant featured the automatic writing of the manager: "Bathed blue light that same 24-hour Restaurant: gleaming chrome handle shifting in the hand Miss Wow Wow twirling in amber plastic and sheep's wool porcelain slicing knobby through fingers. Roar of dispeptic high energy vehicle blue sexy low slung and flatulent on a S.T.P trip. Malibu in back and lots-a-body man. My 1958 Ford 4-door hardtop reminds me of that Same 24-hour restaurant." [45] Another early *Daily* indulged in wandering wordplay: "Jack Dimond smokes rabbit droppings. Paul Evitts drops rabbit smokings... Dropping Paul Evitts will make him smoke rabbitly. Burma shave." [46]

Judy Merril helped set up a Publications Office (the Pub) in January '69 in order to put out Education Supplements. Located on the second floor, the Pub featured experienced publishing personnel

like Merril, Jack Jones, Stuart Hertzog, Stan Bevington, and Victor
Coleman. "You will also find some pretty experienced furniture and
a coffee pot."[47] In the following years, publications which did not
come from the polished performers at Coach House were cranked
out on the equipment at the Pub.

During the same winter, the *Daily Planet* arrived: "the paper that
presents the real truth in a manner that would lead you to believe that
it is all lies."[48] Editor Basil Nardley-Stoades began his wordy career:
"Once again I, your guardian and benevolent benefactor, have pulled
off yet another First in the History of Canadian Journalism. I have
expanded the *Planet* to twice its size in this special, twice-its-size,
edition. This was no mean feat. Not many newspapers manage to
aspire to such gross enlargements so early in their history of distorted
rumour, downright lies, smear campaigns, and subtle propaganda.
But I felt that Rochdale was ready for this. The public policy of Fearless
Honesty and Personal Frankness that permeates this institution and
is practised to some extent among its members is all right for lackeys.
But it is no way to run a newspaper."[49]

A month later, Stoades was writing: "It is this self-sacrificing,
humble attitude of the *Planet* owner and staff that helps to keep the
Planet in the forefront of all regional publications in this Township.
In fact, that help to keep the *Planet* the ONLY publication... etc.,
etc... But this state of affairs will not last. I plan to introduce a rival
to the *Planet*'s orbit: a merely reflecting moon that will only serve
to illustrate the *Planet*'s magnificence. I shall not say how or when
this inferior product will be introduced. But watch out for it. It will
be manned by a team of men, trained in inferiority and all that that
entails. They will be no match for Anthony de Villiers Gibson, Sir
Malcolm and that Schoales fellow, Clarke Kent and Littleman, Jimmy
Olsen, and Emma."[50]

Later *Daily* staff members were no more sedate than Sir Basil.
In *The Hourly Madness-Ghetto News* for September '71, the editor

wrote: "I apologize for the lack of head lines, but I came down." [51] At one point, the plain *Daily* became *"The Imfamous Impartial Unfolded People's Tuesdaily."* [52] Mike Randell, another Govcon president, served on the *Daily* staff and signed an issue dated February 1, 1904, as "publican to the nation." [53] A fellow journalist, 'Dingaling,' said Randell had a "childlike innocent gall and audacity. Some of his verbal sweets ARE convincing and perhaps really valid news items, as well as beautiful entertainment." [54] The "Staph" of the *Daily* in February '73 included the Dragon Lady, the Haunted Typist, Brother Pizza, and The Spirit of A.B. Dick.

The editorial attitude of the *Haunted Typist* would make a fine motto for any newspaper (or book of popular history): "If you wasn't there to see for yourself, don't bitch." [55]

Seeing for ourselves, what can we now say about the artistic legacy created by Rochdale? In the fields of both art and education, however broadly education is defined, Rochdale College created as much as any other college, namely, graduates and artifacts. Some Rochdale graduates have gone on to mature work; some of those will argue that the work developed because of Rochdale. Some others will say it developed in spite of Rochdale. But the work done inside, despite its importance for the participants, has had little direct external effect. Most of it has become artifact, preserved and no more available or popular than the thousands of theses and dissertations in the libraries of mainline colleges. Whether Rochdale was in a League that was Ivy or Poison Ivy depended on quite a different itch than an urge to art.

16

Business Unusual

The official revenues of Rochdale College Incorporated came —
hesitatingly — from rents and minor fundraising. The economics of
the resident-owners, however, were mostly unofficial. A look at the
revenue that reached the Rochdalians themselves, excluding the take
extracted by the external, big drug dealers, shows a mixture of ease
and industry, illegality and invention.

"It is often asserted," says Alex MacDonald, "usually by either
dope dealers or by policemen, that everybody in the building dealt
and that dealing was the absolute and sole economic basis of the
community. This is *not* true. There *were* people who had legitimate
jobs. There were people who lived on welfare. I mean, there were
other sources of money." According to the survey by Lionel Solursh,
close to 10 percent of respondents lived on welfare or unemployment
insurance, but the same percentage had been living that way in the
three months before arriving at Rochdale. Except for a rise in drug
dealing from 1.9 percent before Rochdale to 3.2 percent after moving
in, residents had made no great change in the sources of income.

MacDonald estimates that, by the summer of 1970, "probably half
of the building either dealt or lived off the avails of dope dealing. I
mean, either they were dealers, or middled now and then, or they

operated some non-dope-dealing business in the building which was directly dependent on income generated by dealing." Property Manager Sid Smith tells of one man who told him, near the end of Rochdale: "Quite frankly, I deal in dope and that's what you're evicting me for, also for not paying rent. How do you expect me to pay my rent if I can't deal dope?"

In matters of money and wages, Rochdale tended to be schizoid. One ethic considered work to be tarnished by payment. This was another gap like the one that separated the young from the old — the separation of the worker from his hire, a Generation Gap in the generation of money. By this ethic, it was better to work for a room, for food, for barter, if one had to work at all. Profit could only be unclean.

When Alex MacDonald was a Govcon member, he charged resident impresario Reg Hartt with "gross capitalism" for his film showings at Rochdale and Neill-Wycik College. "I run my films as a labor of love," Hartt replied. "If [Alex] wants to foot the bills, I'll present them free of charge."[1] The same idealistic discomfort appeared when the fourteenth-floor commune opposed a rent strike, saying it "is being encouraged mainly by the conservative, business interests in the building, such as persons who make money dealing to outsiders, bar operators, game land operators, etc., to protect their vested interests."[2]

But criticisms like these couldn't make much difference to anyone since little money changed hands when drugs weren't being passed. The second–floor "Schop" carried an assortment of food and paraphernalia, and invited Rochdalians to "help build up this Dirty Dan Capitalist Conspiracy!"[3] The tease was apt. Small businesses in Rochdale were, deliberately or unavoidably, very small. Yossarian Records on the street-level, for example, sold albums in 1970 at a scant twenty cents more than distributor cost. "We're trying," said one proprietor, "to turn people on to the fact that they don't need a lot of money to live on. Our salaries are $35.00 a week and we are

not lacking." Another way of living without a lot of money, however, was a problem. Not only did customers shoplift, but when the
owners of Yossarian went to a distributor to try to arrange records
on consignment, several friends came along. "When we got inside
there were stacks of albums all over. The three of us went in to talk to
the manager. Then he discovered one of the guys with us had ripped
him off for $40 worth of records. The whole deal was off."[4]

The other work ethic, the one that had made its peace with money,
was unambiguously capitalist.

In November '70, graffiti drew attention to "a startling prolif-
eration of free enterprise in the building."[5] Signs advertised bread,
sandwiches, cigarettes, coffee, beads, soft drinks, health food,
and bootleg wine and beer. The thirteenth floor opened an apart-
ment-based restaurant, "The Rochburger." Two residents of the
seventeenth-floor commune ran a weekend pizza and soft drink
business that paid their rent and expenses. "We work like hell for
three days," they said. "The doorbell rings from early evening to as
late as 5 or 7 in the morning."[6] On the socialist side, the first year
of Rochdale had seen the "Kwop Schop," a food co-op, while on the
capitalist side, now "Co-op Catering" delivered peanuts and pop
to the door or to the movies in the building. "The Same," a twenty-
four-hour restaurant, featured "19 kinds of honey, including linden,
rosemary, and mellona; caviar at 40 cents a portion; 25 kinds of
coffee, from straight Canadian to dandelion; 23 kinds of tea...10
varieties of smoked meats; 22 variations on the theme of jam; and
23 flavors for milk shakes, including anise, bilberry, and tamarind
(a rare Indian date)."[7]

In November '70, the Department of Buildings ordered a stop to
using Rooms 1326 and 1424 "for restaurant purposes," but the industry
carried on. The pages of the *Daily* carried ads for the "True Dough"
bakery, Rochburgers, pizza, and the "Ptomaine Food Store." Three
years later, Ptomaine still existed, offering food, head comics, pipes,

and "a class for children to count change and develop good shopping manners."[8] Meal service at Rochdale depended on The Same until 1971, when the Etherea Family, a commune, opened a restaurant and health food store. On the ground level and with its own entrance, their "Nature's Way Natural Food Store" operated with a 30 percent markup. "It's a better trip than Dominion is on!"[9] And with a mural of mountains and lakes, with thick, rustic wood tables, the Etherea Restaurant beside the food store benefited from the tidy management that the Rochdale bureaucracy had been unable to provide. Remarkably, unusually, the business survived and paid rent to Rochdale right to the end.

Alcohol provided some economic excitement as well. As advertised in the *Daily*, beer sold at "35 cents or 3 hits for 1$$$."[10] One resident remembers that "beer would be delivered to your door anytime, very quickly. I looked in Dave's cubbyhole beside the store on the second floor once. He had cases and cases piled up against the wall." One ashram made a $1,000 profit by bootlegging beer. The group served the ideals of non-profit by buying furniture which was then inherited by a commune.

In addition to commercial brands of beer and wine, Rochdale had its own. One *Daily* promoted 'The Pipe:' "Remember the Pipe!! The Pipe comes to you in three unique brews, DORIC, GOLD MEDAL, and JOHN BULL...The Pipe will get you roaring drunk."[11] At a beer-tasting party, John Bull was judged the best in Canada. "Good Head," they said.[12] The Pipe's operation included "a waterbed filled with apples in the back of a car in the basement."[13] As for homebred wine, a label from 1969 tells the consumer that "Satana red pectore wine is produced and blended in your heart. Contains pure evil of squeezed heart blood. This old wine should get you off, if not, return it and we won't give you more. Distributed by anonymous head and punks together."[14] The word was that "Mother Fletcher had good wine, but it hit like a ton of bricks."

The crafts put some change in some pockets as well. One enterprise was "O Handmade Paper" with Andrew Smith. "O makes the human version of the most commonly produced article. It opposes ecological, artistic, and unemployment hypocrisy. Besides growing food, O hopes to grow its own flax, to be made into clothing and into paper embodied with the graphics that express O's view."[15] By 1972, craftworkers in Rochdale used well-kept studios on the sixth floor, stocked a public showroom, and sold wood carvings, textiles, beadwork, batik, and pottery. Graphics were a continuing favorite: "The family ghost brings a vision: your name or disguise may be warmly colourized. Posters and Door Name Signs by RODON. 4" × 6": 1 dollar and up (door). Posters: 5 dollars and up, depending on specifications."[16] The graphics were not always on such a small scale. In two months, $381 worth of marijuana flags and stickers were printed and sold by "Parthenographic Productions," printers also of 100 Nihilist Spasm Band posters.

One "craft" was key-cutting. Since it was illegal to make copies of master keys, a profitable service could be provided for those who, for their own unquestioned reasons, needed duplicates. "It was just by word of mouth and only by individuals," says a former resident, "but the key machine brought in quite a bit from people on the outside who wanted illegal copies made of any key." Sales didn't exclude Rochdale itself. The rumour was that the cops themselves had master keys to rooms in Rochdale, "which incidentally are going for $7 on the black market."[17]

As we can see, some of those who made their peace with profit would pursue any opportunity. When one Rochdalian had been in Vietnam, he was said to have taken "photos of the ones who had bought it and kept a copy for himself. Soon he had a whole collection of stiff pictures. These he would sell on the black market in Saigon for the people in Europe who got off on that sort of thing. Made a lot of bucks."[18]

In addition to the capitalist ventures, there were businesses which weren't only small, but small, imaginative, and doomed. Inventor Jim

Washington and his "People's Institute of Aviation" head the list. "I got a Rochdale degree in revolutionary engineering," Washington said. "It is the only degree I care to have."[19] By legend, Washington once hovered ten feet above Rochdale's roof on a flying unicycle he designed and built.

The People's Institute of Aviation had a goal in 1972 "to produce and develop ultra-light aircraft for the needs of third world forces."[20] His "Single-Seat Mosquito Gyrocopter... has completed initial taxi and flight tests," and would sell for $600. A more advanced model, the "Single-Seat Phantom Mosquito Helicopter," was not ready yet and thus was "not available for purchase at $1000." Washington's other projects included a "Rigid Backpack," "Trackseat Advanced Electrically-Powered Wheelchair" ($600), "Remotely Piloted Vehicles" that awaited developers' funds, and "Manned Ultra-Light Insurgent Vehicles (classified)."

In May '74, Washington was working on a self-propelled tread wheelchair that could mount curbs. Govcon took a collection for Jim to complete the prototype. He needed $50 and got $28.30. That same year, Washington released a "state of the art development of the bicycle of yesteryear," the 1974 BOD POD. This "people-powered vehicle" was a bicycle "fully enclosed inside a fiberglass body shell."[21]

But Washington had no monopoly on invention. Also high in imagination was an October '68 scheme: "David Hallam and Ian Morrison plus a bevy of young and talented ladies will awaken you any morning. 20 cents for one morning, $1 for one week. Any time of the day or night. Any method you desire will be used to awaken you."[22] A similar offer was adapted for parody after it became clear how chaotic Rochdale government would be. "All you frustrated leaders," the *Daily* announced, "sign up for your followers now and avoid the rush before the next council meeting. This service is on a first come first serve basis for the nominal charge of 25 cents/hour/follower. Uniforms (brown shirts, etc.) must be provided by the leader."[23] Shortly after came a follow-up report: "I am happy to announce that the rent-a-follower service is in full operation. Our list of professional followers includes...the ever-loving chaplain, and many more — Blow in their ears and they'll follow you anywhere."[24]

In the think tank that was Rochdale College, often the thought and not the substance counted, and it didn't hurt that projects like these never, or incompletely, materialized. Ideas were raised in profusion, appreciated, perhaps tried, and discarded. One ambitious, doomed project tried to lift itself out of the tank and onto the ground. In the spring of 1969, resident Bruce Maxwell was helping run a cleaning and employment agency for crashers when he prepared a prospectus for a "Maple Syrup Work Crew." The crew would tap trees in Toronto. "We will be calling seminars all over the building to encourage investment."[25] Stock would be sold at five dollars a share with workers to be paid fifty cents an hour until the selling was completed, then paid retroactively. Twice the rate would be paid to experienced tappers and a bookkeeper, three times the rate to foresters, and five times to fellow organizer Hank Woods ("a [man] with many grandiose ideas," commented resident psychiatrist Bryn Waern).[26] Woods had the backing of the third-floor Crashram, or crasher co-op.

By April, the location for the project had changed. The "Saptappers of Rochdale," eleven strong, arrived at a property in Haliburton owned by John Brown, founder and director of the experimental school Warrendale. "The cabin was practically empty. From nearby houses they gathered some beds and dishes, pieced together a couple of kerosene lanterns and split wood to get the fire going in the small stove."[27] A "Report from 'Crasheurs de Bois'" mentioned that one of them was driven by the local police to the Whitby Mental Institution and — "at the moment we have 8 cans of peanut butter and no bread."

Equipment failures, rip-offs, inexperience, and bad weather ruined the project. Mapletap ended in May '69 with a paltry return and gallons of argument. Under the heading, "Mapletap Mindfuck or Ho

Ho Ho," *Image Nation* pointed to "Mapletap's six gallons of syrup...
now candy-drying on the kitchen table in 905. What happened to the
hundreds of gallons Mapletap was supposed to produce? Who's going
to pay for the $800 debt? Will Rochdale council get their $500 back?
What about the $300 worth of bouncing checks? What happened
to the Reverse Osmosis Processor _____ was supposed to make?...
Should _____ be reprimanded for bouncing $300 worth of checks
or given an award for innovating credit for a creditless class?"[28]

If the inhabitants hungered for funds, Rochdale College, the
official body, slavered. The money mess at the level of mortgage
payments couldn't obscure a smaller but more pressing famine — the
lack of operating funds. Rents could be counted on for some, but the
shortfall had to come from fundraising. From the start, fundraisers
faced both internal hazards and external indifference. The internal
hazards are illustrated by an Indian Institute supper. The posters had
been defaced to read "free" and crashers were turned away — but with
not enough rigor. Alttough forty people attended, the supper lost $20.

Externally, the public didn't know enough about Rochdale College
at that point to give. The Sculpture Shop became an exception. In
December '68, Ed Apt reported that "DOMTAR and CANADIAN GYPSUM
companies delivered twelve hundred pounds of moulding plaster
to our shop, free. Thanks! The Establishment is very good to us. All
it takes is a phone call and the donations just pour in by the tons.
(Remember Toronto Brick Co. last month?)"[29]

In the years after, the public knew too much about Rochdale
College. Fundraising schemes flew like moths against the bright
lights of publicity. The moths, both plain and exotic, tried harder.
One exotic from Rochdale president Mike Randell would have had
blank cheques sent out with postage stamps on them and "three
pictures of Mike Donaghy becoming hysterical."[30]

Despite tiny profits, a favorite fundraiser — though plain —
was the lottery. Rochdale held one of the first in February '69. For

fifty-nine cents, a customer could guess the delivery date of Richard
and Adriene's baby and win $10. Then, in August '70, the *Daily* adver-
tised: "Buy your Roch-Raffle ticket now and win one pound of grass
(or) one ounce of hash."[31] On another occasion, lottery tickets were
offered at $1 for a "roundtrip for two to Rochdale, England, and
spending money to bring value of the prize to $1000, or $1000."[32]
Rochdale had won a license from the city to sell 5,000 tickets, but this
first full-scale lottery sold no more than 1,100. A part-time student/
landlady from the neighborhood won the jackpot — and after her
$1,000 winnings were deducted from the $1,100 take, Rochdale still
had bills to pay for advertising and printing. The winner, at least,
apologized before she left with the money.

Stan Bevington of nearby Coach House Press suggested that
"Rochdale should install turnstiles in the lobby and have people
pay for the amount of time they spend in the building, like parking meters."[33] Bevington was speaking from the Coach House
experience, where "the whole building speaks of sensuality and a
love for the work that's being done." If the atmosphere was tangible enough, perhaps it could become a commodity. But, by the
end, Rochdale had found no magic meters. Was it desperation
that filled one folder in the Rochdale records? The folder collected
money-making literature and get-rich-quick advertisements, including "The Money-Master Millionaires Club," schemes for concrete
fencepost production and hair-clipping, and an application form
for a government grant.

Rochdale tried hardest in the spring of 1970. Just when the rising
level of risky business inside the College might have recommended
keeping quiet, Rochdale proclaimed itself. A "National Share The
Wealth With Rochdale" campaign sent speakers into schools across
the country during one week in April. There, they "gave quite nice
slide shows," and asked as equals, one educational institution to
another, for the funds Rochdale needed. Campaign originator

Jim Garrard confirms that "we spent an awful lot of money on it." In some places, the appeal worked. University students in Nelson, B.C., collected 125,000 bottles and donated $2,500, but although the campaign objective was $100,000, the result came closer to $30,000.

The national campaign, and the press coverage it created, launched what became Rochdale's only dependable scheme — the Rochdale diploma. Handsomely printed diplomas were offered for sale at mock rates: a Ph.D. for $100, an M.A. for $50, and a B.A. for $25. In case the point were missed, a non-Ph.D. cost $25, a non-M.A. $50, and non-B.A. $100. Requirements varied as the diplomas continued to be offered until the end of Rochdale. The questions for the degrees were specific: "B.A. Name the first Prime Minister of Canada $25 — M.A. Name the present Prime Minister of Canada $50 — Ph.D. Name any Prime Minister of Canada $100." [34]

The requirements for the non-degrees, however, were nonspecific. "The non-B.A. is intended to certify that a person does not have a Bachelor's degree," explained president Mike Randell in February '74. "We feel that not having been educated is in many cases more significant than being educated...the requirements are stiff. We require you to say something useful. This is an adequate test, those educated to a B.A. level have usually lost this ability." [35] For a non-M.A., you must say something logical. If you are "capable of speech," then you qualify for a non-Ph.D. A non-Ph.D. diploma stated in official format that "Rochdale College hereby certifies that _____ does not hold the degree of Doctor of Philosophy." [36]

The original 1970 design for the diplomas was clearly satiric. The doubled image of Elizabeth, our "symmetrical queen," had four eyes. Suggested Latin mottos included "Cum opium optimum operamus optime," "Cannabis amamus," "S.P.Q.R.," and "Lest we remember." [37] A cleaned-up version quickly replaced this, though the discreet, decorative border of marijuana leaves remained, as well as the raised lettering and the gold embossed seal from Grand & Toy Stationers.

The queen regained the normal use of her eyes by doubling her image back to back instead of face to face.

Orders for $6,000 worth of diplomas were collected in the first week they were offered. The initial rush saw 131 sold in April '70 alone. It couldn't have been better; Rochdale would be paid for parody. Coach House Press, which did the printing, charged Rochdale a merely nominal amount: "Formula — $1 for person who does it or $2/hr whichever is more. $1 for overhead. $3 special Dope fund or whatever = $5 each diploma." [38]

During the next five years, requests came from across Canada and the United States, from Surrey, England, and Paris, France. Coach House records show that "one guy from Belgium has ordered eight which he wants to present at a Christmas party on December 10 in Brussels." [39] By June '71, degree sales had dropped to $300 a month and Rochdale had to hope for lottery ticket sales to replace the income. However, in August '72, the *Daily* reported that "a mention of degree availability on an NBC news item a few weeks ago had resulted in $6,000 worth of sales." [40] High-profile advertising was not shunned. After a *Rolling Stone* ad brought in a disappointing $900 in orders, president Peter Turner proposed an ad in the *Village Voice*, followed by *Playboy*.

Degrees were issued as late as April '75. At first, the degrees were conferred for ordinary subjects, then the trend turned towards witty and internally given degrees. Diplomas given out included:

Bachelor of: Building Mythology, Twenty-First Century Mythology (Judith Merril), Financial Manipulations, Oral French, Fortitude, Magical Apprenticeship, Life's Tosses and Turns.

Master of: Criminology, Crisis (Alex MacDonald), Communication of Wrong Numbers, the Art of Caring, Body Language (both to Cynthia Lei), Absenteeism, Technicolor (Paint Crew), Rock 'n' Roll, Herbology, Gaming.

Doctor of: Do-Good, Life, Philanthropy (Santa Claus), Canadian Folk Songs, Brush, Bedroom Engineering, Feminism, Poetic

Justice, Canine Aggression (William Littler), Animal Husbandry (Richard Barnes), Mindfucking, Delirium, Organic Chemistry, Psychopharmacology, Nothing, Hardcore Criminality (Henry Morganthaler), Necromancy, Thaumaturgy in Metaphysics (Michael Randell, dated 1537), Paleolithic Technocracy, Ineptitude, Failure (Jack Biddell, receiver), CIA in Government (Peter Turner).

King of: Arts.

Some alumni of Rochdale come from exotic lands — or exotic imaginations. The roster includes Henry Thornton Scott-Pillow, Siegfried Franz Zitterbart, and Mohd. Zulkifley bin Y. M. Nontak. Dozens of diplomas went to John Dope. Zygmont Fonberg's Ph.D. for the "Fonberg Effect in Shaped Charges" arrived at Coach House with a note: "I hope you can fit all of this in. He's a fine old boy, and really has done work on 'shaped charges' — he's sent me reprints from a learned journal dated 1950 or '51!" [41]

From the start of Rochdale, degrees were taken lightly. Project Co-ordinator John Jordan suggested in June '67 that degrees be granted on entrance to Rochdale College "in order to be eligible for grants." [42] In June '69, Jack Jones anticipated the mock diplomas: "There is no reason why [Rochdale] cannot present a straight face to the straight world...I cannot think of one reason why we should not con the Establishment...give out degrees if we must." [43]

Many people didn't understand the parody, or did and were offended. A few understood and saw an opportunity for fraud. A letter arrived from an employer asking for clarification of a Rochdale degree as "Doctor of Clinical Psychology" presented by a job applicant in West New Portland, Maine. [44] "The Cadillac Freak" wrote requesting a Rochdale student card, "chiefly as a 'Status Symbol' of course, but also (and naturally, only incidentally) to obtain discounts at movies, museums, and — who knows — maybe a trip to Europe!" [45] In another instance, a request was received for no "marijuana trippy-shit on the border," an academic seal of the College, and a Dean's

signature.[46] This special treatment, at twenty-five dollars extra, would
have benefited one Greenwall J. M'Hango (Sales Management) and
one Abel K. Mwonu (Geology) — both of whom should have been
awarded non-honorary degrees.

Rochdale had to continually remind its customers. "Mr. Guemple
would like his degree title spelled out in full," complained one nota-
tion. "Some people are weird. The whole purpose of this trip is to
prove the worthlessness of a piece of paper in terms of education, but
Mr. Guemple just doesn't get it."[47] Rochdale's Nickie Ashley replied
to a letter from Edmonton that "our 'degrees' are really PHONEY
DEGREES. They're not real. We DONT want people to use them to
get jobs...For this reason, we do not issue them in medical or legal
fields."[48] Lionel Douglas reiterated that "the degrees have little more
than satirical significance."[49] And the application form for the degrees
carried a photograph on the back that would be hard to mistake: in
violet ink, a naked man in a trench coat offers Rochdale degrees. At
one time, the form asked the applicant "not to use your degree to convince somebody you can do something unless you can really do it."[50]

Rochdale, however, tried both sides. The program for the 1974
Open House felt it necessary to counter the public perception, and
played it straight. "Rochdale has never pretended to be a degree-grant-
ing institution," it said. "The degrees issued are fancy receipts for
donations (which are tax-deductible)."[51] On the other hand, examine
an ad drawn up in May '70, probably for the *Village Voice* in New
York: "Looking for a college degree? Tuition for the B.A. granting
course is $25." Mention is made that the course length is twenty-four
hours and includes a skill-testing question. "For a Ph.D., the tuition
is $100 and there will be no questions asked."[52] The 8 × 10-inch ad
showed a dog sniffing a fire hydrant. There were no other disclaimers.

The truth was that Rochdalians were genuine in pointing out
what was seen to be fraud, and loved using fraudulent means to do so.
Rochdale was working out a preferred art, and the diplomas were only

part of the art. The masterwork of Rochdale, if it could be created, would be both a fake and an original. What was being refined was parody — and the sense of self-importance that encourages parody, a sense of being a bold voice in a wilderness.

17

A Symbol on Bloor

With Rochdale College, the imagination of the Sixties had acquired —
a little late in the decade — a fixed address and both visible and
invisible means of support. As the highrise was entering the Seventies,
the name "Rochdale" and the concrete box at 341 Bloor Street West
had become a symbol, and the low deals in this runaway college had
blended with high ideals.

Indeed, Rochdale had one resource that separated it from any
other available institution: it was empty. As a building, it was empty.
As a set of rules and expectations, it was empty. Like a vacuum
lowered into society, its walls filtered the mess of ideals that flowed in
and collected a purer form of the outside. When those ideals rapidly
changed in content from whatever had been expected — even by the
idealists — the fervor of the ideals continued.

"Rochdale is one of the healthiest, most genuine things our crass,
sterile society has created."[1] Not an exceptional opinion for one of
Rochdale's supporters, but one held by Barbara Adams, a member of
Govcon who was elected, after the end of Rochdale, to the Toronto City
Council. To drug dealer Syd Stern, his years in Rochdale were "five
years in the Garden of Eden." Sociologist Kent Gooderham reported the
feeling that here "Blake's children [were] building the New Jerusalem."[2]

The opening of this sun-building was handled religiously, ritually: "7 hours and one-half after noontide Wednesday blessed be this building / a caravan of priests visitations inherent god comes in head of red & wonder candles will silence all rules (have one warming your palm) levitation exercises bring down barriers / all in the building will be affected wait cautiously outside your door or group by the mystic motion vertical box doors."[3] In October '68, one resident enthused about the "sun-building, pyramid of parallel sides concrete and whole stretching up to its ridge-pole, face to sky."[4]

Proudly, a resident proclaimed that "we are motivated by the 'WORTH ETHIC' in this Karmic accelerator called Rochdale."[5] "Rochdale should gather to itself all the freaks, all the heroes it can hold…" said Jack Jones in his "Aquarian Survival Kit" of September '69. "Rochdale should make gestures, large ones…"[6] Gooderham concluded that "Rochdale is as North American as the automobile, the hamburger, Sitting Bull, and the Church of The Latter-day Saints. It is as important to our social health and well-being as 'Bay Street' and International Nickel…dope, dog-shit, and dirt are as important as are the I Ching, Zen Buddhism, the Beatles, and Marcuse."[7]

Similarities between the youth movement and the Amerindian were not ignored, especially when Rochdale housed a group of Indians reviving their native culture. Both peoples had been detribalized and were struggling to regroup. Rochdale itself could be seen as a reservation, facing the threat of Indian Wars with the police and prejudice from the majority whites. "Rochdale nation is a self-governing economic satellite of Canada, the most tightly organized hippie-indian tribe in North Merica," said resident Bruce Maxwell in the *Daily*.[8]

In the search for metaphors to give shape and size to the energetic, confusing event on Bloor Street, no scale was too large. Rochdale was, at the least, "an edifice complex," and had "almost by accident created a small town within a large city."[9] To commune member Mike Donaghy, Rochdale had to become "a technically sophisticated 'Kibbutz'" and needed outside support just as Israel did.[10] In this metaphor, Rochdale takes on the proportions of a nation. One Rochdale idealist wanted the College to become "a completely independent country. Run up its own flag. Apply to the UN and go down fighting for the new world rather than to perpetrate the old, the evil, by living within it."[11]

Unlike its educational founders, this young Rochdale was not confined by humility. "The College will fly the United Nations flag exclusive of any other standard," resolved the governing council in April 1970, "and will contribute 0.01% of its income to the United Nations special fund as a gesture of support."[12] This is both spoof and serious — as exaggerated, self-conscious, and heartfelt as a drunken sentiment. One man proposed that Rochdale be twinned with Bombay or Prague and thereby launch a World Community. He, however, made his regrets that he had other business to attend to on "Earth Day." The earthlings, presumably, could take care of the details.

The metaphors had to stop at the stars, even for "the infinite synapse connection that is Rochdale."[13] After the last resident left the building at the end of the seven-year itch, it was said that the "Good Ol' Starship Rochdale" had landed. "We'll just have to get our 'earth legs'... Our children are growing up among the earth children teaching them what it was to fly."[14]

As "Image Nation," Rochdale held a mirror up to society. "Inside is virtually an anti-world, a universe of anti-matter that reflects and reverses the rat-race world outside."[15] The College saw itself as "a liberated zone, secured turf in a political-military-cultural war being waged around the globe by young insurgents determined to bring sanity and humanity to social organizations and relationships."[16]

Gooderham listed some of the "dyads" that contrasted the mainstream culture and the youth-culture: "necrophiliac vs biophiliac, liquor vs dope, deodorized vs odourful, clean and white vs colored and soiled, don't vs do, St. Paul vs St. Francis, election vs consensus."[17] The Rochdale type he identified "saw the car as a symbol for capitalist exploitation" and pollution. Also, "to go naked was an ideal."

A cartoon character drawn in the *Daily* by Rochdale Security member Zipp gave a more specific set of goals. If "Acidman" were elected prime minister of Canada, "the age of consent will be lowered to twelve years, birth control pills will be given to all females age 12 or over, hallucinogenic drugs will be government inspected and sold in drug-stores, pornography will be legalized, churches will pay taxes, jails will close down and criminals will be treated in hospitals, underground papers will receive government grants — pass the joint — all cities will be required to open at least one public beach for nude bathing, the police will be disarmed, homosexuality will be legalized, welfare and unemployment insurance will be increased, discrimination on any grounds will be punished, gambling, abortion, and prostitution will be legalized and taxable, censorship will be banned, each city will set up digger-houses, suicide will be permitted, sex education will start in kindergarten, students will govern schools and universities…yes, it will indeed be a just society."[18]

The original Rochdale in England had been set up in the nineteenth century as an experiment in communal living, but "the new Rochdale is the antithesis of the old Rochdale," as Gooderham put it. "This new world is post-literate. It is different in kind from the literate (lineal) world of Newton and the empiricists."[19] The new Rochdale differed in another way by reaching further back, beyond its namesake. Marshall McLuhan, whose investigations into media were being carried out on the University of Toronto campus nearby, decided that "Rochdale has all the makings of a Utopian flop. They're all hurrying backward into the past as fast as they can go."[20] As "radicals" in the sense of "from the root," many of the young people living in Rochdale were far more conservative than the society around them, so conservative that they skipped into a less organized past that seemed new. "The so-called 'hippy' culture is an attempt to adhere to and build on the root premises and first principles of our culture," said Lionel Douglas, one of the governing council members.[21]

The fortunes of Rochdale mattered to many people who never lived there, people who saw their own tentative values being tested. During a promotion trip for Rochdale to Manitoba in 1969, someone in the audience spoke up: "Listen, you have a responsibility to all the others who are going through the same kind of trip — the dropping out. If you fuck up, we're all screwed...watch your step for our sakes!"[22] *Toronto Life* reported in 1971 that "Rochdale, the idea, is a beacon of hope to young people all over North America...Because of Rochdale, they look to Toronto as the last of the enlightened big cities."[23]

As late as March '74, one writer in the *Toronto Star* argued that "every city must have its Rochdale, and in time, every town. For these are the nuclei of tomorrow's culture, the young are in spiritual training for the apocalypse, due almost any day now. When the economy collapses and with it government and order itself, only they will be able to withstand the shocks of these catastrophes for, in a sense, they have already been there. They will have developed immunity, the capacity to survive in the midst of the rubble. In time they may even rediscover fire, how plants reproduce, the way something called the wheel used to function."[24]

The Rochdalians took their status seriously. The *Daily* proclaimed that "this centre of light, Rochdale and the surrounding area, can extend like a nuclear chain reaction to the entire world!!!...When we say 'Rochdale College' out loud our attention is brought to what we aim for. Count on your fingers the times you say 'Rochdale College' each day. Ten times or 2 handfuls will tune you into this great idea we live in."[25]

Often, practicality seemed less real than excitement. Shortly after his three-man Rochdale Music Department disintegrated, musician Michel Roy planned a twenty-four-hour festival, "Play-On-an'-On":

"We are going to have blimps, an air raid of a thousand colored paper airplanes, a 40-story lit billboard, a mass jam session of hundreds, a pied piper children's parade (maybe 300 children), trained animals, a medieval marching band, 24 hour radio coverage, free food, every conceivable sort of music, etc, etc, etc." As was the case on many high society party nights, "Rochdale is going to wake Toronto from its deep sleep."[26]

And among the inflated plans were simple, ignorant plans. With no thought for the source of electricity, one resident proposed salvation by music. "Let's have music...destroy industry with guitar strings and wire and electricity."[27]

When the high ideals didn't appeal, the low ones did. The low ones caught young adventurers and those too cynical or narrow to be recruited by Image Nations. Rochdale had acquired such an air of depravity and license that it couldn't help but draw line-ups for weekends and matinees. Even while complaining about living in a main attraction, Rochdale promoted its air of sleaze with delight. One internal publication advertised "memberships...plain brown rapper — confidential — no salesmen will call. No minors."[28] At one point, the reverse side of application forms for the college featured a flasher with raincoat and full-frontal nudity. An early *Daily* advised that "WEBSTER SAYS...Rochdale is pronounced with an 'o' like that in comply and a 'ch' like that in chip. However, the Rochdale grammarian prefers the pronunciation of the name as though spelled 'R-o-a-c-h-d-a-l-e', basing the choice on considerations of semantics, aesthetics, and common usage."[29] Or, if pot-smoking were not your choice of double entendre, you could pronounce "Rooshdayle" at "341 Blorp" any way you pleased.

How do we take a symbol that treats itself so casually, and teases to the point of self-destruction? As we have seen with the mock-serious monarchy set up in the spring of 1969, and again with the popular diplomas, Rochdale found its forte in parody. What couldn't be accepted with love could be treated with Strange-love. Parody became Rochdale's stance towards the straight society around it — and easily, the parody turned to include the parodists themselves. For these self-proclaimed prophetic voices, the only intelligent response to a ludicrous wilderness was serio-comic, and it seemed only natural that the small-scale mirror being held up to the wilderness, Rochdale itself, was also serio-comic.

In April '67, *Rochdale Bulletin* editor — and president-to-be — John Bradford wrote with some prescience that "our chance may turn out to be a huge put-on, on 'us,' on 'them,' on us all."[30] If the College was viewed by serious thinker and superficial funseeker alike as a critical joke, then the most serious effort became parody, especially if the ones making the effort used forms that were serious everywhere else.

As a counter-institution, Rochdale delighted in mocking what it was intelligent enough to criticize but not competent enough — nor earnest enough — to change. "Due to recent developments in the United States and Europe," said one press release by president Peter Turner, "Rochdale College regretfully announces it has been forced to devalue its currency, the Rochdollar. It is now worth less than nothing." The Rochdollar, like many of Rochdale's mockeries, betrayed a nostalgia for structure, a nostalgia disguised by a joke. Printed by Coach House Press, the dollar bills featured Queen Elizabeth with an eagle behind, and were "negotiable for co-operative service."[31] As a method of keeping track of the duties owed by co-op members, the scheme was short-lived, but serious enough that each note had a separate serial number.

Similarly, drug dealer Syd Stern had checkbooks with blanks made out to the CMHC — not the Canada Mortgage and Housing Corporation that was demanding mortgage payments, but Stern's "Canadian Marijuana and Hashish Corporation." "I had that name legalized before the government had theirs. Sometimes when I deal, my customers pay by cheque." Again, this was a practical problem with a serio-comic solution. The CMHC wanted money and the "CMHC" got it.

When Rochdale erected its own statue, *The Unknown Student*, the College was again playing ape, but seriously. Sculptor Ed Apt explained that "if the city hall can have its statue [*The Archer* by Henry Moore], Rochdale can too, and we have done it. The city paid $125,000 for the Moore, you paid virtually nothing for yours... Conclusion: make your own children yourselves!"[32] And if City Hall could have its own transit, so could Rochdale. When an Austin Mini went up for sale nearby, Edcon passed a motion that they "authorize and encourage the formation of an 'Inner City Transport Study for the Design of Urban Transit Alternatives.'"[33] This study eventually found its alternative in the Boogie Bus, used for travel to Rochdale's farm. The bus operated under a fictitious "Ministry of Transportation and Communications."

A "straight" answer, a simple "serio" solution, was not good enough for Rochdale. Note this parking ticket, a la Rochdale, from Mike Randell of the "Office of the Thaumaturge" to "The owner of this car": "after due consideration and consultation of the oracles... my first rash impulse is to request that you insert your car in another place."[34]

As with the annual royal balls, opportunities for ritual and semi-serious ceremony were seldom missed. To mark the rare success of a communal effort, Rochdale turned to burnt offerings. "IN FACT! Right now (monday night) on the patio in the grill as an initiation 5 (five) SHOPPING bags of grass (stems) were burnt!!!!!"[35] Rochdale collected several self-ordained chaplains, including Zipp and Rev. C. T. Walker. In January '69, Chaplain Walker wrote that he and his family were "recovering from an orgy fun-fest in the pagan spirit of the season that included the roasting of an ox in the shaft of the broken elevator. He is happy to report that the one thing an Otis elevator is suited for is a roasting pit. Next time we'll try barbecuing a sabbatic goat (Y'all cum down)."[36]

Parody lets intelligence sweeten analysis with fun, and Rochdale played the comedian surrounded by straightmen. As a kind of ghetto, and with the reaction to persecution sometimes developed in ghettos, Rochdale perfected evasive, mocking answers. How could Syd Stern answer a straight question, especially from an outsider? When did you arrive in the building? Syd Stern: "Just in time." Where did you come from? "Just down the street."

An audience with a stimulated imagination, Rochdalians loved a good put-on. "De Fat Daddy Cinema Narcotique," with Dean Martin and Jerry Lewis films, caused a stir in the first months of the College. Who was Fat Daddy? The *Daily* passed on a note that Fat Mama was "very interested in the famous Fat Daddy. I've heard *so* much about you. I just know we could make such heavy, heavy music together." A later issue completed the family: "I'm the Fat Orphan and I lost my parents in the Fat Floods of Florida in fourteen forty-five. Must contact either Fat Momma or Fat Daddy — IMMEDIATELY!"

Editor Sir Basil Nardley-Stoades, the *Daily Planet*'s resident trickster, wrote for a like-minded, mock-minded readership. Stoades insisted that one resident's interview with the *Globe and Mail* was intended "to spread the rumour in the straight press that Rochdale was not really run entirely by that super-intelligent, highly perceptive, super-alien from Cygni 6-I — Sir Basil Nardley-Stoades."[37]

"It is time for me, young as I am, to remind you New Generators, that All This Has Been Done Before. I, too, was radical in my time. Even at school I was somewhat a bounder...the first person to climb Out of College after hours...a member of the revolutionary Seductive Brethren, we founded the equivalent of the Freedom Thing. By George! We used to skip out of those boring House meetings and slip into Hennekey's for a draught of vanilla bitters and spend hours talking of This and That. Yes, young people, you're not the first to rebel against your elders. You'll soon grow out of this stage, as the hard lessons of Life round you out into, I'm sure, fine young people, both men and women. But until you do you're just another bunch of damn twisted Dope Fiends and Long-haired Nits. Piss on you."[38]

As a College, Rochdale held itself up to educational institutions as if it were a funhouse mirror. Howard Adelman, in a sober analysis, could see the parody: "Rochdale reveals itself upon examination as the quintessence of the University of Toronto planning tradition embodying diversity to the point of absurdity...Not need but circumstances, not university goals but individualistic strivings, not a master plan but enslavement to tradition in the name of innovation created Rochdale College; and Rochdale College is but a parody of the University of Toronto."[39]

In January '69, the resource people formed, at least in name, their own Faculty Underground Club (FUC), and in April '69, formal invitation cards were printed up: "The faculty and staff of Rochdale College are pleased to announce the graduation of our first class of forty speedfreaks and the commencement of next year's class. You are cordially invited to attend our first class reunion to be held five years from this date at Central Cemetery, Toronto."[40] Even after Rochdale closed in 1975, its educational theme continued with a Rochdale College Alumni Association.

An advertisement for tenants took the form of a Rochdale College Calendar. The course offered was "Paleolithic Technocracy 320: A field-laboratory course during which the development of action over a distance is viewed in the context of its supersession by the Neolithic womb concept. In the light of the historical ascendency of apparent efficiency, interiority as a life value is de-emphasized to generate political capital. The effects of paleolithic-technological opportunism on community developments are analysed."[41] Like looking into a marbled stone, one can see in this passage shapes that might mean — or might not. Prerequisites in this teasing calendar were "Last months rent in advance." The application form ("Free

Coupon" it called itself) had spaces for "Student no.," "No Student," "Coup," "On," and "Warmth (Degrees)."

Sometimes the parody happened unconsciously. In 1969, the "Utopian Research Institute" offered a program that was both serious and impossibly complex. Called "Comparative Methodology in Psychology," the program wanted to touch on "Society (will) — 0.0.3: Structure (Being) — Will: System 7 — Transformation: System 8 — Completedness: System 9 — Harmonization."[42]

More important than this distortion of academia were the parodies that actively challenged what they inverted. Rochdale Security — just by existing — parodied the Metro police force, as pointedly as the drug dealers parodied Yonge Street merchants. The butt of the joke — Toronto, Ontario, Canada — needed very little imagination to begin calling the parody demonic.

Even for itself, Rochdale as a parody ran out of control. Within the range from serious to comic, the tone of any particular event varied wildly among individuals and even within individuals. The creed of "Do Your Own Thing" included a pop kind of relativity in which anyone could Camp Your Own Camp, and it was common for one person's seriousness to slip on another's banana peel. Both sides of the serio-comic became extreme, with some individuals suffering serious consequences — even death — sometimes for laughs, and more individuals struggling hard for an unstable mix of farce and home and principles.

On its masthead, the *Daily Planet* printed the elusive goal: "Be Bold And Lie Truthfully."[43] Freedom would be tested to its extreme: the freedom to lie, to mock, to proclaim. If parody was a kind of right action in an absurd world, why should it be controlled any more than love, or memberships, or kinds of altered consciousness? But Rochdale was building its parody too well. The comedian/prophet on Bloor Street was eighteen-storys tall, and could not be allowed so rapt an audience.

A garden in the fifteenth-floor commune.

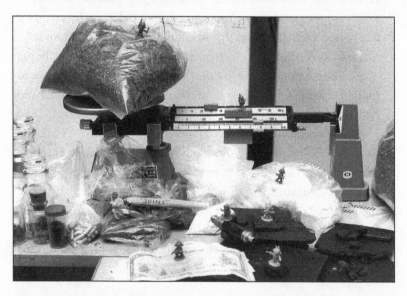

Drug paraphernalia during a "close-out sale" on the eighth floor.

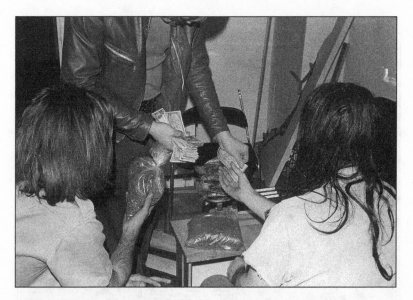

Drug dealing on the eighth floor.

Rochdalians on the sidewalk in front of the College celebrating the withdrawal of police after one of the raids in the summer of 1970.

The late Lionel Douglas, Govcon member and community leader, explaining
in a Rochdale meeting the complexities of Rochdale's financial situation.

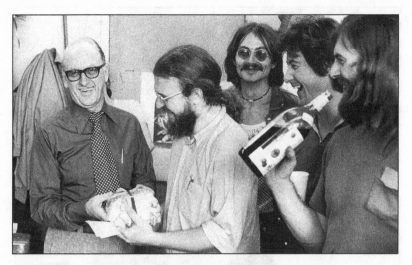

Brian Lumley of Maintenance receives a retirement gift from Property Manager Sid Smith (with tie), early 1974.

The second-floor lounge, home for Syd Stern (at table, facing camera). A Clarkson worker is painting him into a corner.

Rudy Hierck burning an eviction notice that has just been served by a "nameless civil servant."

The last General Meeting, June 1975, on the roof of the highrise.

The second-floor lounge as the renovating company found it. Along the top of the door is written "Just another fallen goddess," and on the back of the wall is "WE SHALL RETURN." (Photo courtesy of R.P.A. Consultants)

PART FOUR:

THE ROCKING CRADLE

18

The Fan

Rochdale had been enjoying moral support from high places, including the federal government. Minister Without Portfolio Robert Andras visited Rochdale at the beginning in connection with the Indian Institute. Prime Minister Pierre Trudeau himself had an ambivalent, even tolerant, attitude towards at least one main component of the Rochdale lifestyle. In August '70, he told a group of high school students that "people who do it [smoke marijuana] I don't judge any more than I judge the person who takes alcohol."[1] The *Varsity* at the University of Toronto reported that officials from the Prime Minister's office "see the college as a useful experiment in counter-insurgency, as a way to keep potentially violent youth off the streets and politically dormant."[2] This resembled the reasoning of the University of Toronto itself, whose administration had offered "its good offices, personnel, and moral support" to develop Rochdale.[3] The founding organization, Campus Co-op, seemed to be "an innocent way for student activists to funnel their energies in a non-destructive way."

In a media-massaged society, the "high places'" that could offer support — or withdraw it — included the newsrooms and editorial offices of television, magazines, and newspapers. And for a long time, the media looked upon Rochdale with curiosity and sometimes with approval. The *Toronto Telegram,* for one, printed mostly favorable reports in the first year. In January '69, CTV filmed for a week for *W5* on national television, and included shots of crafts people beautifying the lounge with murals, paper flowers, and with a carving made from a cedar root. As late as April '69, before the financial shambles became apparent, a staff reporter at the *Telegram* wrote in a full-page story that "Rochdale lives. And like spring grass and flowers breaking through crusty earth, a spirit of exhilaration is pulsing through the chambers of Rochdale College." [4]

For some inside Rochdale, the good press was ominous. In March '69, resident Jerry Ofo submitted "Autoeroticism in the National Press" to the *Daily* and identified a "climax" pattern in reporting on the youth culture: "A good scene happens, an article appears in the national press, the Bus Tour is rerouted to go through the district, more favorable articles, a thousand pseudos show up to dig it, a thousand tourists show up to look at the pseudos and spend money, a little shit happens, the press turns sour, the good people split, the cops come, more bad articles demand the cops do something...I don't expect to be able to convince anybody to keep the press out of Rochdale, but I do hope to destroy the myth that a good press coverage means that 'they' are in favor of us. I suggest that the press is just following its normal cycle and this means that good news today is bad news tomorrow." [5]

Of course, some of the media were trying very hard to find the bad news. The *National Enquirer* took a brief interest in the "Hippie College," but it seemed that they wanted more than they got. The story pointed out the sign on a door that invited: "if you want to come in and make love to me, please make sure you wipe your feet." [6] A photo of some students lying on a floor and some seated (the public areas of Rochdale still had chairs) demonstrated that a "Lecture Hall at Hippie U is relaxed and informal — some drink or embrace as they study."

Another caption, "coeds paint each other before a special Psychedelic Night meeting," matched a blurred shot of a paint workshop.

In June '69, free sex made the *People* in England. The reporter told of visiting one room where "a young couple were lying naked in bed together. There were three other people in the room. One was reading a comic book and two were examining the cover of a record called 'LSD'. Weren't the couple in bed just slightly embarrassed? The naked girl said: 'Why should we? What is important today is honesty.'"[7] And there they were in the photograph, the girl combing the hair of the boy. This was not Rochdale, Lancashire, the paper quickly assured its readers.

Most of this reportage was low-key. It gave a push to the College hard enough to make it rock, and catch the eye of young adventurers, but not enough of a push to tip it over. Opponents of Rochdale in the general public, who were in no hurry to realize they were opponents, seemed to need no more than occasional grumbles in the press. As early as December '68, the Toronto *Globe and Mail* asked editorially, "Is [Rochdale] Yorkville gone high-rise? The connection cannot be avoided. Yorkville has become not so much a district in Toronto as a word in Toronto's argot. It has only to be uttered. It requires no adjectives, no expanded narration to conjure all sorts of repugnant images in the public mind."[8]

One major opponent of Rochdale — the police department — was not at all satisfied with the opposition. Law enforcement would be both mocked and crippled if the good burghers of Toronto the Good didn't learn that hundreds of young people in the heart of their city were sharing a fantasy that was Restricted, even Triple X. The fantasy should be exposed as violent, concerned with sex and nudity. Exchanged at the concession stand were illicit drugs and freeloaded, if not ill-gotten, gains. Worse, the citizens of Toronto should see that the kids were enjoying the show and that some of the kids were their own.

And if vice was not gripping enough, the money would be. The police anticipated that not only would Toronto discover a den of dealers, smokers, dodgers, and free-lovers, but it would realize the den was organized like a syndicate and was permanently housed in a $6 million dollar building bought with Good Burgher government money. Because the loan wasn't being repaid and because it looked like it never would be, a lot of good money had been thrown after bad.

Indeed, it looked as if the citizens were paying for political, as well as social, rebellion. The conservative city of Toronto would need little encouragement to fear the onset of trouble. In this hot, restless summer of 1970, political extremism in the United States had already led to the Kent State killings, the Fred Hampton assassination, the March 6 New York townhouse explosion, the Chicago 12, the Weathermen, and talk of "Weathernation." The F.L.Q. in Quebec were posing a threat that would soon result in the Pierre Laporte assassination and the War Measures Act of October 16, its panic reflex. To the wary observers of Rochdale College, who already had dossiers on this as-yet unexploded bomb, the College might yet play a role in political turmoil.

If nothing else, there were all the American exiles gathering at this one address in the heart of the city. One former resident says that "there was an arrangement with Amex [Union of American Exiles] involving free rooms or, if Amex couldn't do it, Rochdale would send a car down to pick someone up at the border. They wouldn't usually be on the run, but it was rumored that Mark Rudd stayed in Rochdale, and Bernadette Dorn. Toronto seems a natural place to lie low."

With the exaggeration that Rochdale inspired, another informant confirms the large numbers: "What proportion of residents were American? — About 75%. — Draft-dodgers, were they? — I would say all of them." A visitor to Rochdale from California commented to the *Globe* that, during the first large disturbance of the summer, "the ones who started [the near-riot] were chiefly Americans. We were the ones who first ran after the police. Americans are much more activist. Canadians don't seem to do much." [9]

At times, the Canadians in Rochdale resented the American presence, but the resentment never became active. "Canada and the Canadian is a vacuum," resident Mike Donaghy complained in the *Daily*, "that can be moulded by Americans and intelligence — against its apathetic will. Americans have misrun Rochdale and intellect is remoulding Canada." [10] The *Daily* printed another dissenting voice in October '68: "It is my hasty impression that all faces are facing towards Berkeley and the Great U.S. of A. and all the bums are bumming toward the North. We have been invaded once again from the U.S.!... The SDS and other rabble-rousers are going to fuck things up. If that's the purpose: A. I question it; B. They are going to be successful." [11]

Openly, Rochdale was being invited to join the unrest. In February '69, Jerry Rubin visited Rochdale and spoke about the yippies in Chicago, telling Rochdalians that "the cops rioted... We are indicted under the federal anti-riot law because our long hair incited cops to violence against us." [12] Several months later, a note in the *Daily* announced to "COMRADES" that "4 revolutionaries from Sir George Williams U. need a crash for a few nights." [13]

And Rochdale was accepting the invitation: what else could the police think when Rochdale seemed to sponsor the violent May Fourth Movement in May and June of 1970? The May Fourth Movement, or M4M, was "Toronto's equivalent of SDS [the radical Students for a Democratic Society]," and hoped to use the summer for revolutionary gains. [14] M4M "demanded accommodation" from Rochdale in May '70 and were admitted after "lengthy debate." According to Kent Gooderham, not only was the Movement suspect because of its associations with violence and American student political movements, but also because its support for Women's Liberation "appeared irrational to Rochdalians." [15]

However cool the greeting, Govcon gave the Movement a free room for the summer and granted temporary use of the Publications Office. The project? A demonstration against the Vietnam War at the U.S. Consulate. M4M busied themselves with a "great deal of printing." As the date approached, they reacted to a police statement that "someone could be killed" at the proposed Consulate demonstration as a "flimsily veiled threat," but after the Kent State killings, no one could be sure if threats were bluster or truth.[16] From the Rochdale office, M4M sent out an invitation: "We Announce the Death of the Silent Majority. You are cordially invited to The Funeral Wake, with us. Riots, macings, clubbings, fights, killings, and a splendid time is guaranteed for all."[17] After the demonstration, M4M tried to backpeddle, and suggested they had meant something milder: "M4M opposes violence initiated against people but we support violence against private corporate property: the banks, the trusts, and the consulate."[18]

The May 9 demonstration at the U.S. Consulate attracted 5,000 people to the street. As M4M had guaranteed, the splendid time began. According to an eyewitness, at first police made ten or fifteen scattered arrests of "people caught throwing stuff at the Consulate. There was a lull of about 45 minutes and then the police suddenly drove a wedge with their horses right through the crowd, dividing the people standing in front of the Consulate. These two groups stood about for a while and then some began throwing junk at the insurance building. Police charged again. There was a mass exodus — people were driven against the wall. There was another pause and people began leaving, assuming the demonstration was over...

"For some reason, the police did not leave it at that, but charged with their horses, pushing people back toward Yonge Street. Two thousand people ran, shouting and yelling and overturning garbage cans. Then bricks were thrown at Eaton's windows. Cops came on horses, motorbikes, on foot, chasing kids everywhere and arresting 40 or 50."[19]

Other versions laid claim to the assault on Eaton's as a "march" that protested the hip capitalist takeover of the youth culture. It was aimed, they said, against the "Metropolitan Toronto Pig Department," Eaton's, the Canadian Imperial Bank of Commerce, and "Yonge Street plastic." [20] "If we had been more together we could have taken Sam's [Sam the Record Man] and liberated our music…maybe next time."

An "M4M guy" boasted in the *Daily* that "the police are angry because they know they were routed in Saturday's rally. By now they have found out that the people smashing windows at Eaton's was a diversionary contingent. Meanwhile the main M4M contingent was busy planting bombs in the bridges for the Spadina Expressway. Eaton's is but one of the corporate powers behind the Expressway. There is more to come." [21] "Don't forget, folks, when you smash the state to keep a smile on your lips and a song in your heart…when we trashed thousands of dollars of windows at Eaton's on the 9th, it was token revenge for the sweat of thousands of Eaton's workers." [22]

M4M had scored ninety-one arrests in its first big foray, and freely claimed vandalism as political action.

Meanwhile, local radicals of many persuasions were hoping for a grassroots movement, and were trying to nurture it by occupying vacant lots in the Rochdale neighborhood. The series began in April '70 when Rochdalians helped claim the Huron "People's Park," an occupation protesting expansion by the University of Toronto. Then, on a Sunday in May, the "People" reclaimed a lot at Huron and Washington. Some residents of Rochdale "tilled" the earth while The People's Revolutionary Concert Band played and "Huron and Washington (a newly-formed local effort) [did] Chicago numbers." [23] Two black musicians yelled "Power to the People," and the People took up the chant. In June, M4M occupied a lot at Sussex and Spadina where eight homes had been demolished for an air-conditioning plant. Sandwiches, Kool-Aid, and "a box of corn muffin crumbs" were provided. Police stopped the concert at 11 p.m. and firemen extinguished the bonfire in the middle of the lot. Yet another time, Rochdale moved beyond its walls when it joined Project Spadina, a seizure of land for a political purpose, this time to stop the building of the Spadina Expressway that would bring increased traffic into the city.

By now, the police had watched long enough; they had been taunted long enough. Not only were associates of Rochdale seizing or violating property in the name of politics, but drug-dealing itself, another kind of grassroots rebellion, had taken over real estate within the highrise. "In the spring and summer of 1970," says Alex MacDonald, "the police stopped dealing with Rochdale as a police operation and started dealing with it as a military operation." A decision was made to open a war of publicity, and the tactic? — well-staged, well-witnessed drug raids, as well-witnessed and better-staged than the U.S. Consulate demonstration. Each of these raids, conducted for camera and press, would be an establishment version of a political demonstration, featuring police helmets and clubs as visible and message-laden as the placards of radicals. If drugs and druggists were caught as well, so much the better. At this point, no one knew how successful the raids could be, but they knew the fan had been turning too long and too fast. They would throw at it all they had...

What better stage and time for a premiere than a warm, street-filled summer weekend? Whether the scale of it was planned or precipitated, the opening came on a Saturday night, August 15, 1970. On that night, as one resident described it, "we had a monster raid that...included 125 uniformed and plainclothes police officers who charged through the front door and advanced upon the 15th floor." [24]

By another account, the raid began with a foray. Eight or nine RCMP officers entered and searched a fifteenth-floor room "after flashing what may have been a warrant," and caught Rochdale by surprise. "The Horsemen [Royal Canadian Mounted Police] were wrong, dead wrong," said resident "B.N." "We knew it and phoned the 52nd for assistance." [25] The Metro police apparently sent one car at first. However, as the crowd on the street grew and as 150 officers arrived to face the shoving and shouting, it became clear that it was not so much the two Rochdalians being arrested who were important, but the performance being played out for the press.

"Their track record is as follows," the first account continued: "19 broken doors, 31 rooms searched, and two people arrested, ha ha, one fellow had just middled a Hash deal and whose 2 grams of profit were in his mouth, while he was counting his coin, ran into all of these cops in the center stairwell and was immediately arrested, handcuffed, and taken to a waiting car. The other guy was just in the way and was charged with resisting arrest and taken down to join his unfortunate friend in the squad car... people from [Yorkville] village were aware of what was happening within five minutes. The village people, amounting to about three hundred people, joined with the building people who took to the streets in protest and gave the police a reasonably hard time."

"The first action of the masses was to surround the police, to free the guy who was charged with assault, and [then they] proceeded to demolish about nine police cars, including throwing a brick through the roof of one of their cars."[26]

"I don't want to see a shit eating grin on the faces of the RCMP agents who originated this whole thing," said B.N., "and are then exonerated because a lot of us overreacted. I don't want to see a lot of good people, ideas and cool go up the pipe because a number of pricks who may not really give a damn are unprepared to make distinctions, are crazy for a fight, or consciously want Rochdale to blow itself wide open. A lot of people got mad, Security got shoved around, got mad because they've got balls, and shoved the Horsemen back. But when the situation really blew, with the assistance of a lot of action hungry visitors, we were treated to the lovely sight of Security fighting us and them, while yahoos bounced more stones off of Rochdale heads than bull heads."[27]

The police department included a description of the raid in a report released to the press much later: "A man at the front entrance, on observing the police, ran inside. A member of Rochdale Security demanded to see the writ of assistance in the lobby. He took time to examine both English and French versions. The fire alarm sounded, and almost immediately about seventy-five persons gathered, calling the police 'pigs,' and spitting at the officers. Upon reaching the elevator with the security man, the lights went out and, after some difficulty, the officers finally reached Apartment 1509P and found it empty. In the apartment was found a piece of paper on which was stated the price and weights of hashish." The police decided to return by the stairs. "On reaching the ninth level, they observed five males, one of whom had a 3/4 inch square of hashish in his mouth. He was arrested and removed from the building; he was also found to be in possession of an offensive weapon (12 inch blade)." Harassment by the crowd was "stimulated by Rochdale Security who were drinking beer... When one of the officers boarded a police auto parked some distance away, with the crowd following, he was hit in the face with a lighted cigarette, and spat upon." [28]

Tires on a police cruiser were slashed and the activist newspaper *Guerilla* reported an (editorially enhanced) exchange between "thirty cops and fifty residents": "The spokesman for the Division 14 boys charged 'you slit our tires.' 'Well, in the last one and a half years you've busted 2,000 kids on pot charges. Four tires don't stack up as much against 2,000 fucked-over lives.' 'We're just doing our job.' 'Well, it looks like someone else is doing theirs too.'" [29]

For at least one Rochdalian, the raid had long-term effects; the resident was given a free room by Govcon "until he regains sight in an eye injured during the first major cop/Rochdale clash." [30] This compensation lasted for several years — until Rochdale had no rooms to give.

In quick succession, police marked two more weekends with raids: Friday, August 21, and Friday, September 11. The September raid matched 400 on the street with 50 policemen. It is a sign of the ambivalence in high places that the Prime Minister's executive assistant was inside Rochdale College during one of the raids and, according to Rochdale officials, was "displeased" at the tactics used by the police.[31]

But while the gloves were off in the public ring, kid gloves stayed on in private. An anonymous writer recorded on a loose sheet in the Rochdale files that the Rochdale executive "arranged a War-Peace council with Jack Ackroyd [later to become Toronto Police Chief] and some other Police Heavy Staff, and tried to reach an agreement as to how we could co-exist without some of the heavy shit going down and the endangering of life and property on both sides."[32]

Exactly when this meeting took place is not clear. Upon his retirement as Police Chief in 1984, Jack Ackroyd still worried about his handling of Rochdale. "It seems to be my Achilles heel," he said. "Some thought it showed weakness to talk to them but I have always believed that was the way to handle many problems."[33] The extent of the talking and agreeing is hard to determine, but in November '69, one Rochdale resident felt he had reason to charge a Rochdale president with co-operation. "Hard drug users," he said, "are *reported to the police* and evicted in exchange for the freedom to use soft drugs."[34]

Throughout this time, the police maintained liaison people within the College. "I was always upfront with them," one of them said afterwards. "They'd ask, 'Who are you?' and I'd say, 'I'm a cop.' . . . It got so you couldn't go in if you had a uniform, even to go in and get someone out who was ill. I would get called." This particular policeman performed so well that "the police busted in one time without telling me. They thought maybe I was a sympathizer or an informant." Other policemen inside Rochdale were not always so 'upfront' with their targets. As early as November '68, Dennis Lee warned the residents that "there are clearly police agents involved at Rochdale, and there is probably very large trouble brewing."[35]

The newspapers wrote lengthy reviews of the performance by the police. "1500 People Confront 150 Policemen at Rochdale in Near-Riot After Arrest" was one *Globe* entry, with "Mob Wounds Three Policemen After Rochdale Drug Raid" for the *Star* and "1,000 Battle Police at Rochdale" for the *Telegram*. After the shock of those stories, the mainstream press tended to regain its normal calm, as shown in the bland *Star* header, "Rochdale Raided Second Time in Week," and the major newspapers followed once again the debate on both sides: positives such as "Rochdale Guards Win Popularity Poll" (*Telegram*) and "Rochdale Chief Says Drug Pushers Quitting" (*Star*) versus the negatives, such as the *Star*'s "Big-time Drug Peddlers Threaten Rochdale's Future."

Of course, the cheap papers indulged the sensationalism that the more serious press handled carefully. *Tab International* screamed: "Blow the Joint Up! Phoney Rochdale College Spreads Dread Asian VD!" That was just the headline. "Think of all the filth," begins the story, "rot, decadence, and immorality that has infected this world during the past five thousand years. Put them all together and you have only the surface of the biggest cesspool the world has known: Toronto's Rochdale College...Rochdale is a dope den to equal the entire Chinese colonies of all history."[36]

Great stuff, at least as good as another strident farce that was being appreciated by hip audiences across the continent: the movie with the killer title, *Reefer Madness*. Rochdale printed a copy of the *Tab* article in its advertising.

Disease became the favorite opposition metaphor. The same *Tab* article displays the metaphor for us with particular flair. "The main problem in the VD crisis is an Asian type venereal disease brought to Canada by deserters from the United States teenagers who shack up in Rochdale College...the little female teenagers soon take off on the highway to points east or west to spread their newly found VD to other hippies they meet along the highways. It's driving the

Departments of Health across Canada out of their minds!"

A slouching beast indeed. All the way from Asia it comes, Rochdale College bringing the anguish of the Vietnam War into Canadian homes. The war that, on the liberal side, was supplying Rochdale with ideology and members, was now giving Rochdale, on the conservative side, a new dread.

For Rochdale, the raids and their publicity were still melodrama. In an attempt to turn some of the media to good account, residents wrote letters supporting their alma mater. One letter in the *Globe* gave hypothetical comments by police press agents on the conducting of a successful police raid: "If your aim is to maximize press coverage... a minimum of 30 plainclothes and 30 uniformed men are necessary. Allow at least 45 minutes for curious residents to assemble and arrest two or three on non-drug charges. Of course the raid must be planned for 1 or 2 in the morning to allow residents' blood-alcohol level to rise to 'drunk and disorderly.' Next the press agent swings into action. Two or three obnoxious residents become the mob. Ignore the fact that they are calmed, disarmed, and/or removed from the situation by the remainder of the onlookers. You see? First we supply the situation, then we supply the news...It's all so simple really, press agentry, but sometimes I wish I'd entered a more honest profession, like politics..."[37]

19

Danger Zone

Now that the College and the city had begun to spar in public, one question could not be downplayed: just how violent would a Rochdalian become? The more the authorities looked at the youths inside Rochdale, the less they could depend on a Sixties ideal of peace. A number of these flower-children were in love with old-style brutality.

One of their own, resident anthropologist Kent Gooderham, concluded that the Rochdale type "was irrational, undependable and intractable...he could just as readily arrange to have somebody beaten up as to arrange for a rescue."[1] One *Daily* printed a warning, "FROM: Rochdale Resistance TO: Uberfuehrer I. Griggs / Beware / Take care / You will be followed / You are always watched / We are small but we are many / We have our methods / This is your only warning / Beware / RRR Hood and Men."[2] The issue here may be unclear, but the method is not. On another occasion, one resident was reported to have said he "personally believed that words are more harmful than actions so he felt justified in settling his disputes with violence."[3] Within the year, the same man was barred from the building for armed robbery that arose from a poker game in the fourth ashram. And there were more brutal solutions to small problems. One worker in the Rochdale cafeteria lost sight in one eye when he was beaten by someone who wanted in without a ticket.

Rochdale's solution to violence had been the creation of Rochdale Security using members of the motorcycle gangs, and the threat was always there that the protectors of the college would become what they were enlisted to oppose. In one security log entry, Chico of Rochdale Security wrote that, at 5 a.m., "two young men, one of them _____, approached the door and asked for [restaurant manager] Wu. After being told that he was not in the restaurant, Mr. _____ became very obnoxious and proceeded to pull a knife. At this time, I also pulled my knife and escorted both of them out of the building (rather abruptly). The person with Mr. _____ will be allowed into the building while Mr. _____ will not be as he was the aggressor. Wu has been informed of this, seeing as they are friends of Wu. NOTE: As far as I am concerned, the doorman and his assistant are not competent to handle the job seeing as while I was hassling with these people, they stayed far enough away so as not to be hurt."[4]

Though the presence of guard dogs was publicly denied, Rochdale Security had them at hand. In March '71, some "right-wing bully-boys" attacked some members of Rochdale Security. "This explains," said the *Daily*, "the addition of some large quadrupeds to the force."[5] The dogs, if not attack-trained, were attack-intended. A resident confirmed that "the symbols of power at Rochdale were the police dogs. They were clean and well-fed at a time when a lot of people were living on ketchup and water."[6]

The people working for Rochdale had to have fighting instincts, and those instincts could themselves become the problem. In October '70, a resident reported that he saw Rochdale Security grab a seller of the leftist newspaper *Mass Line* who wouldn't leave the front lobby. "A security member came charging into the melee with a sawed-off shotgun converted into a pistol."[7] Four of them took the seller into their office and closed the door. The resident looked through the letter slot and then through the outside window, and saw the seller bound with a belt and struck. Two police officers arrived and took him away.

Then, too, the drug traffic invited violence. At one point, a man wanted in Philadelphia for four murders saw a youth come out of Rochdale with a package of dope and go to his car. Plainclothesmen had the car staked, however, and examined both the package and the man's wallet. The murderer thought that this was a dope deal and, with a gun, demanded both the money and the dope. He was promptly arrested. In another case, two neighbors of "Miss (Blank)" complained about regular visits at 2:30, 3, 4, and 5 in the morning. When Rochdale people told her to stop selling drugs, Gary Segal was pushed down a flight of stairs — while his back was turned — by a person wanted by the police. Faced with more pressure from Rochdale, Miss (Blank) moved out "of [her] own accord" at 2 a.m.[8] The two neighbors stayed with friends when they received threats over the intercom.

But how much of the violence was bluff? One incident will point out the tempers that could flare, and the exaggerations that followed. As property manager Sid Smith tells it: "One afternoon the maintenance man came to me and kept me talking for a while, which was unusual for him. I said, 'you look a little nervous'. 'No, no,' he said, 'it's okay' The next thing I heard a scream and a yell. We both rushed out and this guy was coming out of the maintenance office. Quite literally, his hands were practically hanging off. Blood was going all over the place. Syd Stern was seen walking away with a knife, cleaning it on his back. When the police arrested him, he said he picked the knife up, he didn't do it. We know who did it, but the guy who was stabbed wouldn't give evidence. They reckon he'll never have the proper use of his hands again, he was so badly chopped up. We believe the maintenance man was told to leave his office for a few minutes. That's why he kept talking with me, so he could not be blamed."

For a different version, listen to the man himself. The fight started when _____ pretended to give money to Big Al while wagering in a game, but Al wouldn't give it back. Stern says that, judging by his eyes, Al was "right out of it." _____ left the room to get a knife. Al said, "Where's _____?" He had the brass nozzle of a fire hose tucked under his shirt in the front. As _____ was opening the door, Al swung with the hose. It hit the doorframe, or it would have smashed his head in. They fought until _____ had slashed Al three times in the back and had cut his hand [Stern indicates the little finger almost off]. Al just looked at his hand with the blood coming out. "What did you do to my hand, _____?" he said. Stern grabbed _____'s knife hand and ordered, "Give it to me." It was a machete. He did.

"There were two cops watching...they didn't step in at all. I walked toward them with the knife pressed between the palms of my hands, in front, so they could see I wasn't going to use it. One of them said later he had his hand on his gun and he would have shot me if I had the knife in one hand. Of course they said I was wiping the fingerprints off the handle." _____ was acquitted and Stern got thirty days for obstructing the law.

Stern doesn't talk to Al anymore because he went to the police about the knifing. "The guy is psycho for that."

In a later article, the *Globe* referred to an unspecified murder attempt "when a man was dripping blood from slashed wrists and a stab wound in the back, while still kicking his attackers off."[9] This was seen, the newspaper said, by several police and tenants. Could that have been yet another version of Al's cut? What was it — a little finger, a wrist, a whole hand? A machete — or a butter knife?

With violence, exaggeration is as good as fact when it's time to face a threat. If someone comes at you with any kind of knife and says, "I want your little finger," you're going to assume he wants your whole hand. For the people who were being asked to face these unknown assailants, the police, the danger couldn't be slighted.

"The police were fucking afraid," says one policeman. "They didn't know what these weirdos were about. Were they going to get killed in there? And they knew that Rochdale harbored anyone who asked to be harbored. We had the urban guerrillas in there."

Whether they were urban guerrillas or apolitical toughs, it was clear that more was at stake than fistfights. "They had a store of guns in there," says the policeman, "that would put Hercules [an Army surplus store] to shame." Property manager Sid Smith confirms that "they had a complete arsenal. The RCMP used to sift through the garbage every once in a while and they'd come across empty cardboard cartons from brand-new rifles, high-powered rifles." In February '69, the Nightwatch complained in the *Daily* about "Crippies with Guns... Most of these guns are revolvers, usually .22s, .38s, or .45 caliber... Right here in our home, Rochdale College, we have violence freaks, hippie cripples, crippies...no one has been shot, that we know of, however; one individual in the building has a .38 caliber pistol with a silencer on it, but if he has used it here in the building, we have not found the body, yet." [10]

Smith describes one incident among several: "There was a knock on the door and a fellow came in with an army greatcoat they used to wear in those days. He said, 'I wonder if you'—and he opened his coat and brought out this shotgun—'have ever looked down the barrel of one of these before?' I said, 'Many times. I was in the British Army overseas.' He said, 'Oh, you're a smart motherfucker, aren't you.' 'If you fool around with that thing, you'll be a motherfucker.' He said, 'Yeah, maybe you're right', and he put it back and walked out. Two policemen were coming in. They saw the gun and arrested him. It was fully loaded."

"The bikers routinely played Russian Roulette," says a policeman and former resident. "We got a call and went to Huron Street and found one of them stretched out dead. It was a friend of mine, one I grew up with. Everyone just took a look as if this was normal, this was life."

With Rochdale's normal mixture of fact and fantasy, the *Daily* printed a notice in October '68 for "anyone interested in forming a Rochdale cadet corps, to train in the use of modern weapons, logistics, transport, etc., contact T.W.S. Belford Lieut. (ret.)...Sign up now for the 17th Rochdale Irregulars. STOP THE HUN." [11] Interested irregulars were not hard to find. Chico, the Rochdale Security man, drew portraits of guns like other young men draw hot rods. His 1814 Spanish Dragoon pistol and .22 Derringer showed both love and talent.

"Then there was Dale, the gun freak," as a former resident recalls. "The guys went outside over some drug thing, some argument, and the next thing anybody knew Dale was outside blasting away. The police came, but the others had pulled him inside and stashed the gun. They got him later, though, some weapons charge. He was always waving it around."

The Rochdale community tried to control the possession of guns, but always with a knowledge that the control wasn't tight. In March '69, Govcon appointed Gary Segal to collect guns and place them in a safety deposit box. At this time, gun control was confused and often in the hands of Rochdale Security men who themselves loved firearms. "A gun's principal function is to kill or wound," the *Daily* editorialized in April '69, "and Chico may have erred in his approach to gun control. He made it his business to know where most residents' guns were kept and usually found out whenever somebody brought a new piece into the building." [12]

By May '70, eviction rules had been extended to cover all firearms, including fringe weapons such as BB or pellet guns, starting pistols, blank guns, and flare guns. Possession of any firearm had become evictable due to "volleys of gunshots in the middle of the night, blanks or otherwise, woundings by pellets and BB's and other asinine actions by trigger-happy freaks." [13]

At times, more serious weapons added to the feeling that violence was close at hand. On December 15, 1969, a bomb threat was phoned in at 7 p.m. for an 8 p.m. deadline. Since fire alarms were routinely ignored, it was decided that the building couldn't be evacuated soon enough. "In the nick of time," the searchers found a device with "some acid type timer" that they dismantled. Acid from the device dropped into a garbage can and started a fire that, though never out of control, smoked and smelled.[14] Even if Rochdalians were not the ones threatening to use a bomb, they were attracting and confronting those who were.

Or destruction could come just as easily from an arsonist. The *Daily* printed in December '68 a fantasy inspired by the fact of a fire: "I saw that the garbage could be fired easily by dropping a lighted paper or rag from, say, the sixth floor into the disposal chute. Entry to the chute access room was easy. The guard was not on duty and succumbed easily to a jam and peanut-butter sandwich. The match lit first time and the specially-liquid oxygen and polyeurethane carrier flared with that lovely, hungry, erotically-electric blue and yellow flame. I watched for a few seconds as the fire dance grew. Then I opened the shut chute, shouted, and shat. Shall I? Yes?... NOW! NOW *F*C*R! Events followed in perfect order. The garbage bag caught perfectly, the fire alarm worked perfectly as did the sprinklers, the smoke, and the fire-brigade. What fun! See Barry Luger run! See the people come! See the damage done!"[15]

Playing with fire. The dangers in the Danger Zone could rebound on the residents — or they could be used offensively. One source of danger was uniquely Rochdalian, and became the saddest, most visible case of the double-edged weapon that strikes out, but strikes back. The danger — both a weapon and a curse — was "dropping."

For an eighteen-story building filled to the top with iconoclasts, "dropping" had a fascination inspired by the highrise itself. "At 2:30 p.m. on October 12th [1968]," in response to a contest, "a green projectile was dropped off the 17th floor terrace. Five seconds later it hit the second floor terrace with a velocity of 960 i.p.s... The proto-type projectile protector consisted of two water-filled garbage bags with an [uncooked] egg in a third bag...Exploding on impact did not shatter the ovoid, calcate structured payload, giving designer Peter Judd complete vindication of his theories. And so the first Rochdale space programme was a complete success...The payload was held aloft to the amazed multitude who were staring out of the building. After photographs were taken, the egg was taken back to the building, fried, and eaten."[16]

Dropping may have had innocent beginnings, but it quickly got out of hand. One of the early missiles, a snowball, had a guidance system with a nose for irony — it hit Property Manager A. Raney. "I would like to talk to the person who threw the snowball off the roof on Sunday night at 7:15 p.m.," he notified the *Daily*.[17] "This is serious — because it hit *me* — bring your lawyer, you will need one."

Govcon tried to stop the rain. "IMPORTANT AND OFFICIAL: Will those persons who throw garbage from their windows (including the blond 6' male with a blue nylon jacket) please report right away to the office on the second floor for some important information. THIS IS URGENT. If you are such a person, please report in RIGHT AWAY!"[18] Somewhat naïve — and useless. In March '69, Govcon evicted a resident because "beer was thrown from the window in your room on March 17 at 5:15 p.m. and hit two passersby who, unfortunately, happened to be the Registrar and his secretary of Rochdale College."[19] In the same month, eviction criteria were expanded to include "throwing animals and garbage on the terrace."[20]

In May '70, Govcon swore to evict persons who even removed the screens from their windows, but swearing was as far as they got. Items dropping at a seventy-five-m.p.h. terminal velocity became such a problem that Rochdale members were urged to stand watch outside and report to Rochdale Security. Thus, ironically, the first outside surveillance on Rochdale was proposed by Rochdale itself.

Once the police began attacking Rochdale, from August '70 on, dropping graduated from negligence to a crude, sporadic line of defence. The objects heaved during police actions at Rochdale were light or heavy, solid or breakable, vegetable, animal, or mineral, including full cans of paint. In one incident alone, police responding to a burglar alarm at one of the ground-level stores couldn't check the rear doors "due to a barrage of bottles being dropped from the upper windows." [21] The missiles were not always randomly chosen: a "Rochdale Double" consisted of two beer bottles joined by a length of piano wire.

If the number of guns within the College remained unconfirmed for the police, heavy objects fell without a doubt. Sid Smith remembers that "in one apartment on the 17th floor, we found as many as twenty concrete blocks, all ready in the windows to throw out. All the police were advised never to park their car in front. One officer forgot or didn't know the order. He parked his cruiser there and when he came back, two concrete blocks had cut right through the cruiser into the street."

As late as June '75, as reported by the *Toronto Sun*, "a police officer managed to jump away from an object dropped at him from about 14 storys up at Rochdale. The object? A brown-and-white Persian cat. 'It makes you sick just to think about it,' said the police spokesman, 'but back in Rochdale's heyday every police officer was wary of a stretch outside Rochdale we now call missile alley... Hell, they had concrete blocks piled sky high on the roof to toss down on us during police drug raids... I couldn't count on both hands how many 500-pound stoves and fridges were dropped on us from the top of the building. After awhile you'd build up a sixth sense. You'd sense something was about to fall on you and when you'd look up, there it was on the way down — a fridge, a stove, a cat, anything they could get their hands on.'" [22]

The police were targets and intended victims, but the actual victims of the Danger Zone were youths themselves. By May 1971, a combination of drugs, lawlessness, suicidal confusion, and accident had killed at least three young people. In October '70, Thomas Kelpe had been found at 3:40 a.m. below an open sixteenth-floor window, twenty-seven feet out from the wall. An American draft-dodger, he had been treated for psychiatric problems. In December, twenty-two-year-old Maria Bulfoni, identified as the fourth victim of a fall that year, died after dropping from the twelfth floor. In March '71, Toronto newspapers carried front-page reports of two youths who fell through a window on the sixth floor while fighting. Kevin Yallop, a seventeen-year-old visitor to Rochdale, died on the way to hospital.

Between January 1970 and March 1971, according to an official report, Metro ambulances answered 124 calls from Rochdale. Drug overdoses accounted for 58 of those emergencies. Out of the 124 calls, 3 people were dead on arrival.[23] At this point, references to death at the College included a fourth, unnamed suicide. Indeed, whether accidental or deliberate, caused or self-inflicted, the deaths came to be summarized as suicides.

Accurate estimations are hard to find for the Danger Zone. Official figures don't include the incidents left unreported by a population that tended to dislike police as much as crime. A police report added up the offenses and damage for 1969 and 1970. Aside from drug charges, there were six robberies, eighty-one thefts, thirteen assaults with bodily harm, and twelve charges for weapons. However, it was the falling, the four attempted suicides and four completed suicides, that began to give a morbid dread to the building in the eyes of a public that was still absorbing the extent of the violations happening on one of their placid downtown streets. Nor were the deaths and injuries about to end.

20

To the Wall

If the summer raids were seeds planted by the police in the media, a letter from a Toronto Alderman was the first firm, green spear of an angry harvest. In October '70, Alderman Tony O'Donohue wrote a lengthy letter to the people who mattered: the federal government. O'Donohue itemized for federal Housing Minister Robert Andras a number of crimes committed, described chaotic living conditions, mentioned suicides, and asked that Rochdale be closed down. He "emphasized the milieu" of Rochdale by noting a "male person excreting in hallway while his girlfriend stands beside him," "cats thrown out of windows," and "a conversation between two young 'inhabitants' while a 10 year old girl present, in presence of police, describing perverted sex acts in which the female had taken part and others that she hoped to take part in."[1] His letter was quoted extensively by the press, and with a concise phrase, O'Donohue gave the Rochdale image more pep. Rochdale was, he said, "an 18 storey flop house."

Against this new-found enemy, Rochdale raised its own spokesman. Peter Turner had arrived from the States with Judy Merril in the summer of 1969, worked as a printer in Coach House, and had been elected Rochdale President in the winter of that year. Born in Bolivia, a former student at Berkeley, Turner was "slight, red-moustached, twenty-three, a well-liked and respected American who [had] worked for a year on Eugene McCarthy's national committee."[2] Turner came in "absolutely out of the blue," says Jim Garrard. Turner was "very dry and beleaguered, a Jimmy Carter kind of figure."

Peter Turner faced both the money mess and the media mess by going directly to the top. He had "lots of ideas about dealing rationally with CMHC in Ottawa," Garrard continues. "Turner thought a commonsense, adult presence in Ottawa would persuade them to restructure the financing. It was a good idea, but not in the Rochdale spirit. The Rochdale people backed off and said, 'okay, if this guy wants to put all this energy into this, then let's give it a chance.'" Turner made several trips to Ottawa and aided the campaign with his book-length explanation of Rochdale, *There Can Be No Light Without Shadow*.

A decision by the government was being pressured by media exposure, but by one estimate, Peter Turner's lobbying staved off that decision for at least six months. "Peter stuck at it for ages," Garrard says. "He never had a sense of humour about what was going on, of the joke that was being acted out. It was too bad that it began to get serious to him at the same time that the community started to become unattractive."

The effort to "sell" Rochdale, for public sympathy now instead of cash, faced formidable obstacles within Rochdale itself, namely, its attitudes. Rochdale was not equipped to deal with a loss of favor. As a counter-institution, it was designed to poke and probe, not please. However, a court jester quickly finds the border between the joke that entertains the king and the joke that loses a head. As with the other boundary disputes that the College faced and couldn't solve, Rochdale couldn't find this border either.

The attitudes of a foolish fool were most apparent when they poked the police, or "pigs." Only on rare occasions were relations with the police anywhere close to harmonious. On one of those occasions, a detective commended Rochdale Security for its handling of the scene that surrounded the discovery of a stabbing. Security had blocked off areas in Rochdale, controlled onlookers, and with the help of parents, collected children from the Day Care Center that was located on the same floor.

Bill King announced plans for "Bustday Parties" that would have amused both sides: "Cops will be showered with confetti, streamers, and balloons. Cake and ice cream will be served with party favours for the cops. 'Pig is beautiful' T-shirts will be sold with the proceeds going to the police college."[3] These plans were a gentle kind of laughter, but they still had a tactical value. As "Brother Ersatz" described it, "Pigs know violence and are experts in dealing with it. What they can't handle is non-violence and laughter, 'cause no matter what they do then, they can't help but look dumb and fuck up."[4]

Many Rochdalians, like young rowdies anywhere, viewed police with a mixture of fear and contempt. In December '68, residents were invited to the preliminary hearing for one of the first Rochdale busts. "During their stay in the Don [Jail], [the arrested residents] picked up some pointers on how our own institution should be run. So come on Monday and be excited by the police telling baldfaced lies, marvel at the narcs' ability to read from their tiny notebooks, and watch the four or five freaks guaranteed to be there laughing."[5]

Faced by "pigs" with the law on their side, the youths in Rochdale valued any successful ridicule. When narcotics officers were searching suspicious characters, a resident named Simon "regularly crept from the building in a poncho and a leather hat," in order to attract a search.[6] His contraband? A Bible in a paper bag and a toy duck. Residents must have also enjoyed the hyper-reaction of *Tab International:* "Overheard in one of the sleazy hamburger joints frequented by hippies in the Rochdale area was a plan to completely foul up the Metro Toronto mounted police division... The hippy gang sitting at one of the tables laid out a plan to feed mounted police horses with sugar cubes loaded with LSD! Can you imagine a HORSE on a LSD trip running wild in a crowd of protesters, police, and innocent bystanders? Action must be taken immediately by the police, even if it means putting a muzzle on the horses."[7]

Then too, Rochdale had been provoking a wider target with its ridicule: the white middle-class culture of Toronto. As bad news led to increasingly bad reactions, Rochdale faced its reception in the community with some good humor, some defiance, and some sur-prise. Relations with the surrounding city were "all a border dispute / That can be discussed when we / find the border," as expressed in a poem by resident "Mrs. Dan."[8] But as a leading edge of the new generation, didn't Rochdale deserve more? Attempts to raise money were failing horribly. "Believe me, it's not easy," said one canvasser for a fundraising drive. "So far, I've raised 25 cents by selling 1 (one) Rochdale button to my girlfriend... The posters were ripped down, and when I told people what the [bottle drive] was for, they slammed their doors in my face."[9] In March '72, "Mother Fletcher" reported on more unsuccessful public relations, this one a goodwill trip to fellow students at the University of Western Ontario in London. "Finally we get into the main building stoned out of our trees and expect everyone there to run up and offer us songs of praise, as well as the keys to their Radio Station and be just as stoned as us with no dope."[10] Five did try to take over the radio, but were turned back.

And rejection by Rochdale's immediate neighborhood — what could you do? Rochdale had a party going and had trouble under-standing why the neighbors didn't join in. In September '69, one resident enthused that it was "time again to raise Saturday stereo-phonic arms with the frat rats next door and holler down to the football followers streaming home from varsity stadium, and paper airplanes lining the Bloor Street curb, and wandering through stoned orange hallways."[11]

Stereophonic arms… "Noise complaints were relayed to the Police Department by the hundreds. Rock Bands performed on the patio in the late morning hours and Police Officers were plagued with these calls."[12]

Ten members of a "Committee to Close Rochdale Now" demonstrated in front of the building one early April evening. As they began speaking on the north side of Bloor Street, more than 200 residents came down from their rooms, "some wearing 1930's style press cards in oversized fedoras and surrounding the demonstrators with cameras clicking and pencils scribbling in a parody of a press conference."[13] Confetti was thrown, and firecrackers from the windows. Then six policemen arrived and plastic bags filled with paint and water began to fall around them. The good humor of the confrontation seemed threatened. Just in time, a loudspeaker began putting out music and drew people back across the street. Thus began the first street dance of the year.

Loudspeakers and amplifiers made few close friends of close neighbors. A "Summer Solstice Fair" for 1973 took place on the front patio so "noise would reverberate north and west on to buildings where few people live."[14] The block-busting spirit of previous parties would be tamed, if possible. Cindy Lei was a main organizer. A writer for the *Daily*, "The Dragon Lady," reported that "I saw [Cindy] pushing herself for days, and falling down with fatigue, getting the whole thing together." In vain. The performances of dance, theatre, and Tai-Chi started an hour late, the crowds were small, and midway through a dramatized story of Rochdale, people in the windows screamed for music, one screamer breaking a window. Music they got. On the following days, aldermen, city hall, and police listened to the noise of noise complaints.

This time at least, the city got an apology from Rochdale. An apology? From the Symbol on Bloor? The College was being backed to the wall, and was trying out the small sounds of submission.

Equally endearing to neighbors were the falling objects. A police report tells of "a hole, still visible in the roof [of the service station next to the college], caused by a heavy steel object that had previously been thrown from a window of Rochdale while the police were there. This missile had penetrated an asphalt covering, wooden roof boards and down through the plaster." [15]

The more the city saw of Rochdale, the less it liked. As the bad publicity increased, Rochdale's name became a liability. An owner of houses on nearby streets would not rent to anyone associated with Rochdale, and car insurance companies began cancelling the policies of some residents. Rochdale charged that a cerebral palsy victim inside was refused meals by a service group because of the College's reputation. And in September '70, after the first fanfare of publicity, "4 of metro's men in arms came up no shit saying some cat done called headquarters saying at 12:00 sharp hiphaven would be blown to some proverbial hell." [16] The highrise was evacuated until after 12:00.

If, however, Rochdale College indulged some attitudes that taunted and led to trouble, at least one attitude worked in its favor. The defence of Rochdale College led by Peter Turner had to prove, and could, that Toronto need not have feared any sustained political challenges from the College. In each case of political activism, Rochdalians seemed to treat the event much too lightly. Indeed, Rochdalians preferred the good effects of a party. While some were occupying vacant lots, others infiltrated the Toronto subway, passed out candybars, sang, clapped hands, and acted before the stolid riders "in hopes that this hovering cloud of alienation hanging over Toronto can be extinguished." [17]

The May Fourth Movement was finding that support from its host could be distressingly loose, maybe even apolitical. True, "when it was rumored that the Edmund Burke society was about to attack (M4M had earned the enmity of this ultra-conservative group), 300 Rochdalians left a triple bill movie on the 17th floor terrace to defend 'the revolution.'"[18] However, the "revolution" seemed to last only as long as an attention span, and the Rochdalians who did think about it, demurred. "The New Left group," which included M4M, "was the smallest, the least powerful, and the least respected segment of the society."[19] The *Daily* complained in June '70 that M4M was "pretty heavy on the venom and kind of short on compassion."[20] Then Rochdale Security added their voice against the radicals: "M4M has a room upstairs and they should be keeping their politics and propaganda and newspapers in their office, not in the Art Gallery... it is for art, not politics."[21] At the same time, word went around about the $20 sale of hash to three girls by M4M that proved to be "monkey shit." The hash was defended by M4M as Afghan that had undergone a "funny curing process."[22] An M4M slogan on the walls of Rochdale attracted new comment: "'Political power comes out of the barrel of a gun'...Beside it, someone in political disagreement with the M4M has graphically suggested another use for the gun."[23]

Something was amiss, and M4M had reason to feel thwarted. Rochdale had its own idea of revolution: it wanted to knock over bourgeois straw men. It would have loved the founding of a marijuana republic, but it wouldn't help staff and run a street barrier.

Before politics could be exported from Rochdale College, the internal politics had to be put in order; yet, behind the official councils and the unofficial lobbies of such groups as the drug dealers, leaned a massive majority. The apathetic.

In the attempt to organize the most elementary political structures, Judy Merril felt the frustration of what she called "responsibility droppages."[24] "So maybe it's quaint and little-old-lady," she said, "but by the scruff on my tennis shoes, I do believe in this old thing about an informed populace and self-government." The average Rochdalian avoided the sober side of politics and had little talent for working for a common end. "Collectivity is a totally alien concept to North American society," said Sarah Spinks.[25] "What happens

to an enormous project like Rochdale is that its people never see
themselves as part of a social whole...The slave-resident comes to
the master-management asking him to change his behaviour, not
realizing that he is expressing both his lack of confidence in his own
power and his disbelief in the communal forms..." This can be seen
in the build-up to the first General Meeting in November '68 when a
preliminary meeting decided that "not enough people are working
hard enough at the 'administrative level' and/or we need 'TWELVE
STRONG MEN' to take the blame!"[26]

"The 'them and us' syndrome partially developed from Rochdale's
lack of any notion of social activism...The residents were true North
Americans, out of the tradition of Hobbes and Locke — bourgeois
freedom and self-determination. They didn't understand that one's
freedom is integrally tied to the freedom of other people."[27] The *Daily*
took a saying by Che Guevara — "it is the duty of the revolutionary
to make revolutions" — and gave it a turn more suited to a skeptical
Rochdale: "It is the duty of the revolution to make revolutionaries."[28]

And in Rochdale, before it tried revolutionaries, a revolution
would have to make plain, common leftists. In May '70, Publications
Office worker Stu Roche attacked the internal politics of Rochdale,
which he said were right wing. Rents on the Aphrodites that Govcon
people preferred, he charged, were kept reasonable by "exorbitant"
rents on the east units. Those who were sent by airplane on expense-
paid speaking tours were close friends of the organizer. And "Andy
Wernick was engineered out of his job as treasurer because he tried
to unionize the staff."[29] If Roche was hoping for left-wing support
in Rochdale, it didn't come. Stu Roche too was quickly "engineered
out of his job" in the Publications Office by Govcon...unopposed.

From the start, Rochdale intended to challenge the educational
system, but it had no political ambitions. The founders declined the
label "free university," John Bradford said, because "the free universities then in the U.S. were pretty doctrinaire politically and we

didn't have that idea."[30] Instead, Rochdale wanted to solve political problems such as poverty, not by confronting, but by transcending. "If you want to lower rents," wrote one contributor to the *Daily*, "don't picket landlord pigs. Just build another two Rochdale Colleges... you'll have all the slumlords taking gas when there are no students to rent hovels to. So far this one co-op has taken almost 900 people out of the rat race. That's a total of $13,000 every week that no longer flows into landlords' pockets...Already, the downtown vacancy rate has gone up."[31]

One writer at a 1968 Canadian Union of Students conference in Winnipeg recorded a split in its ideologies. On one side were the "wheelies," the strategists who believed that "mainstream middle-class Canadian students placed in the intense hot-house of a 'free' community and prodded a little by radical ideas and experiences, are but ten days from revolutionary consciousness."[32] However, the writer also reported on a second group: "The Hippy 'feelie' element believed in personal liberation, aesthetics at the expense of politics, individualism at the expense of social action, and salvation through a purified theory and practice of interpersonal relationships."

When Rochdale College opened its highrise, it absorbed this second group in masses. In October '68, "Rochdale was nearly read out of the Canadian Student Movement at the recent congress in Guelph because we are not actively involved in overthrowing the imperialist institution which dominates us."[33] "Toe-to-toe campus confrontations" were missing.

The "wheelies" wanted militant, political solutions; the "feelies" wanted individual freedom to find peace. Susan Swan of the *Toronto Telegram* recorded one toe-to-toe confrontation of the type that kept Rochdale off the streets politically. "Just walking into the cafeteria," she wrote in November '68, "getting a look around from this blonde called Georgia and here was this guy with a great shaggy beard kind of flowing out to sea and this other guy who I remember from last year as a skinny kid who didn't know Mao Tse-tung from Chiang Kai-shek but was pretty sure of one thing, that he wanted to be radical.

"Now he's sitting there with all the polished side effects, beard and army surplus coat...yes, yes and he's very intense and he'd like to see the young learning guerrilla warfare...so that when the establishment comes looking for a hassle they'll get theirs and that's a very different thing, I mean, from going into the streets with your sten gun ready to blaze truth at the man on Finch and Steeles Ave.

"At which point Georgia is getting very uptight, just rolling her own, pulling away at her hair and speaking: 'oppression, who's oppressing you, I can't buy all this paranoia, who's out to get us, come on, things aren't that bad, they just aren't' and she gets up and starts to bounce around a bit because she doesn't want to leave when they haven't cinched on to what she's saying.

"All the time the beard is telling me things are that bad, that he's had a gun pointed at his head and a knife at his neck by The Man of course and it's a different scene when you are in short hair and button downs." [34]

The continuing skepticism about radicals at times became more vehement. One resident warned: "Don't try and lay any of that crap on me, buddy. I'm sick and tired of having political trips laid on me." Another resident didn't like socialists "because they're always running around with some cause or other, pretending they're better than everybody else." [35] After the first large police raid, "John the Peace Freak" placed a message "TO — All the weathermen and Violent People who threw insults Saturday night — and will in the future — GET THE HELL OUT OF HERE AND GO FIND A BATTLEFIELD SOMEWHERE ELSE...Each person should be in charge of himself and his dope — NOT MOBS." [36]

Self and dope prevailed: by the time of the October crisis, the May Fourth Movement had been expelled from the College, and with it went the exaggerated threat of aggression. From this point on, the lawlessness of Rochdale swung within the narrower limits of pleasure, profit, and self-defense.

In the publicity struggle that followed the police raids, it became important for Rochdale to advertise this absence of politics. Not only did Rochdale assemble the apolitical and apathetic; it could say it was taming the few who were experimenting with revolution. "Contrary to popular opinion," said Peter Turner in November '70, "violent organizations have not developed here. They've come into here thinking they would get a certain amount of support. But the thing is, that after an extended period of time in this building, most radical groups have completely dissipated... Here they're spending all their energy fighting each other, in a sense, to keep each other from screwing up the building. Here they're fighting to preserve something that is theirs and that is part of the system. I mean, you've co-opted them, they're on the defensive." [37]

According to Turner, by acting as a model of outside society, Rochdale retrieved people who would otherwise be lost to society. "[Radical groups] are a leadership," Turner continued, "that does not have that full a grasp of societal functions: the government levers, the potentials for change and the potential for non-change. Either you're going to have these people in your society sharing your leadership, or you're going to have them outside of society leading factions against factions." Turner couldn't understand why the authorities wanted to destroy Rochdale and, with it, the taming effect that would help to prevent worse street violence. "Why do they want to wipe out the moderates in the youth culture?"

21

Drug Pros and Cons

As Rochdale evaluated its chances under the scrutiny of hostile media, it became clearer that the health and survival of the College depended on drawing borders, borders that excluded both hard drugs and the hard sell of soft drugs. The community had to decide what kind of dealing was "cool" and how to stop the dealing that wasn't. The ideal of the Open had led inexorably to a need for the Closed, and if many outside minds were planning how to stop the drugs, so were many minds inside.

With a difference. For Rochdalians, it was enthusiasm for drugs that separated "us" and "them," the insiders versus the ignorant bourgeois outside: but the drugs had to be soft. In October '71, a twelve-page publication for high school students written by someone familiar with Rochdale, writing as "Baron von Freeko III," advised its readers to "avoid all needle drugs — the only dope worth shooting is Richard Nixon."[1]

Marijuana and hash, as soft drugs, were automatically cool. Even Rochdale's enemies had kind words; at the end of Rochdale, one of them said that "[liquor] was our biggest trouble here...The heavy drinkers caused the disturbances and violence. The pot just kept them at ease."[2]

Legalization of marijuana was a recurring, favorite issue. At one point, in order to make marijuana an election issue, a group called Chapter 1 organized a rally to begin at the foot of Yonge Street, and then a few devotees were to move on to Ottawa. "These people, under God, are going to walk 243 miles to Oz in an effort to legalize marijuana."[3] On the way, they "slept in ditches, a pastor's home, and even across from an OPP station." Their publication, called Chapter 1 with the "1" in the form of a joint, cited Genesis: "GOD has given us all the Herbs. Is GOD guilty of trafficking???"

But though the soft drugs themselves were cool, many of the dealers of soft drugs lost support. It took a while, but Rochdale finally identified the big business dealers as exploiters and, worse, capitalists.

"Some guy in High Park making a lot of money by bringing the police into my home is not necessarily the coolest and grooviest person in the world," says Alex MacDonald. "A lot of us thought that there was a really important difference between dealing to family and for domestic supply, and corporate level mega-dealing where tons were moving...Even without the police raids, you had five thousand drippy nose punks from Scarborough coming in to buy their fucking ounce of weed or quarter of hash and they didn't care about the education projects or the rest. It was a department store. They just came."

Opposition to the dealers had to overcome a mystique they had as romantic, successful rebels. "Security and the dealing community," says MacDonald, "and a fair amount of the people on Council were of the old guard, were for free enterprise." The dealers could be seen as free agents, businessmen that turned the system around for their own benefit. And for those who didn't want to acknowledge that kind of success, they could interpret dealing from an opposite viewpoint, that of the political left. "Dope dealers have the almost perfect organization for world wide revolution...They remain anonymous, and acquire the weapon of the ruling class."[4]

Though the uncool dealer took a while to unmask, hard drugs were easily identified as undesirable. Perhaps because they threatened the smooth trafficking of soft drugs, and because the threats to community could become unpredictable and violent, hard drugs could excite extreme reactions. In one case reported by Pat Shafer in the *Daily,* "a twenty-one-year-old woman was thrown out of Rochdale by Security. She cracked her head on the pavement and two [visiting] women tried to assist her. They were told to leave her alone. She was a heroin addict and was being 'wiped off the human list.' A bystander said, 'She used to be a really good woman.'"[5]

The brutality may have been that of Rochdale Security, but the attitude was one that reappeared for years. Its preferred target was amphetamine, or "speed." In October '69, seven Rochdale members visited the federal Commission of Inquiry into the Non-Medical Use of Drugs (the LeDain Commission) and, while urging the legalization of marijuana, warned about amphetamine. "I'll take you to any high school in Toronto," said president John Bradford, "and you'll get speed before you'll get grass, any day of the week. One of the reasons people do speed so much is because there isn't much grass around, and the reason there isn't much grass around is because it's illegal."[6] In contrast, possession of speed was not a criminal offense at that time. A member of Rochdale Security testified that it took only five or six hits before a person was hooked, and that eleven-year-old girls had been in the lobby asking for speed. "Speed freaks are about the most dangerous people around. They're paranoid and they're sometimes armed. If you argue with them while they're on speed, they have no compunction about shooting you."

Speed was made illegal in Rochdale College before it became illegal in Canada, and the position Rochdale took towards the chemical helped prevent its spread. Rochdale had more success than the official organizations in discouraging the use of speed, said Bill King, because "adult organizations just don't have any credibility with potential speed users because they take a similar position on pot and fun in general."[7]

The campaign to control speed expanded into a campaign to control outside and outsized dealing. The first major anti-speed resolution was passed by council late in February '69 and steps were taken in the summer of 1969 to police the dealing. This was John Bradford's "get-tough" council. The council held "speed evicting parties" and, according to Bernie Bomers, sixty-five speed freaks were "permanently graduated."[8] *Change* magazine reported that "informers are paid to put the finger on speed and heroin pushers, and informers are no longer timid about coming forward."

By March '70, evictable offenses had expanded to include "possession of needles, syringes, points," "putting up crashers, runaways, underage chicks, etc.," "selling bad dope (burns)," and "pushing stop button on elevator."[9] But "evictable" did not mean "evicted." By July, steps had to be taken again. "Last summer we stopped speed freaks, crashers, bikers, and narcs from destroying Rochdale," Bruce Maxwell said in the *Daily*. "This summer we have to stop the traffic from outside coming in to cop dope."[10] Now, Maxwell charged, "dealers are a powerful and entrenched invisible government. It will not be changed without a struggle... The dealers, of course, say that the building will go bankrupt when they leave. Many dealers live in one room, deal from a second, and stash in a third... The suggestion to tax the dealers $35,000 a week was agreed to at a dealers' meeting one week and abandoned the next."

In August '70, as the police began hammering on doors, inside voices were raised against the dealing with new urgency. Resident Pat Shafer charged that Rochdale was divided into "the pushers and the pushed... I saw two self-declared pushers exploit and rape a meeting of the Rochdale Community which was attempting to solve the problems pushers have created by centering their capitalistic exploitation at Rochdale... The pig may be a policeman, he may be a president or a premier. He may be your local businessman throwing an elegant catered buffet on the 6th floor serving spiked punch to your Security Officer of the evening."[11] Bruce Maxwell claimed that ninety rooms were rented by dealers, and that Rochdale Security was "unalterably opposed" to their removal.[12] Because of walkie-talkies used to alert dealers, he warned, "dealers won't be busted at Rochdale, only users, residents."

With the issue fast becoming the survival of the College, an Evictions Appeals Board, or Eviction Committee, was set up "as a judiciary system."[13] Of all the attempts at culling the worst from the bad, this three-person tribunal lasted longest and evicted best. "We do have a screening process at Rochdale," President Peter Turner explained. "However, it operates in retrospect and not on prejudice. Any individual is allowed to reside here until he proves to be detrimental to either the physical structure or the community or both."[14] If the person proves to be a problem, "our police force (security) serves him with a notice to appear before our Court of Appeals (affectionately known as the Trafficking Court)." With the squirming of forms and identities that typifies Rochdale, the Evictions Appeals Board too changed name and number: for a time, "court" consisted of five residents plus a permanent chairman. The maximum penalty was eviction within twenty-four hours.

Alex MacDonald and Inga Hansen served on the Evictions Appeal Board from September '70 to January '71. MacDonald says that "Inga was the chairman of the Eviction Committee during its only period of true effectiveness... She was tough as fucking nails — I loved her.

"Evicting dope dealers was very popular in that period. That continued for about six months until all of the sacrificial lambs had been used up. It was very easy to evict your average sleazy twit, but much, much more difficult to evict somebody with political clout. Any eviction that was not supported by the community was unsuccessful.

"Judgment and connections separated the cool dealers from the uncool ones," says MacDonald. "[By January '71] it was still possible to deal to outsiders, but you couldn't just be a commercial dopey, you had to be someone like Syd [Stern] who came in and got involved with the building." Stern had a humanistic, "cool" approach that overcame all other grounds for eviction. Stern: "But why would you want to evict me?" MacDonald: "Because you were the symbol of all evil, terribleness, dealing. You sat there on the second floor in front of the windows with a scale on the radiator weighing out dope and did this completely flat-out scene that grossed the shit out of all kinds of people on Edcon and in the communes." Stern: "The Eviction Appeals Board hardly threw anybody out." MacDonald: "Yes, they did." Stern: "Bullshit. I was up in front of your stupid Eviction Appeals Board, Alex, I've even got the paper at home." MacDonald: "You could have gotten evicted 15 or 20 times, but that's a special case." Stern: "I never got evicted."

Clearly, eviction of a favorite dealer was not supported by the community. Indeed, none of these decisions or measures had a binding effect and they had to be renewed as new dealers arrived, or as residents changed their minds. A survey in July '70 showed that Rochdale was almost evenly divided on whether the dealer business should be stopped: 149 against the dealers and 119 for. The sixth floor, site of the dealers' "fortress," counted 23:6 against stopping, while the fourteenth floor, site of the Peace Center, had 16:3 in favor. In the fall, anti-dealers won another building-wide referendum "by about 55–45." The "intensely conservative faction" opposed to dealing, as Alex MacDonald calls it, included _____. In my interview with them, Stern objected that "_____ used to buy his dope from me. What was conservative about him?" MacDonald: "Because he always wanted to evict all the dope dealers. _____ was not troubled with consistency."

Several times, deals for dealers were tried. In August '70, a compromise was reached whereby the "30 or so" dealers would stay, but would set up "milk routes" to make weekly deliveries to customers.[15] Orders would be passed to the dealers by Rochdale Security without the customers going inside. A shortage of milkmen ended this plan quickly.

Shortly after, a draft on "Psychoactive Chemicals" was prepared by which the dealers would agree "not to combine or restrict trade in any way that artificially inflates their cost. We agree to share freely information concerning the properties and subjective effects of given chemicals, places where they may be found, and comparative price information. We agree not to 'push' chemicals, i.e. to someone who has not first asked to buy; nor to engage in advertising."[16] To be cool, a dealer had to be willing to compromise. "Instead of five thousand people every weekend, we were going to have two thousand," says MacDonald about yet another anti-outsider decision. "That didn't mean wiping out dealing, but the people who were doing it were going to have to understand that it was now a restricted market."

The debates continued as if patches were being nailed on a roof while water flowed through the door. Once again, in a General Meeting in January '71, Rochdale officially adopted a policy of no dealing with outsiders. Peter Turner, who had resigned over the issue in the fall, was returned to office as president. Big Al's sixth-floor Fortress, that had reached its peak in the previous summer, had alienated the community with its iron door, hard drugs, and excessive selling, and didn't survive the winter. By April '71, most of the sixth-floor east wing had become "resource" space, with half of the wing "unrentable." "They were eventually evicted," says MacDonald, "or just picked off by the police. The whole sixth floor east wing was literally gone, I mean, there were holes in the walls, there weren't any windows left, the pipes were—I mean, it was GONE."

But after all the complaints about hard drugs and hard selling, after dealer deals and evictions, the results were never more than mixed. Police Officer Dean Audley states that Rochdale "kicked out the speeders because they became too violent and hard to control, but they didn't stop selling the speed to them." "You could buy anything even though it wasn't officially allowed," says a former maintenance worker, "heroin, speed, pot, hash, acid, THC, MDA, opium, mescaline. Besides the marijuana salvaged from the garbage, [my friend] bought balls of opium, little bits of this, tabs of that." MacDonald confirms that "there were no black and white finalities. Coke was illegal, but a lot of people in Govcon did coke."

22

The Great White Fathers

By the end of 1970, groups of police had entered Rochdale at least eight times. Small counts of violence accompanied most of the raids. In one September raid, "an egg splattered against a reporter's leg and a security man grabbed his eye as a bottle shattered nearby. 'Their aim is lousy' complained one witness. 'They're supposed to be hitting the cops.'"[1] On at least one occasion, residents threw cups of urine at police.

"At 3:15 a.m. fire alarm bells began to clang throughout Rochdale College, then cut off abruptly," reported another resident in November. "A raid. A quick glance out a 17th floor window...it is possible to see a small group of men in street clothes piling out of an unmarked car and heading for the building on the run. Shouts begin rising from the building's central stairwell as occupants hang over railings to demand news of what is going on. Residents of both sexes move higher and higher up the stairs as police are reported on the sixth floor, the eighth, the 10th, the 12th...Twenty police, seventy, a hundred. They were using taxis this time, they've got one cruising up and down the street giving instructions or something...They got Newfie. Then, abruptly, the police are gone..."[2] It had been the third raid in eight days. Newfie was taken away and charged with possession of marijuana.

Sporadically, police staged a half-dozen raids in 1971. One of them, on May 27, was seen by a small underground newspaper, *Tabloid*, through one eye (the political left): "The column of burly men wound around the corner of the highrise with mechanical determination. They moved stiffly, like zombies — arms swinging only slightly at their sides, eyes staring straight ahead. The men were spaced evenly, about two yards apart...inhabitants counted 79 policemen."[3]

Then, by July, the big raids stopped. Even the straight press had begun to feel that too much muscle was being used and the results — in drug charges — had been disappointing.

"The police had no intelligence about what was happening in the building," explains Alex MacDonald. "They didn't know who was who. Anything they knew was usually six months out of date. They were always crashing down the wrong door, empty rooms, rousting people out of bed for no reason. I think they threw dice for the room numbers." The tactics of a besieged garrison had succeeded. A formal lecture on "Drugs, Society, and Education," for example, had been alternately titled: "When the fire bell rings, who swallows the jay?"[4] The residents had helped thwart the raids by running up and down hallways and stairs and generally creating chaos.

According to MacDonald, only once did a raid end successfully. "Instead of sending in eight hundred guys, they sent in four cops who knew what they were doing and presented their warrant to security right at the desk. They got all the security guards BAM right there and hustled them into the elevator before anybody could pull a fire alarm. They were all the way up to the thirteenth floor before the alarm sounded. The lights on the floor went out but they already had flashlights. They knocked down the door and hit the jackpot — scales and dope and money and names. That was the biggest haul they ever made because they did it with style. And we got caught flatfooted."

If that was the way to get results, it's clear the police wanted different results and a bigger jackpot. The take in drugs may have disappointed some of the takers, but the take in publicity did not. *Toronto Telegram* reporter John Gault wrote his publisher that "the press has not given Rochdale its due as an educative facility, and I have taken it upon *myself* to give that other side. But it is a pretty lonely business. Probably only in the *Telegram* has this other side been given."[5] The *Globe and Mail* made its position clear in a 1970 editorial: "Much of the history of this evil-smelling edifice," it said, "is written on police stationery."[6]

The publicity fight looked even grimmer when the contents of Alderman Tony O'Donohue's October letter, which had relied on police information, reappeared in an expanded form as an official police report released in April '71. Now O'Donohue had a companion voice, Inspector John Wilson of the Morality Squad.

Rochdale President Peter Turner parried the police report by pointing out that many of the incidents listed originated as calls from the College. "Every time we call, help, or co-operate with the police in such a case [runaway juveniles], it is written up as a police incident. Any 'factual police report' that merely lists incidents will damn all hostels, hotels, drop-in centers, and schools in Metro... With all that is written on telephone booth walls, why is it that Bell Telephone is not the victim of gossip insinuating that they run booths of prostitution?"[7]

In a letter given to the press, Turner objected that figures on Rochdale were being published without comparisons, for example, to the same area before Rochdale opened, to crime increases in all of Toronto, and to police activity on Wellesley addresses. There were suicides on the University of Toronto campus as well, but where were the calls by O'Donohue to close the campus? Deputy Police Chief Jack Ackroyd sympathized that the report was not comparative, but said that the police had given only what they were asked for.

In the agitation after the police report, Rochdale took stock of its allies. As friends on Toronto City Council, they counted John

Sewell — the man who would later become mayor — Karl Jaffary, William Archer, William Kilbourn, and possibly Ying Hope. Federal Member of Parliament Peter Stollery was also thought to be sympathetic. However, public opinion outweighed whatever support those representatives could lend. For four years to come, words warred in public, with Rochdale complaining that "we cannot fight the immense volume and hatred of the media."[8] Govcon heard, uselessly, that Stollery said he could "help with the Liberal Caucus, but to make it work we have to get just one good story in the *Globe*."[9]

Later, when Tony O'Donohue was running for mayor, Govcon tried a small stab by endorsing his bid. Their support, the press release said, was "in recognition of...past interest and involvement in the affairs of Rochdale College."[10] If Rochdalians had the kiss of death, they felt they should at least plant it.

In the spring and summer of 1971, Rochdale waited for the bad words to work on their creditors and final bosses, the federal government. As often happened, Rochdale responded to a mess with a parody. If the federal government was going to take over the College, "it can be expected that Rochdale will eventually emerge as a separate, self-sustaining Crown Corporation reporting directly to Parliament... This will finally bring all lazy and non-productive youngsters into the Civil Service, where they will feel more at home."[11]

Financial failure allowed a neutral means of eliminating Rochdale, a means that stepped around questions of morality, choice, and politics.

After Rochdale couldn't meet its $26,000 monthly payment in November '69 — when the Bradford Council wanted to sell — CMHC allowed token payments of $1,500 a month while it did a feasibility study. Rochdale did its own scrambling for order, but in February '70, CMHC reached their decision: Rochdale College could not succeed financially. Soon after, as MacDonald puts it, "you started to get into serious PR problems and the chances of renegotiation, which was what was necessary, went down the pipes."

On May 21, 1971, the President of CMHC met quietly with a full complement of Toronto authorities to decide Rochdale's future. It was the fifth meeting of the Interdepartmental Committee on Rochdale College, and of twenty-five officials invited, twenty-four of them made sure they attended. The Metro Chairman was there, the Mayor, the Police Chief, the Medical Officer, the Commissioners of Buildings and of Social Services, the Director of Housing Standards, and the Fire Chief. For the federal government were representatives of the Secretary of State, the Privy Council, the Solicitor General, and National Health and Welfare. The provincial government sent officials from Trade and Development and the Ontario Housing Corporation. The meeting lasted all day, but no announcements reached the public.

Inside Rochdale, a united front was becoming less possible. President Peter Turner, for one, became estranged. During the August 1971 General Meeting, a motion opposed by Turner was passed that "all members attending a council meeting be entitled to vote and that Council be bound by the decision taken." [12] As a result, "all of these meetings include participation by a great number of people outside the body of council; in fact, the last two or three meetings have been largely formed and contented by 'externals.'" [13] In addition, although Turner had taken other Rochdalians (such as Bob Naismith), along with him on his diplomatic trips to Ottawa, his "to-the-top" approach seemed to concentrate political power in his hands. Disagreements on how to save Rochdale as well as suspicions of his style of leadership were coming to a head.

As an example of the internal dissension, watch how little peace the Peace Center engineered from the fourteenth floor. Never very friendly with Govcon, relations reached their low point when, in July '71, the Peace Center sent a telegram, written by one of its leaders, to the federal Cabinet Minister deciding Rochdale's fate, to tell him that Rochdale's current governing council had been elected by a scant sixty members and was "not representative." [14] "The 14th Commune," the telegram said, "is internally Rochdale's longest established project (over 2 years) and is directly/indirectly responsible for all future communities and educational projects that have developed." The telegram asked for a meeting with the Minister and Govcon's resignation.

The commune itself broke apart over these tactics. One member accused that leader of "innuendo, filibuster, and paranoid obstructionism" that drove away all but "toady sycophants who will toe the [leader's] line." [15] Half the members left. When he tried Ottawa again, this time with the backing of the University of Toronto Students Council, an epithet thrown at him was: "one snaky, power-tripping bastard." [16]

Then it came — a federal decision to foreclose on debt-riddled Rochdale College.

The decision was announced on August 5, 1971, and confirmed when Rochdale met with the "Great White Fathers" on the following Sunday morning at the Royal York Hotel. "We're the Indians, as usual" said Rochdale, "and whitey wants the property." [17] Rochdale was represented by King James I, a few council members, and a few residents. Housing Minister Robert Andras refused to call off the municipal tax case that was still squatting in the courts, refused to allow part-use of the building at reduced rates, and refused to rule out mass evictions. According to a Rochdale flyer announcing another General Meeting, the minister also said: "Good Morning; Pleased to Meet You; That was a Good Meeting; Hi, I'm Bob Andras; I'd Underestimated the Size of the Dinner Party; What's Your Name?; Steve, Phone for Pizza, Won't You?; Hang-up (8 times); Straight (5 times); Sometimes I get Too Far Out — Steve has to Watch Me — I Don't Like to Go There." [18]

For Peter Turner, the frustrations of government had become too great. In the fall of 1971, Turner resigned and moved out. Before he left, he released a press statement on the foreclosure as a parting shot: "One of the other major concerns of our government is the takeover by outside interests. Countries like Canada have been the most blatant exploiters…we are 90% owned by a Crown Corporation whose home offices are in Canada, and are in no way located in this premises…The opposition has been calling for nationalization or 51% ownership…If the economic situation has not changed in the next 110 days, we will have to foreclose on our mortgage on City Hall." [19]

With the announcement of foreclosure, the 800 current residents of Rochdale College — and thousands of past and potential members — had lost heavily. Instructions were distributed for turning lights in the rooms on or off, on both the north and south sides of the building, to display an eighteen-story "Fuck Off."

The College had had a good run with its dream and now the city had a dream of its own—the end of Rochdale. The federal government had said nothing about how it would carry out this clean decision. It was apparent they didn't know how.

PART FIVE:
THE FALL

23

Invasion

Rochdale would be foreclosed, that was the prospect. Could the foreclosure of Rochdale College as a financial organization lead to closure of Rochdale as a building? Could Rochdale be eliminated all at once? The defenses seemed too strong; the potential violence too great. As with castles throughout history, an alternative was a siege.

But before a siege could be effective, the authorities needed Greeks inside the gates of Troy, a beachhead among the heads. It was agreed that the first wave of head-hunters would have to arrive through normal practice, though perhaps a souped-up version of normal practice.

With Canadian respect for due process, the government would appoint a receiver.

As the government searched for an accounting firm with a sense of adventure, Rochdale College continued running its own affairs in its own eccentric way. The news of impending foreclosure was both good and bad — bad because Rochdale had taken one long step towards extinction, but good because the announced foreclosure "started the Golden Age," as Alex MacDonald calls it. "After CMHC foreclosed and before a receiver had been appointed, there was no real reason to continue to pay mortgage payments. In the period

1968 to 1971, we paid every mortgage payment we possibly could and that meant there was no money around for anything else. After foreclosure, suddenly we had a budget."

The picture of Rochdale College before the Fall is one of increasing stability and efficiency — not surprising when the figures come from statements made after the receiver arrived, statements intended to show that foreclosure of Rochdale was unnecessary and wrong.

In that picture, we see the population of Rochdale peaking way back in January '69 with, by the highest estimate, 1,250 people, of whom 650 were students and 350 were crashers. In June '69, at the end of the school year and at the time of the new Bradford council, the figures dropped suddenly and continued to decline until their lowest just before September '69. At that point, fewer than 400 people were in the building, of whom about 175 were students and only a couple dozen were crashers. By January '70, numbers were back to full occupancy at 850.

From May '70 to April '71, occupancy stayed poor at 70 to 85 percent, with one estimate as low as 60 percent. Then Rochdale decided that part of the problem must be the rental structure itself and, in April '71, changed it by putting fewer tenants in some of the suites. Rochdale accountant Jay Boldizsar pointed out that the original plan for student housing meant substandard housing. Occupancy of the overcrowded Kafka suites ran at 30 percent until hot plates were added and the double rooms converted to singles. The "rent equalization scheme" corrected some of the imbalance that had subsidized the west wing at the expense of the east. Rents were lowered further the following year, in April '72. As a result of these measures, occupancy rose to 98 percent for the first time since April '69, and remained so through to the end of the summer. "Full occupancy" now meant 650 residents and, in contrast to the rent-dodging of the first years, rents were successfully collected from 96 percent of the tenants. Alex MacDonald confirms that "[by summer '72], we were collecting something like 95% of the rent. Your average highrise collects about 98%, so we weren't as good as the average, but it was definitely within reasonable limits."

As usual in the history of Rochdale, no one was really counting though many were numbering. However, even if dirty percentages were trimmed up and laundered for the public, they spoke of a competence that Rochdalians were developing. "By that time ['71–'72], the nature of the building was changing," says MacDonald. "In the first year and a half, the average tenancy was six months. With the passage of time, the element of the population that was stable and domestic and interested in art and families and education just got larger and larger and started to crowd out the itinerant dealer population." MacDonald sees foreclosure as the premature ending of that process. "Had Rochdale been permitted to continue to manage the building until the present, it would have gotten more and more quiet."

As the community stabilized in 1971–72, MacDonald says, it started "to get more and more difficult to establish a franchise in the building. You couldn't just come in and deal, you had to have a connection, you had to understand how the system worked because a growing number of people thought that living in the drug dealing center of North America was not necessarily — I mean, it was a nice party except for the police and the broken facilities and the traffic."

But if the traffic was now following some set of rules of the road, were the roads any less jammed? As late as January '72, the residents of Rochdale received 1,350 visitors between 3 p.m. Friday and midnight Saturday. Seven fights in the front lobby set "a new record."

The dealer organization, too, seems to have survived into Rochdale's "Golden Age." Once again Rochdale Security was being charged as an accessory, this time by Rochdale Treasurer James Newell: "A sweet lobby-Security protects [dealers] from the police, Rentals rents them stash rooms, _____ argues for them at Council meetings." [1] There were at least thirty dealers, as recorded in a *Daily* report that Govcon had rejected a request for special locks. "If a dealer doesn't trust the Rochdale Administration enough to have a regular lock, he can fuck off and go to Yorkville." [2] And the deals with dealers continued. The latest, in February '72, began when a couple of dealers persuaded a Rochdale Security guard to put in a remote control device. The device, installed in the fire alarm room, made it possible to turn on the alarm from a transmitter at the front desk when police arrived. Govcon discovered the set-up and took the batteries away.

But what could anyone do? A mock plan proposed in May '72 would have caught "pope peelers" by using cameras in the garbage rooms and by searching the garbage for "empty boxes of baggies." [3]

"We compromised by letting 'cool' dealers continue here," continued James Newell, "until now we have 80 cool dealers and the same problems with the police as we did in 1970." [4] After Newell spoke out against the dealers, opponents added a swastika to his name. The most articulate reaction from the dealers, if only because it was written, came from "Pete": "Those council mentioned their intense dislike to dealers... Far out. You members involved in fucking up the alarm thing are a bunch of fuck fucking hypocrites... You won't fuck me, pukes."

So, as Rochdale waited for the axe, it continued to ask for it. Whatever diplomacy the College had lucked into with figures like Peter Turner, it threw away heedlessly. In a letter to Robert Andras in January '72, Rochdale Treasurer Newell said that a proposed Advisory Group with two Rochdale reps was "sheer tokenism." Newell mentioned the possibility of rent strikes if Rochdale lost its own management. "Translated into ordinary speech from Newellese," said the *Daily*, "[the letter] says 'Watch your ass, honkey poop.'" [5]

A year after the foreclosure announcement, a last-ditch meeting with CMHC failed to change their mind about a receiver. In preparation, Rochdale residents were encouraged by Govcon to sign leases before August 8, 1972.

Going into September, Rochdale looked healthy. Rentals had only eight units left to rent and was turning away ten to twenty people a day. When Edcon reported that seventy-five units were not generating rent, a Space Commission was set up ("Space Duck Rides Again") to review the problem. The rentless rooms included twenty-two units on the sixth, where the dealer fortress had been, twenty-three units on other floors, thirteen units given by Rentals in return for such things as clean-up, and seven units "granted by various people and full of Syd Stern and so on."[6] Space Duck was also charged with checking into the matter of dealer stash rooms which, though rented, were "useless to the community."

"The last great political discussion before the Receivership," says Alex MacDonald, "was Space Duck, which was the space committee. There had always been empty space in the building, a lot of it because it had been so severely vandalized that you couldn't rent it. The unrentable space was given to Edcon so that you could put people in there to clean up the mess. And that was okay as long as there was a surplus of space. In August of 1972, we were 95% to 98% full. There started to be a lot of pressure to re-evaluate certain Edcon projects. There were people with worthwhile ideas and people who were just holding space and not doing anything with it."

The expected appointment came on September 13, 1972. Clarkson, Gordon, and Company — the straightest of the straight — would be Rochdale's new masters.

Clarkson Gordon accountants included Lester Pearson's ex-Finance Minister, who had once said that the art of receivership consisted of "plucking the goose to get the most feathers with the least squawking."[7] The firm had been involved in the pending takeover since early May, with a new, external security force for the building a priority. Police Chief Harold Adamson had recommended a former

Deputy Chief of Police in Toronto, Joseph Thurston, and his outfit, the Community Guardians. Thurston, although "reluctant," accepted the assignment, hired special staff, and trained them for several weeks in June. Later, members of the Community Guardians identified themselves in court as licensed Special Investigators.

All seventeen Community Guardians, or "Greenies," arrived on the first day, "probably as a show of strength."[8] It was Thursday, September 14. The new security got as far as the lobby before they were stopped by a crowd. "Tempers were high," the *Daily* reported.[9] "Behaviour at times seemed indicative of Rochdale's recent degeneration into a booze culture. One well-known dealer was heard telling a rent-a-cop that we could not tolerate his mercenary values! It was reported that later a woman was grabbing the guards by the balls and took off one of their shirts. A few other ties and a pair of cufflinks were taken also. One person said that out of 40 people in the lobby, only about 5 lived here. Today the guards seemed scared."

Sid Smith, who took over duties as Property Manager for Clarkson Gordon soon after, says that "most of the tenants, the militant ones, came into the lobby, the girls stripped in front of the guards and some of the tenants peed on the trouser-legs of some of the security. They did all the harassment they could." Other persons unknown were also busy. "After the mob scene," said the *Daily*, "some ashes were found in place of the Rochdale records. The records were elsewhere however and recovered by Security. It is rumoured that some of the dealers who instigated [this] went home to the West End afterward in their 7,000 dollar auto."[10] The theft of the records angered James Newell, who had become, in the meantime, Rochdale President. He resigned and told Rochdalians that "the appointment of an Interim Receiver should be irrelevant to this community. Management is management is on floor two, and people are people are on floors 3 to 18."[11]

Another reaction to the arrival of the Community Guardians, "a high-priced, police-trained private gang," was Rochdale College

Community Referendum No. 1: "As a self-governing community, Rochdale College claims the right to deny entry to any employee of an external 'security' force who is not the guest of a resident or in possession of a proper warrant for entry."[12]

"Every night at two o'clock," says Alex MacDonald, "just like a ritual, the bars in the building would empty and people would pour into the elevator and bring bags of shit and rocks and eggs and haul out the fire hoses and drive the Greenies out of the building. This went on until they pulled out and subsequently negotiated their way back in. No one was actually hurt, but they always from that point on lived in stark terror of whatever physical forces existed in the building."

The Community Guardians had been unable to go further than the front lobby on September 14, "and five days later, the Receiver removed its servants and agents for reasons of safety."[13] Clarkson planned another attempt and expected no less trouble. The accountants prepared for action with a September 20 court order for police assistance. Rochdale council met with Clarkson president J. L. Biddell on September 21 and discussed conditions for re-entering the building. Biddell insisted that "maintenance people must indicate messy residents" and that Clarkson "must have all the keys," but he also assured Govcon that the Community Guardians had never made a drug arrest.[14] Most importantly, Biddell came armed with the threat of a mass invasion by police.

After a council meeting later the same day, Govcon recommended co-operation. Mike Randell wrote in the *Daily* that "any scenario leading to excessive violence will result in the presence of Metro cops. Metro cops are capable of over-escalating us to an extent of 5 harness bulls to every hippie. This is similar to a nuclear attack."[15] Govcon agreed to disband Rochdale Security (it didn't) and improve "cleanliness and conduct" in public areas. In return, there would be no routine patrols in the halls and Community Guardians would stay on the first two floors except by request or breach of the peace or to investigate a fire alarm or "an object dropped from an upper floor where such an investigation might be expected to locate the source." Biddell wanted the garage locked to thwart the supply route for marijuana and hashish for the "three or four people who are thought to be serious commercial sellers," but seventy tenants also used the garage. As a compromise, the garage would be patrolled, but not locked.

When the Community Guardians re-entered, the police expected trouble and cancelled weekend leave. At 200 per shift, as the *Daily* estimated, 800 policemen were affected. However, according to the Daily, no external security men were scheduled to work within the building that first weekend, so police staff "heaved a sigh of relief and sent the men home."[16]

After a gradual, cautious injection of Community Guardians, Clarkson set up an office on the second floor on October 6, 1972. The virus in the community now had its own virus.

The *Daily* turned to Tennyson for comfort: "Tho' much is taken, much abides." The External Affairs minister for Rochdale, Mike Randell, said Rochdale should adopt a stance for the media "that there is no legal mortgage to CMHC, that we are not a party to the mortgage (technically true) and that *they* owe *us* back any money we have already paid them."[17] The *Daily* pointed out a weakness in the opposition — the need to save face. CMHC had to treat Rochdale as if it were a student residence, it said, "or else it looks to the public as if they made a stupid decision. Well, they did."[18]

24

Sirens at the Rock

By October '72, the city had won the gates of the fortress in its midst. Until the following spring, that was all the winning it tried. "[Clarkson's security] occupied the offices," says Smith, "but from there they were not allowed since the security of Rochdale was still there, they were not allowed to go any higher than that floor." The receiver entertained the idea, at least publicly, that the College would continue, although in an altered and tamed manner. Bidden assured the tenants in a letter in March '73, that "it is not our intention to close down the Rochdale building," but he stressed that "dramatic evidence" was needed that trafficking was being eliminated.[1]

Meanwhile, Rochdale Security had been decaying as the restrictions on it increased. Zipp, for one, had left due to family problems and "lack of faith in him by the community," and another had resigned due to "association with known speed users" and "undue use of intimidation."[2] In the first winter of occupation, 1972, Govcon tried to finance its ailing Rochdale Security by an informal system of neighborhood collectors. "The person collecting for Security wages will keep no records. There are no reprisals for failure to contribute (that's called extortion)."[3] Two months later, the weekend collection continued, but "publishing names of collectors has been discontinued so they don't get heat."[4]

As the internal police declined, the external police took heart. Drug raids had publicized the need to close Rochdale, but the authorities felt they had a better plan. Now that Rochdale was being weakened from inside, police could begin the outside half of the strategy — a siege.

According to Inspector John Wilson of the Morality Bureau, Rochdale had become the drug distribution center for all of North America. Such was the fame of Rochdale, Wilson told the *Toronto Star*, that dealers came from California, Detroit, New York, and Chicago.[5] The occupying forces inside Rochdale confirmed the volume. Sid Smith reports that "one time we gave our security hand-counters at 6 o'clock on a Friday evening, to count until 6 o'clock on Sunday evening as to how many people came into Rochdale who were not residents. Over two thousand young girls and boys, 16 to 18, came in to buy dope on that one weekend."

The siege began early in 1973, when twelve men and one sergeant were assigned as a permanent surveillance force. According to police files, this special squad laid 974 drug charges on 794 people in the first four months of the year. The charges involved 27,074 grams of marijuana (54 pounds), 8,646 grams of hash, 32 grams of hash oil, 16 vials of hash oil, 85 grams of opium, 188 grams of MDA, 974 tabs of LSD, 370 caps of THC, 8 grams of cocaine, and 103 caps of mescaline.[6] Of the people charged, 244 came from outside the city, from 77 communities as far away as Mexico and both coasts of North America.

Later that year, the policeman in charge of Rochdale affairs, Deputy Chief Jack Ackroyd, also reported on the activities of the squad. "Under the new program we arrested more than 1,000 people over a period of three months. We arrested people from 59 cities in Ontario, from practically every province in Canada, people from three states and Mexico, all of whom were there to buy drugs. At the same time we seized about $250,000 worth of drugs, mostly soft drugs."[7]

The siege was working well. One former resident tells how, after being given "an ounce of very nice marijuana as a birthday present" in a room on the sixth floor, he immediately went out of Rochdale, joined two friends, and all three got into the front seat of a car. "We got pulled over by guys in toques, plainclothes guys, and they said, 'get him, the one in the middle, his lefthand coat pocket.'" The resident believes the police must have been using binoculars in a hiding spot in a three- or four-story bachelor complex just south of Rochdale.

The following year, the squad resumed its blockade. Had the customers and salesmen of Rochdale learned a little prudence? In two weeks, fifty-nine persons were arrested on seventy-six drug charges. From March to August, 1974, 600 drug charges were laid on 445 people. The take included 45,595 grams of marijuana (91 pounds), 887 grams of hash, 158.5 grams of MDA, 160 hits of THC, 2 grams of LSD, 281 grams of methadrine, 2 grams of opium, 76 caps of tuenol, 5 grams of cocaine, 1 vial of morphine, 232 caps of valium, and 32 caps of mescaline.[8]

Even as part of a police campaign to close Rochdale, the previous figures have not been inflated. Rochdale records themselves confirm the scope of the dealing, even in the face of invaders. In one example, the Course Catalogue for 1972 said that, as a legacy of "the dark ages of early 1969 . . . marijuana dealing became a major source of income for some residents, with millions of dollars worth of free advertising appearing in the Toronto newspapers, usually on the front page."[9] "We take responsibility," said the *Daily* in January '75, "for all the hash to have entered this country in the last seven years." Rochdale's reputation became fixed and vivid. One Toronto cabbie exclaimed years later that "Rochdale was the center for pot and such — and they weren't even ashamed of it!"

Far from shame, Rochdale had counter-measures. One former resident tells how he lived in a house across the street from the College and "an unmarked car with two men would be there *always,* 24 hours a day, in the alleyway looking towards Rochdale. I would take down the license numbers whenever they changed, give the list to a friend, and he'd give it to Rochdale. Sometimes he'd come over when some stuff was going to be moved and keep an eye on the car. If it moved, he'd phone over and warn them."

With the police squad waiting outside the doors, exporters tried every resort — including the Property Manager. "One day," says Sid Smith, "I was approached in my office by a member of Rochdale who said, 'We know how you go home, where you live, what time you leave there,' etc. etc. 'We have a briefcase exactly the same as yours, with your initials on it. We're asking you to go home in a normal way one evening and put your briefcase down while you're waiting for the subway. Your briefcase will be swapped and in the new briefcase will be $50,000 in cash, in small bills. The next night there will be another swap, that's all.' The briefcase would have contained cocaine, whatever. I flatly refused."

Among the more legal resorts that Rochdale tried were a few publicity moves of its own. The media battle had become a matter of debits and credits in a credibility account. Public accusations were tendered by Rochdale as if they were cheques, subject to all the suspicion that a bad risk excites. The accusations said Police Harassment and Brutality.

One early accusation — during the period of the raids — came from an Eastern European refugee, "Associate Professor of Economics," and resident of Rochdale. In a letter to the *Globe,* he complained that "I heard blows of a hammer on my door and saw five or six gentlemen who, after having broken in, invaded my room and started searching it without any introduction, question, or explanation...I was finally told that they were the Metro Police...and I was assured that they had the warrant — however without being able to see it...in my former country, even during the worst times of Nazism and Stalinism, the police used to knock or ring the bell first." [10]

As the conflict between Rochdale and the "police state" heated up, accusations were made that have to be seen in context of the loathing that had been encouraged between youths and "pigs." One such instance occurred in the spring of 1974. The siege, renewed for a second year, was effective enough that, in response, Rochdale presented a 300-name petition to the city in March demanding a stop to "police harassment." Just before a delegation went before the important Metro Toronto Executive Committee in April, an arrest entered the newspapers. By his account in the *Toronto Star*, Robert Higgins had been walking down the alley behind Rochdale when four officers jumped out and pushed him against a wall. "They hoped I was carrying dope — and I wasn't, only books. I told the guy beside me I didn't have anything and he said, 'If we don't find anything we'll put something,' and I was frightened because there were no witnesses." At the police station, said Higgins, he was stripped and abused. "They kept calling me, 'You Commie,' and everything was 'f... this or that,' like a boys' locker room..." First he was told he would be charged with possession of LSD for the purpose of trafficking, then "an officer walked in and said, 'Well, Mr. Higgins, you've just been April fooled.'" [11]

The *Daily* printed warnings about just such tricks. One resident said he found two pounds of marijuana in his car after he had parked it unlocked in the garage. He cautioned others to "lock your car and look over it before you leave; you may just find something that the blue elves have left." [12] Likewise, the *Daily* warned about a plainclothes cop at the Bathurst subway station: "the game is to leave a crumpled baggie with about a dime of blonde hash part way up the inside stairs and watch who picks it up." [13]

Besides the Higgins affair, the Metro Toronto Executive Committee heard another accusation. "At 1:30 a.m., the morning after the presentation [of the petition to the city], police followed a resident...into the garage at 341 Bloor Street West. It is his contention that the police car came from the parking lot across the street when he opened the garage door. A man, later identified as a plainclothes-man, appeared out of nowhere inside the garage and pointed a gun at him without showing any identification. [The resident] then struck the gunman, knocking him down, and kicked him. Even before the other policemen from the cruiser could get the handcuffs on, a total of 31 policemen had appeared on the scene. The fire alarm went off, waking all the residents who had not already been awoken by the screeching tires of police cars. The fire department appeared almost immediately, almost as fast as the police. The garage door had extensive and costly damage done to it by policemen forcing it open...Few of the policemen wore badges."[14]

Rudy Hierck, another resident, confirmed that four police cars, one unmarked, pursued a vehicle with a resident into the Rochdale garage at 1:30 a.m. While the man was being arrested, more arrived until there were twenty-three uniformed policemen, eight plain-clothesmen, and three firetrucks. Most hid their badge numbers and "milled around for about 20–25 minutes telling residents (who numbered approximately 15) to 'fuck off, mind your own business.'"[15] Some residents were pushed. The incident, said Hierck, was "a strong incitement to riot."

In the fall, the *Globe* reported extensively on complaints made by two suspects taken to 52 Division during the same period of public accusations and possible reprisals. Richard Hemingway, an eighteen-year-old U.S. army deserter, and Susan Wells, a twenty-one-year-old free clinic counsellor, were stopped on March 28, 1974, while entering the St. George subway station after leaving Rochdale. Hemingway was carrying a shopping bag full of saw-dust shavings for his pet guinea pig. "I asked if I was under arrest,' said Hemingway, "and the officer said, 'No.' I refused to let them search my pockets. I was wrestled to the ground. One of the offi-cers kneeled on my chest and applied a handcuff. The other officer stood on the tips of my fingers and began to kick me in the lower side of my back." [16]

At the station, Hemingway sat cross-legged on a chair. According to the *Globe* account, "one detective walked into the room and looked puzzled at the yoga position in which he was sitting. The detective suddenly kicked the front of the chair flipping it upside down. Mr. Hemingway said he landed face-down on the floor, unable to protect himself in the fall because his hands were still cuffed... Then Mr. Hemingway said a detective got out a loaded service revolver, placed the barrel against his forehead between his eyes and threatened to shoot him. Mr. Hemingway said he could see the bullets in the gun as it came toward his face. 'The detective told me, 'You know I could blow your ------ head off," Mr. Hemingway said. He said it twice. Finally, a detective removed a fistful of sawdust from the shopping bag and forced it into Mr. Hemingway's mouth."

The *Globe* arranged lie detector tests that indicated the complaint was truthful, though with one qualification: Hemingway was "involved in yoga and perhaps this could affect his results in a way unknown to this examiner."

One of the last cheques written on Rochdale's credibility came in the final month of Rochdale. Resident Bill King wrote to the Law Reform Commission, saying: "John John came in with a black eye, cut cheek, cut/swollen lip, sore balls, and bruises almost everywhere else. He was walking one block from his new home when he heard a voice say 'Hey, Rochdale!' He turned into the punch that drove his glasses into his cheekbone. As the Metro police were kicking him on the ground they said, 'You Rochdalians are a cancer and we're going to wipe you out one at a time.'" [17] The reply, a form letter, was courteous: "I am very pleased to know that you have been keeping up with the work of the Law Reform Commission."

Each time abuses by the police were charged, the charges were passed over by public silence and skepticism. What the public was hearing, what destroyed the possibility of sympathy with these unwelcome complainers with their unwelcome complaints, was the sound of sirens quite different from those of the law. They were hearing the sirens of ambulances.

As usual with Rochdale, the numbers are uncertain. One estimate of the victims taken from the Rock by ambulance counted four suicides and two drug-deaths by March '74. Another placed the toll at one murder and eight suicides for the whole seven years; yet another said that nine people died between 1970 and 1974. At the end, police said there had been one murder and six suicides; press reports indicated as many as eleven suicides.

Rochdale argued that it was responsible for none of those deaths; it had inherited people from outside with problems that reached a conclusion inside, and for the size of its population, it had no worse a record than elsewhere. In May '71, President Peter Turner objected that a seventeen-year-old who had just died had not been a resident. Another fatality, a twenty-four-year-old woman, "had only come into Rochdale a few minutes before her leap" and had come from the Clarke Institute.[18] After two youths fell through a window while fighting, killing one, the *Daily* commented that the dead youth's problems "came of living in the beautiful, well-run towers of Cadillac, Greenwin, and Meridian [management companies]. When his emotions finally boiled over, he brought his troubles to Rochdale."[19] Troubles such as the ones faced by "Dave," a resident, were also imported: "Some people say Dave died because Rochdale drove him to it. He was feeling fine when he deserted from the army. His parents refused to claim his body."[20]

Rochdale acquired its share of suffering, disturbed people, and the drugs that were available amplified the disorders that were already there. Even the well adjusted felt some tax being taken from their mental energies. One resident referred in the *Daily Planet* to "the complete oppression of always being stoned; different, tender, jaws."[21] Bill King wrote that "it's gotten so that you can't say the word paranoid

too loud or the guy across the hall will think you're talking about
it." [22] Paranoia returns as a theme in several of the Rochdale poets
published in 1971's *Flophouse Poetry*: "finally all come under the law,"
"Jay B." says in "Paranoia Passion." "Total enforcement, total police.
/ The badge is one eye; the buzzer of terror." [23]

According to the 1971 survey by Lionel Solursh, 20 percent of the
sample had been seen at some point in a hospital for psychiatric reasons. [24] Sharon Kingsland of the Rochdale Free Clinic gives a sketch
of one of the characters that could be found in Rochdale: "Crazy
Arnold would come by in the middle of the night. He was psychotic,
but harmless. He went around town spray-painting 'O Sperm, O Egg'
on the sidewalk. He would come in and say things like, 'I'm going
to masturbate now.' Okay, Arnold, just sit down. We'd let him into
a closet and he'd come out and tell us 'I just finished masturbating.'
Or he'd say, 'I'm going to kick your face in.' Of course he never did
anything."

In addition to the help offered by the Free Clinic, a psychiatrist, Dr.
Bryn Waern, provided counselling from her room on the upper floors
that was "especially good for women with trouble talking to male
psychiatrists." [25] The Edcon catalog for 1974 explained that, "because
of her unusual techniques, [Dr. Waern] has trouble collecting OHIP
payments for work done in Rochdale, but is medically recognized."
Since 1969, she had been both resident and available to help — despite
often heavy demand. At one point, calls at three in the morning for
colds and the flu brought Bryn Waern to the breaking point. "Due to
physical and mental exhaustion," she announced to the *Daily*, "it no
longer makes sense to try to operate a free-for-all-at-any-time-of-the-
day medical thing out of 1823 (my home)... The simple demands of
the Zombies are easy to deal with (pills, downers, etc.): much easier
than committees, space, and sickly middle class colds." [26]

But if some of the time Rochdale helped the ones in trouble as a
grassroots social agency, at other times it ignored or made the troubles

worse. On one occasion told by "Miriam," a girl came knocking on Miriam's door asking for tranquillizers for another girl who was freaked out on acid. When Miriam held out the bottle to give her a couple, the girl grabbed the whole bottle and ran down the hall. "'I'm going to kill myself!' the running girl yelled. 'I'm going to kill myself!' Not a soul tried to stop her," Miriam said. "That's how much love there is here. Guys looked at her and said, 'Groovy, man. Let her do her thing.' She ran past doors and past 100 people. Nobody made a move. She took them. But she didn't die." [27]

How could Rochdale deny that overdoses were easier to obtain in Rochdale than anywhere else? "One girl, Linda, hadn't been seen for a while," recalls Sid Smith. "I went up to the apartment and the door was jammed for some reason. By the time I pushed in with security, we found her in bed, in a foetal position, with earphones and the music still playing. She died of an overdose." When drug dealer Syd Stern was asked about suicides on acid, he first checked whether the question referred to acid alone or acid and alcohol. Acid alone, he said, accounted for two deaths. "Two out of three million — that's not bad! Three million — that's how many hits of acid went down in Rochdale. I should know; I had a million of them."

The one indisputable murder associated with Rochdale may have happened while the College was being used as a shelter from the police. As reported by the *Toronto Sun* in December '71, the body of Marika Sokoloski, twenty-two, was discovered stabbed once in the chest by a kitchen steak knife on the third floor of the highrise. The discovery of the body, dead for two days, came after detectives interviewed two men in connection with the attempted robbery of a nearby bank. One of the men still wore a tee-shirt with a bloodstain. Sokoloski had died, the detectives found out, in an argument over drugs. Her husband told the *Sun* that his wife had left him two years before. "She started hanging around Rochdale and taking speed — she seemed to be high all the time — and she didn't want to work no more, so we split up." [28] The two men were charged with robbery and one with noncapital murder.

After its report on the stabbing, the *Toronto Star* received a letter from a non-resident. "I went to college in the United States," she wrote, "and this place had five suicides in one year, thus outdoing even the Abominable Rochdale. Yet to this day, the school enjoys the reputation of being one of the best colleges in the country." [29] The writer's highrise near High Park had a murder, arson, and numerous thefts, without a media report in which "nearly six inches of the story was devoted solely to the damnation of [the] place...Unless the walls of Rochdale have weapons with which to kill, and perhaps its furnace room actually contains a malevolent guiding brain, I hardly see how the past history of the building can have anything to do with a recent death of one of its occupants."

Sokoloski had died a private death, with a public revulsion. The most damning, however, were the public deaths, the falls from the windows and the roof. "We found an American boy in the courtyard at the back," says Sid Smith. "He was splashed all to hell. Because it was wintertime, when daylight broke we found his body frozen to the ground." Jim Garrard witnessed what may have been the same fall. "A kid had been sitting for quite a long time in the laundry room window on the 18th floor and he'd been having conversations with people during the daylight hours. He didn't seem to be unhappy or dispirited. He didn't live in the building. That morning around four o'clock, I was walking around the 2nd floor. There was a lot of activity downstairs. I had just walked out in the hall and there was this klunk behind me and I turned around. The kid had slipped and fell — or maybe he decided to jump. The doors were locked to the outside deck. There was virgin snow, not very much of it. He had landed on his back and there was this blood coming out from his head, like a halo. A man on security got an axe and got through the chain. A stream of young girls came down the stairs with coats to lay over the kid, who was nearly dead or died shortly after."

It would have been easy to fall accidentally from one of Rochdale's windows; the sill was low and sloped at an angle like a chute. A building inspector noted in his report that "some screens have been removed from windows. One young lady was seen sitting on window sill on 8th floor with her legs dangling on the outside."[30] The cats that fell to their deaths had trouble enough with those sills. "When you walked outside," says a former resident, "you took care not to walk close to the wall. Peyton alone lost three cats out of the window. Any morning you could look down and see a little kitten corpse, and it was normal to hear 'my cat took the big dive yesterday.'"

So were the falls accidental? Or were they deliberate? Were they suicides?

"So-called suicides," scoffs Smith. "One time, a young fellow was found in the garbage compactor at the back with just his legs hanging out, his back broken. He came of quite good parents in Mississauga; the mayor of Mississauga knew his family very well. We firmly believe that he was thrown out of the bloody window, for dope dealing… Another one went up on the 18th floor, supposedly high on LSD, and thought he could fly to the moon and went off that way."

Most damaging for Rochdale, to its enemies, were the falls clearly associated with drugs. A well-publicized incident in March '72 left Rochdale with an image it could never completely dispel. "As to the naked 14-year-old girl," resident Mary Anne Carswell wrote in reply to a story in the *Globe*, "yes, she was naked, 14, and high on drugs. No, she did not believe she could fly. Here's what actually happened. In the first place, the person she was visiting thought she was about 18. His room was on the 4th floor. She looked out of the window at one point and noticed a convertible, the hood up, parked directly under the window. She said she thought if she jumped out the window she'd bounce on the roof, like a trampoline, and not be hurt at all. Her host, anxious lest she be serious, went next door to get help. When he returned, his room was empty. The Rochdale security guard who found her reported that when he found her she was lying on the pavement, laughing." [31]

One resident added details in his own notes. "Front page news in the *Globe and Mail* of 14 year old girl jumping bare-assed out one of our windows, but the authorities knew what to do for her — they sent her back to the convent she'd escaped from the day before. It seems we'd driven her to think. The last thing she said before she went out the window was, 'I bet if I jump I'll land on that green car and be okay' — she was until they arrested her as she tried to run away." [32]

Here we see the "us" and "them" separation that both defined and broke Rochdale College. Despite the nearness of tragedy, the onlookers are still trying to score points for freedom, points for a tiger in the midst of his mauling.

Rochdale was producing one stage of a morality play, a moral struggle over the ownership of consciousness. Who can say whether mind should be the property of a producer/reproducer society or of a consumer/iconoclast individual — and who can say now? But unfortunately for Everyman inside Rochdale, some of the members of the play were dying on the stage, and the audience was blaming the play.

Rochdale needed a cause that the public would accept, something that would override the tragedies. With all the sirens threatening its survival, it tried to use some of those sirens to arouse a wider, political fear, but the College was never given its clear shot at credibility. More people would have believed the charges of a "police state" if a mass invasion of the College had taken place.

Mass invasion almost happened on two occasions. The first threat of mass invasion, as we have seen, accompanied the entry of the receiver into the building in September '72. The second marked a great leap forward for the occupying Community Guardians.

In March '73, the Greenies were still confining patrols to the first two floors. The powers inside were roughly balanced. "[Rochdale] would not let us use our own people for cleaning," says Property Manager Sid Smith. "They would put their own stool pigeons in for the jobs. One day they wanted to clean the security office, so we moved the filing cabinets and chairs out into the corridor. While the things were out, an engineering type put a bug under the chair. After a while, Rochdale Security seemed to be finding out too many things, so our security searched and found the bug." In March, several members of the Rental Staff were fired and Sid Smith took control of move-ins, locks, and keys. Then Clarkson fired yet another Rentals employee for "security leaks" and started to maintain duplicates of all rental files.

In a Masters Court session called to examine possible overspending by the receiver, Clarkson president J. L. Biddell admitted that "we do not have effective control of the building above the second floor and basement." He complained that "I did not hire the Community Guardians to go on a drug hunt... There is not too much security considering the type of people who live there... They are difficult in the extreme... The arrests outside the building are a result of Community Guardian presence... If we don't curtail this activity public authorities will close the building down... In order to correct it I'm going to have to get the right class of tenant in there."[33]

Gone was at least one symbolic obstacle. After years of contesting, in March '73, the court finally upheld the original assessment that, indeed, Rochdale was not a college.

On May 5, 1973, Biddell issued an ultimatum to the residents: either the external security men be allowed access to the whole building, or access would be taken by force. "It will either be Clarkson assisted by Community Guardian personnel as required, or Clarkson assisted by the Police of Metropolitan Toronto."[34] "Mr. Biddell had the jurisdiction of the court to take whatever measures he needed to clean that building out," says Sid Smith. "He had a high-level meeting with all the top police and the RCMP." The police plan for "quelling disturbance," the *Daily* reported, involved 900 policemen in five shifts of 180.

Threat came closest to force on May 16. "There were two or three busloads of policemen in riot gear," Smith continues, "parked in the Medical Arts Building parking lot across from Rochdale, but the inspector in charge would not give the order. I never knew the reason."

Would that have been a mass eviction of the whole building? "Yes." Would that have been beneficial in the long run? "It would have been a complete riot, people killed."

Later, in a presentation to the Metro Toronto Executive Committee, Rochdale explained that "the Clarkson Company called off the police invasion only after Rochdale officials, under duress, agreed to the demands of the ultimatum."[35] The Committee heard that "Rochdale officials were afraid for the safety of residents and children...this ultimatum coupled with threats of police invasion amounted to nothing less than blackmail in which the police department allowed itself to be used as a tool of intimidation."

Eighteen unrestricted floors had been won, floors that outside authorities had been trying to reach for years. In a press release, Biddell implied that Clarkson had been supplied with names of traffickers by members of Rochdale. Talks with Biddell set up a "Rochdale Joint Security Program" that cut Rochdale Security to five or six persons, with one member of Rochdale Security per shift at the front desk to "offer advice as to identity and condition."[36] From that reduced role, Rochdale Security declined to two members and then died within a year.

Biddell also told the press that Clarkson had initially taken "token possession" of the building and through "intelligence gained by the Receiver's security force," had now enough information to proceed with "a planned program of evictions."[37]

Now that Rochdale had a pig on its back, it would never be the same. The story of the College becomes one of increasing entropy, with some opportunists putting large amounts of energy into increasingly poor opportunities as the whole affair wound down. What had turned into a school for social rehabilitation, changed again into a school for complex, lost causes, causes that are well documented because the struggle needed paperwork and detail. Rochdale became reactionary with smaller and smaller results, responding to a war of attrition in which they could call very few shots. And while lobbyists for the College gained time for the sake of lifestyle, drug dealers used that time for last ditch profits. Rochdale had lasted too long: it was a Sixties phenomenon that was already deep into a foreign decade and heading for a prepared death.

25

Eviction

From one perspective, the history of Rochdale is a history of evictions. The removal of external management in June 1969 was the major and most formal eviction in a series that saw the original academics forced out of their own project. A second sporadic series of evictions, mainly of drug dealers and speed users, marked attempts from within whereby the community tried to gain control of itself. It was a purging that some say could have succeeded if it hadn't been interrupted by a third and fatal series of evictions — the evictions that came from without as the larger community of Toronto moved to purge itself of Rochdale.

With the arrival of the receiver, Rochdale had turned full circle. Clarkson, Gordon, and Company imposed a management as external as the Toronto Student Management Corporation had been in the beginning. The colonizing by this receiver was slow, relentless, and demoralizing. "There had been a system for getting rid of people who were outright assholes," says Alex MacDonald, "the formal system of the Eviction Appeals Board, the less formal system of security unilaterally throwing people out, and the social system of just ostracism. When the Clarkson Company moved in, the most important thing they did was to destroy that balance because it was no longer possible to evict an asshole because that meant you were siding with the Clarkson Company. It was completely different to have the police chop down your door every couple of weeks than to have them down in the lobby all the time. So the first thing that happened was a breakdown in internal discipline. People started to leave who couldn't be replaced. As the period from '72 to '74 continued, the quality of the population deteriorated."

Occupation by an external government encouraged a resentment towards the "Greenies" that pulled no punches. MacDonald says "there was universal agreement on the motion that Clarkson was evil and had to go. There was considerable disagreement on how best to effect that." At various times, the Community Guardians reported that they had tear gas and fire hoses turned on them, urine thrown over them, and sexual assaults from females. In this state of war, nerves were the first ones shot. On one occasion when a full-time policeman was stationed in the lobby with the Guardians, resident Cindy Lei reported that "I was planning to pat [the policeman's] moustache and tell him how nice-looking he was, but he became frightened (or so it seemed) and grabbed my wrist, telling me not to touch him."[1] Nudity, whatever the intentions, could become both a uniform and a weapon. "I was sitting in my office at 8:30 one morning," Sid Smith remembers. "This girl came in. She used to dress in motorcycle clothes; her father was a top surgeon. She sat in the chair opposite me, a little high on dope even that early in the morning. She said, 'Don't you find it warm in here?' and I said 'Nope,' and then she started stripping. Within five minutes she was naked except for her motorbike boots. I said, 'I think you'd better leave now, I'm frightened of you getting a cold.'"

During the occupation, serious threats couldn't be discounted. "One time they were going to kidnap either Mr. Biddell, or myself, or both, and hold us for ransom," says Smith. "They were watching my house — I didn't tell my wife, of course — and Mr. Biddell's house.

The guy watching Mr. Biddell's house was very, very intellectual. He used to drop acid all the time, something terrible, and was always in fights with the Community Guardians."

The tension that the Greenies faced can be illustrated by a more elaborate incident. Near midnight, a Community Guardian narrowly escaped injury when unknown persons on the fourteenth floor threw through the lobby windows a number of bottles, an eight-foot length of pipe, a radiator core and radiator cover. Investigation on the fourteenth floor found about eight people in the lobby. The radiator had been pulled from the walls and water was flowing down the front of the building and into the elevator shaft. The damage may have resulted from a fight amongst those present, but no one gave information. While repairs were being made, one resident removed a crowbar from a toolbox and was charged in the morning with theft. The resident responded by threatening Manager Sid Smith through a friend. The friend advised Smith that he "should have the charges dropped as he did not want any harm to come to Mr. Smith or the maintenance staff as he was not dealing with a normal human being but an animal." [2]

The rhetoric could turn vicious as well. The Community Guardians were "the Green Mucous Slime of the Clarkson variety." [3] Word was out that it took two Greenies to play one game of solitaire, and that "misery is…being stuck in the alligator [elevator] alone with Bob Green [of the Greenies]…especially if you're Bob Green." [4] "Dingaling" wrote in the *Daily* that "the feeling some of them get when they catch a hippy or reasonable facsimile at a disadvantage, is akin to what most of us feel when we have good cannabis." [5] The movement to discredit the new masters welcomed the news from film-shower Reg Hartt that he could afford to bring in the pornographic hit *Deep Throat* — at $400 — only because someone associated with Clarkson Gordon wanted it for a convention.

For some, the rhetoric against the Greenies went too far. Mike Randell cautioned that it's "sort of silly to say [the Greenies] turn on all fire alarms, splash paint, throw things out of windows, put sugar in their own gas tanks, etc." [6] At one point, the *Naked Grape* opposed a rent strike and gave rare support for the Greenies: "On a personal level, we have found that the Greenies are a little less piggish than the Rochdale Security people. Both groups are difficult to stomach." [7] Mother Fletcher of the Rochdale Free Clinic agreed and spoke out: "If Rochdale Security taunted, harassed, and intimidated the residents the way the residents do to the greenies, they'd be called pigs." [8] The *Daily*, too, had good things to say after several months of occupation. "The guardians have proved," an editorial said in December '72, "to be tactful and reasonable, and our people have accepted their unobtrusive presence." [9]

As usual, no one could speak for all of Rochdale. The people who found the presence obtrusive directed a lot of resentment specifically at Property Manager Sid Smith, the enemy within. In an interview five years after the end of Rochdale, Alex MacDonald and Syd Stern talked about him as if the issues were still current. MacDonald: "You have to bear in mind that Sid..." Syd Stern: "Would you please call him Smith." MacDonald: "Okay. Smith's job in the hierarchy was to smile, lie, and otherwise be deceitful. At which he was very accomplished, very accomplished. So he was always making friendly and chortling and being buddy-buddy in the hallways. And we sort of went along with that because everybody knew it was a war zone but you've got to have diplomats to talk to one another or it gets really bizarre...He had so many faces. He was quite decorative." Stern: "The only time I ever saw him actually laugh—it wasn't a laugh, it was a chortle—was when the building was completely closed after the police had thrown everybody out. That was when he chortled."

Rochdalians attempted to unnerve and discomfit the man as often as possible. "We came back from court one day," says MacDonald, "and Sid was in the hallways being his usual self—Smith in the hallway—and suggested that this battle could go on indefinitely. It could

be twenty years from now and we'd still be hobbling through the
hallways fighting this court battle. [Mike] Randell was standing there.
He has a very disarming bright smile, very bright-eyed, up-tempo.
He raised his eyebrow [to the older man], went from bright-faced to
straight deadpan, and said 'Yes, we may be here in twenty years but
you'll be dead.'"

Despite harassment, Sid Smith did his best to be liked. One
Christmas, he composed a friendly parody for the *Daily* that ran, in
part: "may everything go placid, without any of your family dropping
some acid...so here's to you and yours from all of us on the floors,
and if you go short of that stuff called 'cash', you can always get a
job slinging 'hash.'"[10] Even so, Smith was referred to at least once
as 'Mr. SS,' and inspired a cartoon with Smith as a fat buddha with
glasses. "I evict," said the caption. "Therefore, I am..."[11]

And evict he did. Until the May '73 ultimatum, Clarkson Gordon
operated "at the sufferance of the tenants," but after winning access
to the whole building, the receiver used its greater powers to quietly
reduce occupancy. Rooms were left empty when residents moved
out and prospective tenants were discouraged. Clarkson had been
issuing small groups of eviction notices — thirty-five in March '73,
thirty-six in April '73 — and now was able to pick off offenders with
greater accuracy. By November '73, 130 of the apartments — or one
third of the highrise — had been emptied.

Not all of this emptying needed Clarkson. One-time Rochdale
president James Newell, for example, had joined Rochdale in 1969
as a fourth-year dropout from the University of Toronto and served
as treasurer from 1971, quitting his job as computer programmer.
Disillusionment with Rochdalians led to resignation from Govcon
when the receiver arrived, and by May '73, it was time to go: "There's
so much in apartment 1003 that I want to bury — drugs, politics,
astrology, perhaps a certain kind of irresponsibility...I have already
moved out, in the spirit."[12]

The removals by Clarkson had to be done unobtrusively. How would it look if a management seemed to be dismantling the very thing it had been assigned to manage, increasing debt instead of dissolving it? Wouldn't this be seen as an extreme, even aggressive case of dismanagement?

At this point, Clarkson had no authority to try anything more than small bites at the College. Ironically, Rochdale was being protected from its new internal enemy by the system it had most scorned. Of all its scattered allies, Rochdale wouldn't have suspected that the legal system would become its longest and strongest. Though some direct lobbying by Rochdale may have prolonged the life of the College, a good portion of its lifespan came as an inadvertent gift of the courts.

Even two years after the intent to foreclose had been announced, the foreclosure was still deadlocked. Was this a case of skillful man-oeuvring by Rochdale? No, a dividing of conquerors. The court action to foreclose was being contested by the developer, Revenue Properties.

Revenue had reason to distrust financial dealings involving Rochdale. From the start Rochdale had missed payments to the developers, an oversight not noticed by Revenue until February '69. "Since [they] finally seem to have realized that this amount is due," said a memo in Rochdale, "we should pay it quickly."[13] The payment was never made. By spring of 1970, a writ had been served and one response was to threaten to counterclaim against "the quality and timing of construction."[14] Uncertain that sale of the building would cover their second and fifth mortgages, Revenue Properties sued to have CMHC's first mortgage declared invalid. If successful, their second mortgage would become first.

Revenue's suit against CMHC gave Rochdale the luxury of a court's sense of pacing. Unhurried deliberation and an unhurried deadlock continued until finally, in February '74, Revenue's suit was rejected and Rochdale was awarded to CMHC. This decision allowed tough instructions to come direct from the Federal Government to the receiver. Urban Affairs Minister Ron Basford told Clarkson that "every effort must be made at this time to change the type and character of the occupants of the said building."[15] By this time, after a year and a half of attrition, Clarkson had already served piecemeal 309 eviction notices and had terminated 219 leases.

Clarkson responded to the federal instructions by public statements made in court as it asked for additional operating funds. Memoranda Numbers Two and Three presented by Clarkson in March '74 reported 135 cases of "involvement in drugs or other anti-social behaviour" (minus 22 for lack of evidence, it was conceded), 174 cases of rent arrears (minus 7 for no proof) and 40 cases of arrears that were paid and revived, $52,000 lost in rent owed by untraceable persons, and a $1,000 per unit average for repairs, with one unit alone costing $1,800.[16] In the previous year, Clarkson had refused 167 applications for tenancy. Not only was the building uneconomical, the receiver argued, not only were the tenants unruly, unpaying, and often nude, but there were also "50 attack-trained guard dogs... and constant evidence of defecation by such dogs."

Clarkson asked the court for a $200,000 operating loan and for permission to evict everyone.

Clarkson was asking the court for "vacant possession" of the building. Vacant possession of an eighteen-story building! Even a federal Member of Parliament expressed his surprise. "I don't understand," said Peter Stollery, member for Spadina, "how the Judge could issue an order to the Receiver authorizing eviction of people without due cause. The truth is, I suppose, that objectivity has long since flown the coop."[17]

But, except for surprised single voices, nothing remained of the high-level support that Rochdale College had enjoyed from the federal government early in its career. Embarrassingly, the Opposition raised questions in the House of Commons in April '74, asking, "Is there one law for Rochdale and another for Toronto?"[18]

When, at the end of March 1974, the court granted permission to empty the highrise, the final phase of Rochdale College began. The war changed its character; no longer was the struggle one of management, but one of annihilation. At the same time, Clarkson buried its opposition literally: the accountants took the Rochdale Security desk from 1970 and filled it with earth and potted palms. Immediately the scale of the evictions changed. In May 74, 87 notices were served and in June, 151 more.

As the first large group evictions hit Rochdale, the College's most extended program — the Golden Lake campus — had to be cut off. Sale of the farm was okayed at a general meeting in May '74, and the transfer to a group of resident farmers and Rochdalians completed in September. Faced with losing their building, tenants with an already slack regard for living conditions went completely loose. The downpour of debris during police raids now became objects at intermittent times, the more substantial the closer Rochdale came to its own fall. During one eviction, a window itself, metal frame and all, landed in the middle of Bloor Street. Another time, a couch thrown out the back landed on a truck. At one point, even the maintenance crew threatened to quit because of increased vandalism, deliberate fires, loose dogs, and "rumours that threats have been made to cut elevator cables and vandalize natural gas pipes."[19]

Some Rochdalians capitulated. Cindy Lei complained in a letter to a former resident that, "so far as the 15th floor is concerned, everybody, or almost everybody, has signed a deal with Clarkson to be gone by May 15, so as not to owe the $20,000 when they leave and have jobs...I'll probably be one of the last dozen to be dragged out by the armpits."[20]

Other Rochdalians co-operated. When Clarkson gave the Jesus People a rent-free room, suspicions immediately came to a boil. Alex MacDonald expresses some of them: "Jesus freaks do as they're told. When the Clarkson Company told them to get out, they were one of the very, very few groups in the building who said okay and left. They didn't go to court; they didn't fight it. 'Authority is good.' Certain of their members were on staff — they got down that low."

One of the Jesus Freaks in particular was ostracized for being too friendly with Clarkson. At a meeting of the triclinium, as the assembled councils of Rochdale were calling themselves, it was announced that the person had handed over east wing units directly to Clarkson, including the former chapel. A Tribunal charged him with "Trespassing, Audacity, Impersonating a Christian," and "remanded [him] to the Cross for mental examination, 3 days." [21]

Some resistance to the dismantling of the College made use of the parodies that had been set in motion earlier. The monarchy intervened with a "Rochdale Tribunal Nullification Certificate" signed by Joe Wertz, "a judge for the people of Rochdale." "I HEREBY NOTIFY you," it said, "that in the name of his majesty King James I of Rochdale, the – Notice to Vacate – Notice of Motion – Other (specify) dated _____ and issued to you by Clarkson Company Ltd is NULL and VOID."

However, a new element had entered the Rochdale style: fighting back using highly proper means. Now that the game had become base survival rather than high parody, Rochdale turned towards the recourse that any citizen could use, the institutions and protections that had been scorned. Ironically, the free forms of Rochdale were leading to the ultra-forms of courts, Legal Aid with Area Directors, appeals to Area Committees and Assessment Officers. The avowed contempt of law became in the final stages of Rochdale an eagerness to shelter within it.

After the announcement of foreclosure in August '71, a General Meeting had resolved "to go on with the community, to expand education, to make Rochdale a better place," and legal action against the foreclosure had begun. [22] At that time, Rochdale accountant Jay Boldizsar had argued in an affidavit that Rochdale "has evolved into a low income housing building in which 532 people now are tenants."[23] Govcon had offered two dollars each for names of people living on government subsidies such as Welfare, Opportunities for Youth, etc. The plan was to prove to CMHC that the building was filled with the lowest of incomes. The scheme reappeared in a more substantial form in October '74, when Mike Randell sent a proposal to Members of Parliament in Ottawa. Endorsed by MP Peter Stollery, it suggested that Rochdale carry on as low-income housing with ownership transferred to a tax-exempt agency.

By the end, the evictions were being protested as "violations and breaking of the law...committed flagrantly and with impunity by those agencies administering the law."[24] The legal actions taken tried any angle available, including the argument — dismissed by a judge — that members of Rochdale College Corporation were owners of the building and were therefore not evictable.

Rochdale's attitude had changed since the time of *Tab International.* On the defensive now, they tried to alter its raw image and laugh more carefully. The day after the receiver's report on guard dogs and nudity, they invited reporters to tour the building — and the reporters found nothing to complain about. They reported that "it seemed sort of academic, the way it was put by the portly, bearded chap sitting in the sun-filled living room of the commune... 'If there were 50 attack-trained guard dogs wandering around and you were Joe Average-Naked-Person, would you go out and wander around?'"[25] "Marcia" wrote in the *Daily*: "Dear Clarkson Company...I have not been allowed the opportunity to run naked in the halls and common areas because of the lack of decent heating. Could you do something quickly so that I can romp rampant with the rest of the building."[26]

An Open House two months later provided a handout, *Welcome to the Rock,* that referred to the "50 attack-trained guard dogs running loose. Not true. Only a few attack-trained children playing with the dogs."[27]

A humbler Rochdale tried to enlist wider support. It participated in the founding of the Federation of Metro Tenants Associations (FMTA) in June '74, along with tenants from Kendall Park, the Toronto Islands, and Parkdale. According to the minutes of the meeting, it was decided that "whenever a member of one of our groups was to be evicted, 50 people from all groups would be contacted and would sit in the evictee's residence and physically prevent eviction." [28] The physical support never materialized, but later the Federation gave moral support. In a letter to Rochdale, it said that it was "anxiously aware of the implications of this first mass eviction of an apartment building in Canada." [29]

If the courts and the tenant association became guns for the Rochdale bureaucracy, the finances of the College in receivership were ammunition. In September '74, the receiver's deficit was growing by $50,000 per month. The $2,500 income couldn't match $44,000 expenditures, including $13,000 for security. Worse, a statement by Clarkson showed a deficit from Sept '72 to Sept '74 of $1,279,650. The courts approved loans of $1,000,000 (September '73), $200,000 (April '74), and $400,000 (January '75). Rochdale protested publicly that Clarkson people were "financial undertakers" who wasted "exorbitant amounts on unwanted and inefficient security." At a new high of $19,000 a month, the Community Guardians were "the Expensive Protective Agency." [30] It was pointed out that "Amerika spends about 26% of its money on defence; Clarkson spends 50%." [31]

One weapon in the fight against the receiver was close enough to home to win popular interest among the residents, and add another straight solution to its possibilities. In March '73, Rochdale formed the Toad Lane Tenant Association to negotiate "from a position of strength" by means of a rent strike. In two days, the association collected $2,600 in rents as opposed to $700 that went to Clarkson — and of that $700, $400 went by error or by welfare cheque. Clarkson charged in an affidavit that Toad Lane was "created for the purpose

of intercepting rent payments... to permit the association to withhold rent collected and to bargain..."[32] Clarkson president Biddell
notified tenants that his company would not accept rents from the
association. By July '73, the call had become: "Support the Toads
in the fight against the Green Lizard oppressors!"[33] A year after
its founding, Toad Lane claimed as members two-thirds of the
residents and fifty children, all of whom received a newsletter called
"Toad's Breath."

But Clarkson had paperwork on its side. Because most records
had been destroyed before the receiver moved in, Clarkson had no
prior list of tenants for Rochdale. This gave the receiver a free hand
in determining who belonged and who didn't. For Clarkson to consider a resident registered, the name had to be on their list of May 15,
1974 — and by January '75, only 39 qualified out of the 180 residents
who remained in the building. Tenants would often return from a
weekend to find a new lock on their door. By that time, tenants were
allowed no mail service and no visitors. Mike Randell alleged that,
if the tenant was "thought to be unable, either for financial or legal
reasons to adequately defend himself, he is apt to be prosecuted for
trespassing charges."[34]

As the receiver advanced into more and more territory, skirmishes
continued to be fought using any appeal available, as the Greenies
discovered when they tried to control access to the building. "We
bolted and barred the backdoor," says Sid Smith, "so there was only
one way to go out, but then they complained to the Fire Department
that we were barring the exit, so we had to open it."

Some appeals were less successful. According to resident Cindy
Lei, the Legal Aid Society refused to help, saying the applications
were "frivolous, vexatious, abusive."[35] At one point, Legal Aid was
"freaking out" at the number of applications. "One person at legal
aid is very negative and may try to yell at you and call you names
and tell you that we can't win."[36]

One "evictim" solved his eviction — for a time — by setting up housekeeping on the seventeenth floor by means of a canvas tent. Others were more militant. "Word got around," say Sid Smith, "that I had confidential material on the tenants in my office — which wasn't true — and one Easter weekend my office was broken into and everything was completely smashed. I don't have many souvenirs left."

Then, on July 30, 1974, came "The Ruckus." Residents reacted to a drug arrest by blocking the exit of the two policemen. Anger at 151 evictions that were pending turned towards the Community Guardians. Six of them were barricaded in the second-floor offices. A typewriter and mechanical calculator were destroyed along with office records, and the security desk was dragged outside and burned. "They got the Community Guardian people penned in their office," says Smith, "and turned on the firehose through the mailslot. Downstairs they were throwing full beer bottles and then bottles filled with kerosene against the windows of the office. Then they went outside and burned all the office furniture." Papers taken from the second-floor offices during the riot had not been recovered as late as September. A request for their return promised that "no questions will be asked, about anything."[37]

The highrise had started to become empty and desolate. In November '74, the triclinium reported that seventy-four abandoned suites in the building had faulty or missing locks. Inside were trash, broken windows, and refrigerators with latches that posed a hazard to children. A PR release from Rochdale proclaimed that "THERE ARE 100 APARTMENTS LIKE THIS ONE EMPTY IN A DOWNTOWN BUILDING — AND 300 ROOMS FOR STUDENTS. BUT YOU CAN'T RENT THEM." It gave the unlisted phone number for Clarkson Gordon and suggested calling to "let them tell you why you can't."[38] In January '75, the parking garage was locked and all cars towed away, assisted by the Metro Police, who by then had one officer on duty in the front lobby twenty-four hours a day.

With day-round surveillance and the end in sight, did the users of the College tread softly? No. The drugstore was selling out, a clearance. As late as January '75, the *Daily* reported, Inspector Wilson of the Morality Squad was saying that people from 158 communities of North America, from Miami to Halifax to Vancouver, were going in and out of the building. In six months, there had been 984 arrests on possession. [39] Even in May '75, when vacant rooms far outnumbered the occupied and the last tenants were facing eviction, a trespasser was arrested on the fourteenth floor with a paper bag containing 700 tablets of LSD. [40]

Early that last year, a Grand Jury formally recommended that the Canadian Army be called in to do the final clear-out. The members of the jury had been exposed to years of Rochdale's reputation, as had the majority of sober citizens. Their ability to separate fact from fiction can be estimated from a statement in their report: "It is obvious that a very large percentage of crimes committed in York County are committed either by people in Canada illegally or by those recently granted landed immigrant status." [41] They gave no supporting evidence.

Meanwhile, eviction skirmishes continued. In at least one case, Rochdalians tried using the artistic resources of the College for politics. With a master key, eighteen people entered an office that had been recently taken over by Clarkson. They set up a video camera and then one leader called the Greenies and told them he wasn't going to leave. A guard and a policeman carried him out by feet and arms, and charged him with assault and trespassing. The *Globe* reported that "the other people, who had been talking of the occupation as 'the first stage of the spring offensive,' dispersed to the noisy sound of a bongo drum." [42]

Then, in March '75, the same leader made a stand in a room that had been bailiffed and was arrested for trespass. Five days later, a number of pieces of video equipment were discovered missing from the same room. The security report on what was called a "theft" guesses that the equipment had been "removed by _____ for use in an up-coming TV show (*The Rochdale Tapes*)." Of course, there was "no formal complaint from owner of property."[43]

By late spring '75, life at Rochdale College had become a continual routine of finding trespassers, cautioning, finding doors broken open, more trespassers, abuse, cautioning, and arrests for trespass and obstructing peace officers. Of course, community had disintegrated and support systems were gone. One person in particular needed that community, and her fate shows the pain and loss felt by Rochdalians as Rochdale itself paid its debt and died.

A resident at least since December '72, Cindy Lei served on the governing council as treasurer, on Edcon, and in the Toad Lane Tenants Association, and taught a dance class in the building. In Lei's Explorative Choreography course, "inhibitions re dance are tolerated but not really."[44]

By January '74, Lei was fighting against apathy and backbiting, and charged into projects with high energy, but with unhappy results. As a protest against institutionalized painting by Clarkson, she began a collage of newspaper and magazine cutouts on the pastel paint of the tenth floor. But the wrong people were upset. The residents of the tenth floor scraped off the collage and Cindy apologized for not consulting them. In another set-back, Lei was summoned the same month by the court as the organizer of the noisy, complaint-ridden Summer Solstice celebration in 1973. Lei arrived at court with the Rochdale lawyer a few minutes late. The judge remanded the case and exclaimed as he left, "Rochdale? Hah. A thousand dollar fine. That's what's going to happen to [the case]."[45] Several months later, Lei "ranted about the Edcon energy crisis and suggested that everybody on Edcon get their acts together or move over so we can keep on truckin.'"[46] In June '74, Lei called her lawyer and the complaint department after her room was searched by narcotics officers.

"Cindy really struggled to make Rochdale work," said one of her former dance pupils. "She was always after people to pay their rent and keep the place clean. Her own ashram was a place of great peace."[47] By January '75, Lei was depressed enough to write a list of items that identified a "pig," including a line about "having a big beautiful funeral with all the trimmings, if you decide to make something, someone help you to commit suicide."[48] In May '75, just before her suicide, Cindy Lei lost her appeal regarding rent arrears. In the words of the judge, "the tenant was happy to sit back and enjoy the premises without making any payment on the rent as it accrued due. I have no doubt she was content to have the matter drag on indefinitely so that she could occupy indefinitely the premises which she was then enjoying."[49]

The official takeover date for CMHC was June 6, 1975. In May, seven sheriff's officers with sledgehammers, backed by twenty-five policemen, cleared out and padlocked twenty-one units, with the action (and evidence in case of a fight) recorded by their own video crew — for "a training film."

"They emptied everything on the 15th and 16th floors," said Bill King. "That's about 30 per cent of our remaining territory and that's what we've long known they were going to get... From the court case actions we knew it was time for them to come. I know when they get the writs of possession. I've got eyes everywhere."[50] A week later, sheriff's officers returned with fifteen policemen and Community Guardians and used sledgehammers in an attempt to clear out the last sixty occupants. Some, however, had rent receipts and were allowed back in.

At the same time, the Community Guardians changed the locks on the front door and denied access to all guests of tenants except "family members of the legal tenants, professional services, i.e. legal or medical, and any other person having a valid reason."[51] An angry group assembled outside the front door and later, at least two court actions reached the Supreme Court of Ontario to protest the lock-out. Both cases involved rent arrears as well as a complaint that lawful visiting was not being permitted — and both cases were awarded to Clarkson Gordon. In the first week of the blockade, what had been thousands of outside visitors in the years previous became a very short list indeed: one lawyer, one brother, two girlfriends, two parents, and several city inspectors.

By June, only twenty-one residents remained legally in "Rochdale Prison." The ruined, deserted castle now had an atmosphere that could only be called gothic. Dispossessed residents tried forcing doors and using a ladder to reach the second-floor patio. In one of those attempts, after being evicted from an ashram lounge, "Jojo" sneaked back by the rear door with two others. "All the time we were back inside the building we were forced to sneak around hiding in kitchens, bathrooms, or anywhere if we heard sounds that sounded like a patrol of cops and greenies going through the building."[52] They were caught two days later.

During the last summer, 1975, the few remaining tenants faced the "usual problems of living in prison," as Bill King put it.[53] They had to have permission to leave and enter, and sometimes they weren't allowed to enter. The emergency exit doors were sealed. Any visitors had to be approved by either the Community Guardians or the police, who still had twenty-four-hour shifts at the foot of the elevators.

At the end of September, one of the jugglers of relative value threw down from the roof — in a final ceremony — a shredded copy of Einstein's theory of relativity, and the last three residents of Rochdale College slipped away.

26

Afterwords

The seven years of survival by Rochdale College displays a more important survival — that of Canadian tolerance and good sense in the face of adversity. Few societies would have allowed such a provocation to continue for years while the questions were deliberated. At the same time, Rochdale was a sign of social wealth. For a while, Canadian society could afford a luxury of sorts, a small percentage invested to test the next steps and to let the testers release their pressure for change until they themselves changed.

And how much did this luxury cost?

Imagine for a moment that society is a combination of taxpayers, and satisfied only by numbers. By June '75, damage to the highrise included a by-now-familiar list: toilets and sinks removed from or smashed in apartments and hallway washrooms; extensive water damage from ruined plumbing; floor tiles burned or removed on many floors; holes punched in ceilings and walls; windows broken; cupboards removed; "concrete in toilet"; "clay in bathtub"; interior walls knocked out.[1] Although some of this was Rochdale's idea of decor, most was a scorched-earth policy in the face of evictions. The final inspection report in 1975 listed "398 separate cases of destruction, theft, and deficiencies," and estimated the rehabilitation at $500,000.[2]

CMHC bought Rochdale outright for $8.6 million at a court-ordered public auction in April '75, and by 1976, its financial involvement had reached $16 million. Of this amount, $2.5 million had gone for rehabilitation of the building, $2 million for the receiver, $2 million for taxes, and $2.5 million for interest.[3] The Metro Housing Commission then bought the building for $9 million on the condition that it be used for senior citizens. By the time the repairs were finished, the Rochdale facelift had cost $4.5 million.

Expensive?

With no significant public grants and with a municipal tax assessment, co-founder Howard Adelman estimated in June '69 that "Rochdale College must be considered as the cheapest experiment in education on the continent."[4] In the program for the 1974 Open House, Rochdale downplayed its debt: "The land value of Rochdale has increased since 1968 to more than make up for this deficit."[5] Indeed, if Rochdale had sold the property before the receiver moved in, the debt could have been paid with a surplus. Until 1972, Rochdale College existed — potentially — at no cost to any government. However, the surplus after selling would have remained with the College and another form of Rochdale would have been set loose on the city of Toronto. The authorities decided that must not happen and used the financial mess as a tool to dismantle Rochdale. The costs by the end were the costs of a war, not of a college, and should not burden its record.

Indeed, here we have the true glance. Rochdale could offend manners, decency, morals; Rochdale could mock and tempt; but until it offended money, it was safe. This one weedy garden uncovers the Primal Sin for the society of Canadians in Toronto in a seven-year sample — and the sin was debt.

The building reopened in December 1979 as the Senator David E. Croll Apartments. The bronze Unknown Student was turned around to face the street and continues to dwell on Bloor in place of all the others who had not been known as students. The mural in the lobby, good enough to have survived years of compulsive painters within the College, also survived the scouring that removed virtually all other signs of Rochdale, and exists into the Eighties[*] as a frieze above the tidied doors.

In early 1976, Rochdale College was still incorporated as a group of members without property, and its finances were never healthier: total debts were two, to Bell Telephone ($83) and the Canadian Press clipping service ($79). The residents had been re-absorbed by the city and, in a sense, Rochdale continues in networks of friends, scattered farms, and shared housing.

Did Rochdale succeed as an educational institution as many people swear? The question can't be answered. For every happy, creative graduate, opinion must be divided whether that person made it because of Rochdale, or in spite of Rochdale. The liberal education it started to serve still continues in modified, dissociated forms as educators in various colleges and private schools make use of alternatives that have been pioneered. Interdisciplinary studies have more of a history now, as do courses without grades, self-structured programs. No one could claim these derive from Rochdale, but the early ideals pursued by Rochdale seem more vigorous by surviving a time of distortion.

At its best, Rochdale was a noble experiment. It tested new approaches to education, creativity, and community, and like the testing of new products in industry, the limits of a new product cannot be known until the point of destruction is reached. This product of the Sixties — the mix of ideals and attitudes that Rochdale concentrated from the surrounding youth culture — had to be dropped from a height, pounded, stretched, and put under heat. The accomplishment

---

[*] And still exists in 2019.

of Rochdale cannot be separated from its eventual destruction, and an institution that was not allowed to be self-destructive about such sweeping questions would have tested nothing at all.

Those who disliked the product can take satisfaction that the College and its breakdown helped purge a lot of notions that still haven't returned; for those who liked those notions, the College celebrated them far beyond the point they and their opponents could have anticipated. This double-faced effect, purgation and celebration, returns us to the Middle Ages, to the festivals when a Fool was made King and the social order was briefly overturned for the psychic health of the community. But such inversions and parody repeat another, non-European, tradition. In the lands bordering on Lake Ontario, the Iroquois tribes used to set aside two weeks in the spring for a festival of dreams during which fantasies could be acted out. In three hundred years, the nature of the people on the borders of Lake Ontario changed. The white man, the Bible, written laws, capital, education, the city of Toronto — all came and all changed — but despite locking into reservations all that they could, those repressed white men began their own festival of dreams.

When a troubled, irritating dream lasts seven years, the dreamer must wonder why it hung on as long as it did. Could it be that dreams take too long to begin and face too long a stretch without imagination when they're gone? That running away has become the only way out? In a land of restrictions, there are too few festivals, too few affairs.

The Rochdale festival was possible only in a reservation, a fortress, an enchanted castle besieged and out of time. As a fortress, it allowed a delaying action while all around it, young people passed into disco and business. In retrospect, a sense of waste surrounds Rochdale, a sense of waste similar to the one I feel towards the experimental program at U.B.C. that first turned my interest to Rochdale. As with the Sixties themselves, somehow opportunity was lost and nothing fundamental changed. But isn't the role of a festival essentially comic and conservative? After a festival comes a return to a renewed norm, the binding of the tiger for another season, a comic restoration made tragicomic in this case by the times.

An experiment the size and duration of Rochdale College could not run its course without cost. Undeniably, some paid far too much. Those who paid the most, died. Continually, the residents paid by facing noise, dirt, confusion, danger — and felt those were simply the dues they owed. The customers who were supplied by Rochdale — with ideals, drugs, freedom, license — were sent into the consequences of their choices faster and harder than they would have been without the College. But that adds as much force to the reaction against as the movement towards. The worst opponents of the extremes of the Sixties can thank Rochdale for isolating, purifying, and holding out as a target the things they opposed.

"Fortunately for Metropolitan Toronto," said one such opponent after Rochdale closed, "the Rochdale experiment was such a blatant failure that it was philosophically and politically easy to abandon it, without being labelled reactionary." [6] And so also, the *Sunday Sun* intoned: "Rochdale is dead. It was killed by toxic people within toxic walls. It took seven years to die." [7]

Meanwhile, Bill King spoke optimistically for the lost College. "We have future plans," he said. "Dispersal means expansion." [8] "Rochdale Nation is as permanent as the Jewish religion. They seem to have a better chance of keeping their physical motherland focal point but Rochdale can exist without 341 Bloor Street West just as Judaism existed without Israel." [9]

When it was clear that the game was up, Rochdale published its own wry comment: "Drugdealing is now the domain of the professionals, i.e. lawyers, doctors, etc. Let's hope they never get to live in the same building." [10]

Endnotes

Some of the following references are incomplete due to the disorganized and partial state of the samples available in the various collections. Unless mentioned otherwise, most items can be found in the Thomas Fisher Rare Book Library at the University of Toronto. The *Dailies* in that archive have been sorted chronologically and are especially accessible.

Abbreviations used:

ABS   "Anything But Son of Rochdale," 1:1, Sep 67, FRB

AE   Alan Edmonds, "The new learning: Today it's chaos/ Tomorrow…FREEDOM?," *Maclean's*, May 69

AL   Arthur Leader, "Rochdale," *U.C. Gargoyle*, 16 Jan 69

AO   Anthony O'Donohue, letter to Robert Andras, Minister of Housing, 21 Oct 70, MRL

BJ   Brian Johnson, "The Rochdale Papers," VAR, 7 Dec 70

BZ   Barry Zwicker, "Rochdale: The Ultimate Freedom," *Change*, Nov/Dec 69, FRB

CAT   "the catalog, nov 1972," RC, FRB

CHA   located in the Coach House Press archives, National Library, Ottawa

D   *Daily*, all versions including the *Daily Planet*

DG   quoted by Donald Grant, *Globe*, 23 Oct 75

DP   David Piatt, "Creating the Architectural Project: Rochdale and the Student Housing Co-ops," paper for U of T Architecture, Apr 76, FRB

FRB   located in Thomas Fisher Rare Book Library, University of Toronto

HA   Howard Adelman, *The Beds of Academe*, Praxis Books, 1969

IN   *Image Nation*, several issues, FRB

IR   *InfraRochdale*, several issues, FRB

JK   Joyce Kury, "The Rochdale Experiment," *Random*, U of T, 15 Feb 68, FRB

JW   John R. Wilson, "Rochdale College," 13 Apr 71, known as the "Police Report," MRL

KG   Kent Gooderham, "Come Live With Us" in P. Turner, *There Can Be No Light Without Shadow*, 1971, MRL

LB   Linda Bohnen, "Rochdale Is Alive But Ailing," *Miss Chatelaine*, late 70

LS   Lionel P. Solursh, "A Questionnaire Survey of Rochdale College," Department of Psychiatry, U of T, Jun 71 FRB

MB   Mark Bonokoski, "Rochdale R.I.P.," *Sunday Sun*, 8 Jun 75

MCP   "Rochdale College: A Managerial and Corporate Paradox with Educational Overtones," Fall 69, pamphlet, FRB

MH   Michael Harris, "Few regret having spent time in the 'island of lawlessness,'" *Globe*, 22 Aug 81

MRL   located in Metropolitan Toronto Central Library, Municipal Reference, Toronto City Hall MS MaySay, several issues, FRB

MV   Michael Valpy, "Rochdale's reality is something else," *Globe*, 16 Dec 68

MZ   Marc Zwelling, "Rochdale, seminary-in-a-dormitory, is alive," *Toronto Telegram*, 22 Apr 69

NG   The *Naked Grape*, 21 Nov 69

NOTE   refers to note above, in same chapter

OR   occurrence reports and writs in my own collection

R   Rochdale College

RC   Rochdale College

RCB   *Rochdale College Bulletin*, various issues, FRB

RE   Robert W Ewart, "Rochdale," paper for Anthropology 420
          (U of T?), 23 Apr 70, FRB

SS   Sarah Spinks, "The Rochdale Experience," pamphlet, CHA

VAR   The *Varsity*, University of Toronto student newspaper

WR   "Welcome to the Rock," pamphlet, 11 May 74, FRB

1. The Seven-Year Itch

1. From an interview with the author. All subsequent quotes from original interviews will appear without footnotes.
2. notes, FRB

2. An Ideal Beginning

1. SS
2. SS
3. KG
4. Oct 68
5. Joyce Kury, *Random*, U of T, 15 Feb 68
6. AE
7. *Time*, 20 Sep 68
8. HA
9. RCB, 30 Jan 67
10. pamphlet, FRB
11. *Windsor Star*, Jan 69
12. Kury, op. cit.
13. D, 11 Nov 69, CHA

14. Kury, op. cit.
15. *Time*, op. cit.
16. D, 20 Sep 68, CHA
17. RCB, Apr 67
18. *Toronto Life*, Oct 68

3. The Rock

1. ABS
2. Alan Walker, *Star Weekly*, 13 Jan 68
3. "A Rochdale Handbook," Nov 68
4. ABS
5. letter, FRB
6. HA
7. MZ
8. RCB, Apr 67
9. HA
10. HA
11. BZ
12. D, 16 Apr 69
13. SS

14. MCP
15. D, 24 Sep 68
16. ABS
17. George Russell, *Globe,* clipping, FRB
18. CAT
19. DP
20. KG
21. D, 20 Dec 68, CHA
22. MCP
23. clipping, MRL
24. *Toronto Star,* 1 Mar 80
25. SS
26. Dennis Lee, ed., "Rochdale Handbook," Nov 68
27. ibid.
28. D, 22 Nov 68, CHA
29. leaflet, FRB
30. "Where It's At," Jun 69, FRB
31. minutes, 13 Sep 66, FRB

4. The Rochdalians
1. D, 2 Feb 69
2. for interview quotes that are unidentified, the name has been withheld by request
3. KG
4. 12 Jul 69
5. D, Apr 69
6. *Globe,* 13 May 74
7. D, 24 Oct 68, CHA
8. LB

9. D, 13 Apr 73
10. D, 2 Mar 73
11. LB
12. BZ
13. letter to President Ford, FRB
14. D, Nov 68, CHA
15. LB
16. "Program for aiding American immigrants to Canada," FRB
17. pamphlet, Mar 69, FRB
18. SS
19. D, Feb 69

5. The Changeling
1. D, 20 Nov 69
2. AO
3. D, 3 Mar 69
4. D, FRB
5. D, 14 Aug 72
6. D, 24 Sep 68, CHA
7. "Counterblast by Joel—Listen!," D, 5 Feb 69
8. D, 25 Nov 68
9. D, 2 Feb 69
10. NOTE 7
11. D, Nov 68, CHA
12. D, Dec 68, CHA
13. MCP
14. SS
15. D, 19 Nov 68, CHA
16. LB

17. D, Nov 68, CHA
18. AE
19. BZ
20. D, 4 Feb 69
21. D, 6 Oct 68, CHA
22. D, 30 Dec 68, CHA
23. IR 5,19 Mar 69
24. D, 4 Feb 69
25. D, 7 Feb 69
26. D, 2 Feb 69
27. IR 2,16 Feb 69
28. D, 8 Feb 69
29. leaflet, Feb 69, FRB
30. D, 3 Feb 69
31. D, 14 Feb 69
32. RE
33. MS 6,12 May 69
34. IR5, 19 Mar 69
35. leaflet, FRB
36. MV
37. KG

6. Pass/Fail

1. JK
2. Bob Bossin, clipping, FRB
3. JK
4. D, Oct 68, CHA
5. D, Nov 68, CHA
6. D, Dec 68, CHA
7. IR 2,16 Feb 69
8. "Sunday Thank You Supplement," 13 Apr 69, FRB

9. notes, FRB
10. Art Hendricks, quoted in BZ
11. AL
12. "Rochdale Is," floor plan and curriculum, Mar 69, FRB
13. Tim Inkster, *The Varsity*, University of Toronto, Jan 70?
14. MV
15. Harriet Kideckel, *The Varsity*, 5 Feb 69
16. D, Oct 68, CHA
17. NOTE 15
18. Bill King?, notes, FRB
19. Sue Swan, *Toronto Telegram*, 9 Nov 68
20. "Education Next Year," Dec 68, in D, 10 Feb 69
21. Bernie Mehl, D, 13 Feb 69
22. David Hallam, D, 10 Feb 69
23. John Bradford, in Connie Nicholson, "Rent Debt May Fold Rochdale," *The Ryersonian*, 14 Nov 69
24. D, 19 Apr 69
25. letter, FRB
26. NOTE 20
27. MS 7, 13 May 69
28. "Letter to Members," FRB
29. BZ

7. Govcon

1. MV
2. D, Nov 68, CHA
3. Marc Zwelling, *Toronto Telegram*, 22 Apr 69
4. D, 20 Dec 68, CHA
5. leaflet, FRB
6. D, Nov 68, CHA
7. IR 5, 19 Mar 69
8. Jack Jones, leaflet, 4 Feb 69
9. leaflet, FRB
10. D, 13 Dec 74
11. BZ
12. KG
13. KG
14. 3 Apr 69, FRB
15. IR 2,16 Feb 69
16. AE
17. leaflet, FRB
18. Ruth Hartman, 29 Sep 70, FRB
19. BZ
20. Paul Thompson quoted by Lynda Hurst, *Toronto Star*, 1 Mar 80
21. D, 1 May 70
22. D, 16 Apr 69
23. D, 1 Feb 72
24. Govcon minutes, 17 Feb 72, FRB
25. D, 13 Dec 74
26. D, Nov 68, CHA
27. MS 5, 11 May 69
28. MV
29. BZ
30. D, Oct 68, CHA
31. .D, Jan 69, CHA
32. D, 9 Jun 70

8. Dismanagement

1. HA
2. leaflet, 11 Sep 67, FRB
3. SS
4. LB
5. D, 13 Feb 69
6. IR 3, 24 Feb 69
7. leaflet, Mar 69, FRB
8. IR 5, 19 Mar 69
9. leaflet, FRB
10. CAT
11. CAT
12. Sue Swan, *Toronto Telegram*, 9 Nov 68
13. SS
14. D, 27 Nov 68, CHA
15. D, CHA
16. D, Nov 68, CHA
17. SS
18. AE
19. D, Nov 68, CHA
20. D, 27 Nov 68, CHA
21. D, 30 Mar 71
22. ABS
23. D, Sep 68, CHA

24. D, Nov 68, CHA
25. D, 8 Feb 69
26. D, 24 Sep 68, CHA
27. "Wedaily," 12 Mar 69
28. D, 27 Nov 68, CHA
29. D, 14 Feb 69
30. D, FRB
31. leaflet, 10 Apr 69, FRB
32. pamphlet, May 74
33. MS 2, 4 May 69
34. D, 30 Jun 70
35. D, 23 Jun 70
36. LS
37. D, 5 Sep 72
38. D, 9 Mar 73
39. AL
40. AL
41. Mike Randell, letter to Bloor Street United Church, 16 Jul 74, FRB
42. D, 20 Jul 71
43. DG
44. John Jordan, letter, 14 Mar 69
45. clipping, MRL
46. D, 16 Sep 70
47. D, 27 Sep 73
48. MS 7, 13 May 69

9. Independence

1. IN, 3 Apr 69
2. IN, 3 Apr 69
3. D, 25 Nov 68, CHA
4. SS
5. MS 7, 13 May 69
6. MCP
7. "Who the fuck are TSMC and Campus Co-op Anyway?????," leaflet, FRB
8. ibid.
9. HA
10. HA
11. SS
12. HA
13. SS
14. HA
15. letter, 18 Jun 69, FRB
16. Bill King?, notes, FRB
17. memo, 16 Jul 69, FRB
18. D, Jul 69
19. letter, FRB
20. HA
21. John Jordan, letter, FRB

10. The Money Mess

1. pamphlet, 9 Aug 71 r7
2. Walter Dmytrenko, leaflet, FRBC64
3. D, 20 Jan 69 r298
4. SS c202-13
5. G.H. Ward, "Auditor's Report," 8 Dec 71 rl26
6. Bob Naismith, "The Straight Shit," leaflet, 13 Sep 72 r221

7. CAT r237
8. pamphlet, Jan 67 r271
9. "Adelman: omissions and distortions," VAR, 13 Jan 71 c57-2
10. HA m34
11. *Globe,* 10 Jul 73 c89
12. BJ c56-2
13. pamphlets, FRB rl4
14. Peter Moon, "The student co-op mess," *Globe,* 9 Sep 74 clOO-l
15. DP r255
16. "Omissions and distortions," VAR, 13 Jan 71
17. "Unfair indictment," VAR, 13 Jan 71 c57-2
18. "Don Black Daily," 11 Nov 69, CHA m3
19. NG rl82
20. NG rl84
21. KG m25

11. Hipheaven

l. DG
2. Sid Smith interview
3. Rimstead's Toronto, *Telegram,* 25 Jul 70
4. LS
5. LS
6. DG
7. *Globe,* 26 Apr 77

8. D, Mar? 71
9. *Globe,* 6 Dec 71
10. *Globe,* 26 Apr 77
11. Martin Burns, D, 26 Feb 72
12. DG
13. clipping, FRB
14. *Globe,* 6 Apr 77
15. *Globe,* 26 Apr 77
16. D, 10 Aug 71
17. document in my collection
18. MH
19. clipping, 3 Oct 70, CHA
20. D, 11 Aug 70
21. D, 22 Jul 70
22. D, 12 May 70

12. To Serve and Protect

1. JK
2. D, 13 Feb 70
3. LS
4. JW
5. *Toronto Star,* 23 Feb 72
6. *Globe,* 23 Mar 73
7. "Clear Light," Feb 71
8. D, 20 May 70
9. IN, 15 Apr 69
10. ibid.
11. D, 7 Jul 70
12. D, 14 Feb 69
13. D, 18 Aug 70
14. D, 14 Jan 69
15. D, 14 Feb 69

16. leaflet, CHA
17. leaflet, FRB
18. D, 13 Feb 73
19. D, 22 Jul 70
20. AE
21. CAT
22. D, 24 Aug 71
23. D, 23 Jun 70
24. leaflet, CHA
25. *Windsor Star*, 2 Oct 70
26. Bill King?, notes, FRB
27. D, 20 May 70
28. NOTE 7
29. D, 20 May 70

13. High Society

1. *Toronto Telegram*, 6 Oct 70
2. *Toronto Telegram*, 25 Jul 70
3. D, Sep 68, CHA
4. D, Oct 68, CHA
5. D, 23 Jun 70
6. D, 28 Jul 70
7. D, 18 Nov 75
8. D, 5 Dec 72
9. leaflet, FRB
10. leaflet, FRB
11. D, 4 Jun 71
12. D, 11 May 71
13. D, 20 Apr 71
14. 27 Jun 69, FRB
15. leaflet, FRB
16. JW

17. D, May 74
18. *Globe*, 23 Oct 75
19. D?, FRB
20. AE
21. D, 2 Jun 70
22. KG
23. AE
24. D, 9 Jun 70
25. Mar 69, FRB
26. D, 22 Aug 72
27. D, 27 Sep 73
28. D, May 72
29. D, Nov 68, CHA
30. CAT
31. Bill King, letter, FRB
32. 20 Mar 74, FRB
33. KG
34. D?, 3 Feb 69
35. "IILYDAILYDAII," 16 Oct 70
36. D, FRB
37. Nov 74, FRB
38. D, fall 74
39. D, 16 Sep 70
40. Sep 68, CHA
41. SS
42. KG
43. D, Nov 68, CHA
44. D, Nov 68, CHA
45. John Slinger, *Globe*, 31 May 74
46. Mark Kennedy, *Toronto Telegram*, Sep 70, letter

47. D, 25 Jul 72
48. D, 1 Jan 69, CHA
49. Mar 69, leaflet, FRB
50. "The Naked Grape," 21 Nov 69
51. D?, Jul 69, FRB
52. Feb 70, leaflet, FRB
53. 23 Mar 70
54. *Globe*, 2 Mar 70
55. LB
56. KG
57. NOTE 46
58. D, 30 Oct 70
59. leaflet, 11 May 74, FRB
60. notes, FRB

14. Under the Rock
1. leaflet, FRB
2. "Where It's At," Jun 69
3. D, May 74
4. D, 20 Sep 71
5. MH
6. notes, FRB
7. D, Nov 68, CHA
8. SS
9. *Toronto Star*, Apr 71
10. AE
11. pamphlet, CHA
12. CAT
13. WR
14. 30 Oct 73, FRB
15. CAT

16. pamphlet, 11 May 74
17. HA
18. D, 20 May 70
19. *Globe*, 13 May 74
20. D, 21 Nov 72
21. SS
22. D, 12 Oct 71
23. leaflet, FRB
24. IR 1, 16 Feb 69
25. leaflet, CHA
26. *Toronto Telegram*, 2 Jun 69
27. "Education Brief to CMHC," FRB
28. leaflet, FRB
29. *Toronto Telegram*, 2 Jun 69
30. *Globe*, 24 Apr 72
31. pamphlet, 11 May 74
32. D, 16 Jun 69
33. Jack Jones, leaflet, FRB
34. D, 27 Jun 72
35. CAT
36. D, 25 Jan 74

15. Arts Daily
1. D, 9 Mar 69, CHA
2. Marci McDonald, *Toronto Star*, Mar 69
3. ibid.
4. BZ
5. HA
6. clipping, 18 Jul 69, FRB
7. notes, FRB

8. leaflet, FRB
9. D, 1 Feb 72
10. CAT
11. D, 20 Mar 74
12. D, 3 Jan 69
13. IN 6, 6 Jun 69
14. HA
15. CAT
16. "Exit!" 25 Jan 68
17. D, 14 Feb 69
18. D, 16 Apr 69, CHA
19. D, Mar 69, CHA
20. leaflet, CHA
21. AE
22. D, 20 Feb 70, CHA
23. D, 23 Jun 70
24. JW
25. Kingsland interview
26. DG
27. D, Oct 68, CHA
28. D, Nov 68, CHA
29. D, 16 Jan 69
30. LB
31. MZ
32. D, 13 Apr 69
33. leaflet, FRB
34. CHA.
35. notes, FRB
36. HA
37. notes, FRB
38. CHA
39. D, Sep 68, CHA

40. CHA
41. Raymond Venison, 12 Sep 70, FRB
42. D, 6 Oct 68, CHA
43. ABS, Nov 67, FRB
44. 25 Jan 68, FRB
45. D, 1 Oct 68, CHA
46. D, 28 Sep 68, CHA
47. D, 29 Jan 69
48. D, 1 Jan 69, CHA
49. D, Dec 68, CHA
50. D, Jan 69, CHA
51. D, 3 Sep 71
52. D, 12 Oct 71
53. D, 1 Feb 72
54. "Triclitorium," Sep 74
55. D, 16 Feb 73

16. Business Unusual

1. D, May 74
2. "The Naked Grape," 30 Mar 73
3. D, 6 May 70
4. VAR, 19 Oct 70
5. George Russell, *Globe*, Nov 70
6. ibid.
7. AE
8. D, 30 Nov 73
9. CAT
10. D, 11 Sep 70
11. D, 13 Aug 71

12. D, 5 Oct 71

13. D, 24 Oct 72

14. CHA

15. CAT

16. D, 20 Sep 68, CHA

17. D, 27 Nov 68, CHA

18. from an interview

19. *Toronto Star*, 7 Jun 75

20. CAT

21. leaflet, FRB

22. D, 24 Oct 68, CHA

23. D, Dec 68, CHA

24. D, Dec 68, CHA

25. IR 4, 2 Mar 69

26. IN, 3 Apr 69

27. ibid.

28. IN, 8 May 69

29. D, 18 Dec 68, CHA

30. D, 28 Nov 72

31. D, 11 Aug 70

32. leaflet, CHA

33. SS

34. leaflet, FRB

35. letter, 25 Feb 74, FRB

36. CHA

37. notes, CHA

38. CHA

39. CHA

40. D, 29 Aug 72

41. CHA

42. minutes, 26 Jun 67, FRB

43. "Where It's At," FRB

44. FRB

45. FRB

46. CHA

47. Oct 72, CHA

48. 13 Feb 74, CHA

49. *Toronto Star*, Apr 71

50. leaflet, FRB

51. notes, FRB

52. CHA

17. A Symbol on Bloor

1. D, 24 May 74

2. KG

3. D, 24 Sep 68, CHA

4. D, Oct 68, CHA

5. D, May 74

6. FRB

7. KG

8. D, 14 Jul 70

9. Bill King, *Guerilla*, clipping, FRB

10. MS 8, 15 May 69

11. KG

12. D, 17 Apr 70

13. D, Dec 68, CHA

14. D, 18 Nov 75

15. MZ

16. Stuart Roche, D, undated

17. KG

18. D, 7 Jul 70

19. KG

20. *Newsweek*, 25 Nov 68

21. *Toronto Star*, Apr 71
22. IN, 26 Apr 69
23. Eric LeBourdais, "The Other Side Of Rochdale," Jan 71
24. Dennis Braithwaite, *Toronto Star*, 25 Mar 74
25. D, Oct 74
26. IN, 26 Apr 69
27. D, 13 Apr 73
28. "Clear Light," Mar 71, FRB
29. D, 19 Oct 68, CHA
30. RCB 1:3, Apr 67
31. CHA
32. D, 4 Apr 69
33. minutes, 18 Dec 73, FRB
34. FRB
35. D, 22 Jul 70
36. D, 1 Jan 69, CHA
37. D, 18 Dec 68, CHA
38. D, Jan 69, CHA
39. HA
40. FRB
41. leaflet, FRB
42. D, 3 Feb 69
43. D, Jan 69

18. The Fan

1. *Toronto Star*, clipping, FRB
2. BJ
3. HA
4. MZ
5. D, Mar 69, CHA
6. 4 May 69
7. 22 Jun 69, clipping, CHA
8. MV
9. *Globe*, 17 Aug 70
10. D, 7 Jul 70
11. D, 11 Oct 68
12. D, 1 Mar 69
13. D, 8 Apr 69, CHA
14. LB
15. KG
16. D, 8 May 70
17. leaflet, FRB
18. D, 12 May 70
19. "By Glen who was There," clipping, FRB
20. pamphlet, FRB
21. D, 15 May 70
22. leaflet, FRB
23. D, 1 May 70
24. notes, FRB
25. leaflet, 16 Aug 70
26. notes, FRB
27. leaflet, 16 Aug 70
28. JW
29. Jan Reid, clipping, FRB
30. notes, FRB
31. *Toronto Citizen*, 27 Aug 70
32. notes, FRB
33. *Toronto Star*, 19 Apr 84
34. NG
35. D, 25 Nov 68, CHA

36. 3 Oct 70, clipping, CHA

37. Ian Argue, 24 Oct 74

19. Danger Zone

1. KG

2. D, 8 Feb 69

3. clipping, FRB

4. IN, 15 Apr 69

5. D, 30 Mar 71

6. MH

7. D, 16 Oct 70

8. D, 7 Mar 69

9. DG

10. D, 14 Feb 69

11. D, Oct 68, CHA

12. IN, 15 Apr 69

13. D, 8 May 70

14. D, Dec 69

15. D, Dec 68, CHA

16. D, 14 Oct 68, CHA

17. D, Nov 68, CHA

18. D, Sep 68, CHA

19. D, 27 Mar 69

20. D, 7 Mar 69

21. JW

22. MB

23. *Toronto Star*, 8 May 71

20. To the Wall

1. AO

2. BZ

3. D, 22 Sep 70

4. D, 5 Apr 74

5. D, Dec 68, CHA

6. *Toronto Star*, 7 May 74

7. clipping, CHA

8. leaflet, FRB

9. D, 27 Mar 70

10. D, 24 Mar 72

11. leaflet, FRB

12. AO

13. *Globe*, 18 Apr 73

14. D, 23 Mar 73

15. JW

16. D, 22 Sep 70

17. D, 28 Apr 70

18. KG

19. KG

20. D, 16 Jun 70

21. D, 9 Jun 70

22. ibid.

23. George Russell, *Globe*, Nov 70

24. D, 7 Feb 69

25. SS

26. D, Nov 68, CHA

27. SS

28. D, 28 Sep 68

29. D, 1 May 70

30. D, 3 Jun 69

31. D, Oct 68, CHA

32. Andrew Wernick, clipping, FRB

33. D, Oct 68, CHA

34. Sue Swan, *Toronto Telegram*, 9 Nov 68
35. George Russell, *Globe*, 14 Nov 70
36. D, 18 Aug 70
37. Russell, op. cit.

21. Drug Pros and Cons

1. pamphlet, FRB
2. DG
3. D, 24 May 74
4. D, 3 Sep 71
5. D, 1 Sep 70
6. *Globe*, 18 Oct 69
7. *Guerilla*, clipping, FRB
8. BZ
9. D, 6 Mar 70
10. D, FRB
11. D, 25 Aug 70
12. D, 18 Aug 70
13. CAT
14. *Globe Magazine*
15. D, 1 Sep 70
16. D, 16 Sep 70

22. The Great White Fathers

1. *Toronto Star*, 12 Sep 70
2. George Russell, *Globe*
3. Jul 71, clipping, FRB
4. D, 17 Apr 70
5. memo, FRB
6. *Globe*, 29 Oct 70

7. letter to Alderman Paul Pickett, 26 Apr 71, FRB
8. pamphlet, FRB
9. minutes, 22 Oct 74, FRB
10. D, 5 Dec 72
11. clipping, FRB
12. minutes, 31 Aug 71, FRB
13. leaflet, FRB
14. D, 20 Jul 71
15. D, 30 Jul 71
16. D, 10 Aug 71
17. D, 13 Apr 73
18. pamphlet, 9 Aug 71
19. leaflet, 25 Aug 71, FRB

23. Invasion

1. "Heliofax,"29Feb72
2. ibid.
3. D, 12 May 72
4. "Heliofax," 29 Feb 72
5. D, 25 Jan 72
6. D, 5 Sep 72
7. D, 19 Sep 72
8. Bill King, notes, FRB
9. D, 19 Sep 72
10. D, 19 Sep 72
11. ibid.
12. leaflet, FRB
13. J. L. Biddell, "Memorandum No. 2," 7 Mar 74, FRB
14. NOTE 13
15. D, 26 Sep 72

16. ibid.

17. D, 12 Sep 72

18. D, 25 Jul 72

24. Sirens at the Rock

1. 29 Mar 73, FRB

2. Brian Gilhuly, "operating report," 29 Oct 70

3. D, 13 Feb 73

4. D, 4 May 73

5. *Toronto Star*, 23 Feb 72

6. MB

7. *Globe*, clipping

8. MB

9. CAT

10. *Globe*, 29 Apr 71

11. Mary Janigan, *Toronto Star*, 10 Apr 74

12. D, 26 Mar 74

13. D, 20 Apr 73

14. pamphlet, FRB

15. leaflet, FRB

16. Gerald McAuliffe, *Globe*, 24 Oct 74

17. 5 Sep 75, FRB

18. letter to Tony O'Donohue, 19 May 71

19. D, 23 Mar 71

20. Bill King, notes, FRB

21. D, 10 Jan 69

22. notes, FRB

23. Victor Coleman, ed., CHA

24. LS

25. pamphlet, 11 May 74

26. D, 13 Feb 69

27. Rimstead's Toronto, *Toronto Telegram*, 25 Jul 70

28. *Toronto Sun*, 7 Dec 71

29. Carol Marino, *Toronto Star*, Dec 71

30. J.J. Bradford, 29 Sep 70, FRB

31. *Globe*, 28 Mar 72

32. notes, FRB

33. notes, 1 May 73, FRB

34. pamphlet, FRB

35. pamphlet, FRB

36. notes, FRB

37. leaflet, 18 May 73, FRB

25. Eviction

1. pamphlet, 2 Feb 75

2. occurrence report in my collection

3. pamphlet, May 74

4. D, May 74

5. "Foliage," Sep 74

6. "Foliage," Jul 74

7. 30 Mar 73, FRB

8. D, 20 Apr 73

9. D, 5 Dec 72

10. D, 21 Dec 73

11. pamphlet, Nov 74

12. D, 25 May 73

13. FRB

14. memo, 23 Mar 70

15. D, 26 Apr 74

16. 7 Mar 74, FRB

17. letter to a resident, 17 Apr 74, FRB

18. quoted in a press release by RC, 2 Apr 74

19. D, 26 Apr 74

20. 17 Apr 75, FRB

21. pamphlet, Nov 74

22. CAT

23. 25 Jul 72, FRB

24. "Petition," Jun 75

25. *Globe*, 21 Mar 74

26. D, 13 Mar 74

27. pamphlet, 11 May 74

28. FMTA minutes, 10 Jun 74, FRB

29. FRB

30. Cynthia Lei, pamphlet, Nov 74

31. leaflet, FRB

32. Biddell, 10 Apr 73

33. D, 20 Jul 73

34. pamphlet, 23 Jan 75, FRB

35. "Equivocal Calamities of RC,"Nov 74

36. leaflet, FRB

37. "Foliage," 2 Sep 74

38. leaflet, FRB

39. D, Jan 75

40. OR

41. *Globe*, 15 Feb 75

42. *Globe*, 26 Feb 75

43. OR

44. D, 10 Jan 74

45. D, 10 Jan 74

46. D, 26 Apr 74

47. MH

48. D, Jan 75

49. leaflet, 13 May 75, FRB

50. *Globe*, 24 May 75

51. OR

52. "Petition," Jun 75

53. *Globe*, 4 Jul 75

26. Afterwords

1. OR

2. *Toronto Sun*, 30 Jul 75

3. "Rochdale," 1:3, Charasee Press, Oct 76?, FRB

4. HA

5. leaflet, FRB

6. *Canadian Architect*, Nov 76

7. MB

8. letter, FRB

9. notes, FRB

10. "Petition," Jun 75

Index

DAVID SHARPE teaches writing online and on campus at Ohio University. In addition to *Rochdale: The Runaway College*, he is also the author of the short story collection *Seasoning*.

LIST

The A List

The Outlander Gil Adamson
The Circle Game Margaret Atwood
Moving Targets Margaret Atwood
Power Politics Margaret Atwood
Second Words Margaret Atwood
Survival Margaret Atwood
These Festive Nights Marie-Claire Blais
Thunder and Light Marie-Claire Blais
La Guerre Trilogy Roch Carrier
The Hockey Sweater and Other Stories Roch Carrier
Hard Core Logo Nick Craine
Great Expectations Edited by Dede Crane and Lisa Moore
Queen Rat Lynn Crosbie
The Honeyman Festival Marian Engel
The Bush Garden Northrop Frye
Eleven Canadian Novelists Interviewed by Graeme Gibson
Five Legs Graeme Gibson
Death Goes Better with Coca-Cola Dave Godfrey
Technology and Empire George Grant
Technology and Justice George Grant
De Niro's Game Rawi Hage
Kamouraska Anne Hébert
Ticknor Sheila Heti
Waterloo Express Paulette Jiles
No Pain Like This Body Harold Sonny Ladoo
Red Diaper Baby James Laxer
Civil Elegies Dennis Lee
Mermaids and Ikons Gwendolyn MacEwen
Ana Historic Daphne Marlatt
Like This Leo McKay Jr.
Selected Short Fiction of Lisa Moore
Furious Erín Moure
Selected Poems Alden Nowlan
Poems for All the Annettes Al Purdy
Manual for Draft-Age Immigrants to Canada Mark Satin
The Little Girl Who Was Too Fond of Matches Gaétan Soucy
Stilt Jack John Thompson
Made for Happiness Jean Vanier
Basic Black with Pearls Helen Weinzweig
Passing Ceremony Helen Weinzweig
The Big Why Michael Winter
This All Happened Michael Winter